AF344255

Barack Obama, Post-Racialism, and the New Politics of Triangulation

Barack Obama, Post-Racialism, and the New Politics of Triangulation

Terry Smith

BARACK OBAMA, POST-RACIALISM, AND THE NEW POLITICS OF TRIANGULATION
Copyright © Terry Smith, 2012.

All rights reserved.

First published in 2012 by
PALGRAVE MACMILLAN®
in the United States—a division of St. Martin's Press LLC,
175 Fifth Avenue, New York, NY 10010.

Where this book is distributed in the UK, Europe and the rest of the world,
this is by Palgrave Macmillan, a division of Macmillan Publishers Limited,
registered in England, company number 785998, of Houndmills,
Basingstoke, Hampshire RG21 6XS.

Palgrave Macmillan is the global academic imprint of the above companies
and has companies and representatives throughout the world.

Palgrave® and Macmillan® are registered trademarks in the United States,
the United Kingdom, Europe and other countries.

ISBN: 978–0–230–37199–6

Library of Congress Cataloging-in-Publication Data

Smith, Terry, 1964–
    Barack Obama, post-racialism, and the new politics of triangulation /
by Terry Smith.
        p. cm.
    Includes index.
    ISBN 978–0–230–37199–6 (alk. paper)
    1. African Americans—Politics and government—21st century.
2. Post-racialism—United States. 3. United States—Race relations—
Political aspects. 4. Obama, Barack—Influence. 5. United States—
Politics and government—2009– I. Title.

E185.615.S5838 2012
973.932092—dc23   2011050343

A catalogue record of the book is available from the British Library.

Design by Newgen Imaging Systems (P) Ltd., Chennai, India.

First edition: June 2012

10 9 8 7 6 5 4 3 2 1

Transferred to Digital Printing in 2013

For my mother, who had little but gave me so much

Contents

Preface   ix

Acknowledgments   xi

Introduction   1

Part I   Before Obama

1   Black Politics: Which Way Is Left?   9

2   Race and Money in Politics   21

3   Black Tea: Black Conservatives and the Rhetoric of
    Social Conservatism   45

4   Contradictions in a Latino Moment: Latinos as
    Less Black?   63

Part II   Barack Obama and the New Politics of Triangulation

5   Triangulation 101: The Old Conceives the New   83

6   The New Politics of Triangulation: Obama and
    Post-Racialism   101

7   A Thousand Obamas? Black Electoral Ambition and
    Accountability to Black Voters   119

8   Do African Americans Need a Black President?
    Of Movements, Not Men   135

Conclusion   157

Notes   159

Index   217

PREFACE

I have written about the intersection of law and the political process—and its impact on black politics in particular—for the past eighteen years. During that time, the country elected a black president and increased its ranks of minority officeholders. Yet despite this progress, blacks continue to be an exceptional subspecies of the American body politic. The merits and necessity of majority-minority districts continue to be debated, the United States Senate is still disproportionately white and male, as are the governors of most states, and new forms of black disenfranchisement have emerged to blunt whatever progress has been made. Instead of outright denials of the right to vote, minority access is now hindered by felony disenfranchisement laws, photo identification requirements, voter roll purges, and unduly long waiting times at the polls. Notwithstanding the persistence of these and other barriers to black political equality, an activist United States Supreme Court has hinted that a cornerstone of African Americans' right to vote, the Voting Rights Act of 1965, may be unconstitutional.

Having written about many of these aspects of minority political inequality, Barack Obama's election as the first black president presented a welcomed challenge to me as a legal scholar. Did the election mark a significant advance in minority political equality? Or was it possible for things to get worse, or at least stay the same, for African Americans even as the country performed the improbable act of electing a black man as president? As I observed the first three years of President Obama's term, I continually asked myself how Obama's presidency fit with the larger historical arc of black politics. Some heralded the election as a generational shift, a passing of the baton. I have never been impressed by this analysis, for the so-called new black politics is too reliant on key aspects of the old to represent a generational change in any substantive, as opposed to chronological, sense of that term.

So in writing *Barack Obama, Post-Racialism, and the New Politics of Triangulation*, I set out to explore in an interdisciplinary way the relationship between the "post-racial" politics personified by Barack Obama, Cory Booker, Adrian Fenty, Harold Ford, Jr., and others, and traditional black politics and the problems of political and economic inequality with which it has historically concerned itself. That relationship is in some ways in tension and in other ways is complementary. Importantly, though, that relationship reveals a broader pathos about the association of African Americans to politics writ large. I have selected the frame of "triangulation" through which to explore this pathos, but all frames risk oversimplification if they are abused. Cognizant of this, let me say upfront that there is obviously more to Obama's relationship with black voters than triangulation, and I do not intend that the takeaway from this book be otherwise.

The reader will determine for herself or himself whether I've gotten things right, wrong, or somewhere in between. In any case, I hope my observations stimulate a dialogue in some circles about post-racialism, the meaning of a black president, and the appropriate metrics for black political progress.

Acknowledgments

The fruits of my labor would not have been possible without feedback and encouragement from Sumi Cho, Valerie Johnson, James Fleming, Audrey McFarlane, Richard Delgado, Devon Carbado, Lincoln Pettaway, Darren Hutchinson, Karen Porter, John Banks, and others whose pardon I beg for not specifically mentioning here. As well, my research assistants—Katherine Gillard, Kevin O'Bryan and Damon Rittenhouse—were indefatigable and indispensible. Reference librarian Milta Hall proved to be an invaluable resource, as was Glennis Jones-Marshall for coordination of secretarial support.

Finally, I express my gratitude to the University of North Carolina Law Review for its grant of copyright permission for my article, *Race and Money in Politics*, 79 N.C. L. REV. 1469 (2001), and to the University of South Carolina Law Review for its grant of copyright permission for my article, *White Dollars, Black Candidates: Inequality and Agency in Campaign Finance Law*, 57 S.C. L. REV. 735 (2006).

Introduction

This is a book about what happens to black politics in a prematurely post-racial world—one in which racial disparity persists but race as a national issue falls out of vogue. Thus, it is also a book about what happens to black people in such a world. Finally, it is a book about what happens to politics writ large in a post-racial world. The ideal of colorblindness notwithstanding, Americans' voting and policy preferences continue to be defined by marked racial stratification. The state of black politics defines the state of American politics and vice versa.

Even the most well-meaning individuals can only visualize black politics as a caricature—a narrow, ethnocentric interest group movement. This distorted view is often personified by the Reverend Jesse Jackson. Jackson, however, articulated a broad progressive vision during his two runs for the presidency in 1984 and 1988. In that vision, striking workers could not be replaced, health care was a fundamental right, and affirmative action could operate as a corrective for past injustices. Jackson is just one of a long line of black leaders to articulate an expansive progressive vision not centered on race but not afraid of it either. The Great Society is the paradigm for such a vision. So in discussing black politics, I am not referring to a crude phenotype, but rather to the progressive policies—some explicitly race related, others more class based—personified by President Lyndon Baines Johnson.[1] Many consider the Johnson presidency to be the last era during which the concerns of African Americans were given sustained national priority.[2]

If Jackson and Johnson are the personifications of black politics, then Barack Obama is the personification of post-racial politics. But more central to the thesis of this book, Obama is a practitioner of post-racial triangulation. Political triangulation describes the "third way" between liberalism and conservatism that President Bill Clinton espoused. Barack Obama has celebrated triangulation as "Bill Clinton's singular contribution."[3] Triangulation is the rejection of partisan orthodoxy in favor of supposed pragmatic solutions to policy questions and conflicts. More cynically, triangulation has been described as "co-opting the center to divide opposition and inhibit attack" by "pre-emptive theft of the opposition's (more conservative) attitudes and language, uncomfortably sounding like Reagan on welfare, endorsing everyone pulling themselves by their own bootstraps."[4] The fruits of Clintonian triangulation included the North American Free Trade Agreement (NAFTA) and welfare reform, neither of which is viewed as a policy triumph in progressive circles. As the cynical view and policy results of political triangulation suggest, the strategy involves a succumbing to the power of the Right; triangulation does not starve the ideological Right of its policy preferences to the same extent as it does the ideological Left.

Now imagine a similar strategy of triangulation being implemented by the nation's first black president—not solely in the left-right continuum of Clintonian triangulation, but also as a buffer against the nation's continuing racial divide. Just as political triangulation did not hurt the Right as much as the Left, post-racial triangulation does not hurt white political hegemony as much as it does black people and black politics. Quibble with the choice of analogy if you like, but among African American leaders and intellectuals, one perception of the trajectory of Barack Obama's presidency has become clear: Obama has walked the racial tightrope of American politics in much the same way Clinton negotiated the right-of-center tightrope for his political survival.

Such has been the perception of many members of the Congressional Black Caucus (CBC), a group of legislators who would under ordinary circumstances be loath to publicly criticize the first African American president.[5] And few black public intellectuals have been more outspoken about their disappointment with Obama than Princeton University professor Cornel West. West is blunt: "He can take the black base for granted because he assumes we have nowhere else to go. But we just won't put up with it. He has got to respect us."[6]

West's foreboding aside, the disapproval of Obama among black "elites" is unlikely to translate into a drop of support among black voters. Even after his tumultuous first year in office during the Great Recession, black support for Obama was nearly unanimous at 95 percent versus only 56 percent of whites. Moreover, in the same survey, most blacks believed that Obama shared the values and interests of black Americans.[7] Yet because black support for Democratic presidential candidates and presidents is almost always higher than any other demographic group's support, these numbers may be less a referendum on Obama's actual performance than a reflection of two stubborn realities in American politics. The first and most important is that black voters continue to be captured by the Democratic Party with few if any plausible political alternatives. The second is that national or even statewide black political success remains such a novelty that African Americans quite understandably nurture and protect the symbols of that success.

While these conventions of American politics likely contribute to Obama's willingness and ability to triangulate black voters to the frustration of black leaders, this is an incomplete account of the predicament of black voters under the first African American president. Well before Obama's ascent, "black politics"—the left-of-center, race-conscious brand of politics that has typified black voters and candidates—was under assault by forces of post-racialism. Supreme Court decisions alleging "reverse-racial gerrymandering" had "whitened" many majority-minority legislative districts. Even districts that continued to be majority-minority were confronted with what had been an open secret in black districts: even when black voters have controlled the votes, they did not finance their preferred candidate. White dollars did. White donors, however, had begun to choose candidates other than the ones supported by most black voters. The license that the United States Supreme Court had long given to big money in American elections had finally begun to influence—or distort—the electoral outcomes in black districts.

The ramifications of legal doctrine were not the only forces stymieing traditional black politics. Black conservatives had begun a concerted effort to fracture blacks' unified support of the Democratic Party and to contrive an alliance between black voters and culturally conservative whites. Meanwhile, Latino voters were attempting to forge their own alternating alliance with Democrats and Republicans, one of convenience in which they would act as coveted "swing" voters, similar to the much-heralded political independents who consume an inordinate amount of candidates' and the media's attention. This meant that, despite their shared socioeconomic—and in some cases racial—disadvantage with blacks, Latinos could not be counted on to fortify the voter cohesion exemplified by African Americans. The traditional model of black politics was under stress, perhaps even on the verge of ossification.

Enter Obama. At a time when traditional, left-of-center, race-conscious black politics was already being vitiated by multiple forces, a telegenic black candidate whose politics were facially progressive, even if not race-conscious, could offer a credible alternative to traditional black politics, and, less obviously, could compound its difficulties.

And compound he has. Black voters remain race-conscious. For example, a 2010 Pew Research survey revealed that 8 in 10 believed the country needed to continue to make changes to ensure black equality. By contrast, 54 percent of whites felt that the necessary changes had already been made.[8] Despite their beliefs, blacks supporting Obama must repose their hopes and aspirations in a brand of politics that so calibrates race that it disappears from the national policy dialogue. Consider Obama's response to questions about epidemic levels of black unemployment: "The only thing I cannot do is, by law, I cannot pass laws that say 'I'm just helping black folks.' I'm the president of the entire United States."[9] A more stock, race-neutral response would be difficult to elicit from a conservative Republican. This was typical of Obama's strategy of post-racial triangulation.

These are, one hopes, matters of style or modulation, a diplomatic wink-and-nod by a black president who "gets it" when it comes to the issues affecting blacks. But style can impinge on substance, and, moreover, it can obscure simple truths. Even during more normal economic times preceding the Great Recession of 2008, the official black unemployment rate routinely doubled that of whites, as did the poverty rate.[10] And a host of other socioeconomic indicators, from wages to accumulated wealth, have long relegated black citizens in America to second-class status. In short, race matters. It matters far too much for any politician of any color to respond as Obama did: "What I can do is make sure that I am passing laws that help all people, particularly those who are most vulnerable and most in need. That in turn is going to help lift up the African American community."[11] This is merely an attempt to address racial disparity without addressing race. This is post-racial triangulation.

Focusing on Obama is not meant to suggest that African Americans were not among the targets of Bill Clinton's political triangulation. They certainly were.[12] In this regard, as in many others, distinctions between race and politics where the two strongly correlate can be artificial.[13] Nor is the focus on Obama's triangulation of race intended to suggest the absence of a broader strategy of triangulation by Obama, as some commentators have already observed.[14] Yet, as the first African American president, Obama has had extraordinary incentive—indeed imperative—to practice post-racial triangulation. Keith Reeves, among others, has persuasively documented that when race is invoked among majority-white voters, the minority candidate suffers electorally.[15] White voters simply do not punish white politicians for invoking race, or even racism, to the same extent as they punish minority candidates for being identified with a racial issue.

For example, although former Virginia Senator George Allen was widely thought to have lost his reelection in 2006 because his anti-Indian slur ("macaca") was caught on video, a majority of whites still voted for Allen.[16]

Some may argue that Obama's "third way" on race is distinguishable from Clinton's third way in political triangulation. That is, Obama may truly be seeking to redress the condition of African Americans in a race-neutral fashion. This argument ignores another dimension of the relationship between political triangulation and post-racial triangulation. In his most explicit pronouncement of political triangulation, Bill Clinton famously declared in a State of the Union address, "The era of big government is over." Remember, Obama has celebrated Clintonian triangulation as Clinton's "singular contribution." To the extent that Obama has adopted this page from Clinton and from the Right, government's capacity to address racial disparity in a race-neutral fashion is severely limited. One cannot on the one hand argue for remedies that would benefit large non-race-specific swaths of the disadvantaged and at the same time argue for substantially less government. Obama's third way on race is no less triangulating than Clinton's brand of triangulation.

Even if all that I have said thus far is true, some may ask, why would Barack Obama ever undertake the politically suicidal feat of identifying with race? But the mirror image of the same question is this: who will save race from extinction in our national policy dialogue? If it is unrealistic to expect Barack Obama to be Lyndon B. Johnson to black Americans, perhaps it is not unreasonable to expect that Obama will not participate in the marginalization of black politics.

Or perhaps that is one tightrope too many. A hydraulic conception of black politics, in which African American issues percolate from localities and congressional districts to the national sphere, is a theoretic possibility that relieves a black president of the laboring oar on race. But this is not possible when black politics has been weakened by legal doctrine and parasitic forces intent on devaluing the group cohesion that lies at its core. Furthermore, it is not feasible when Obama's post-racial triangulation is viewed as a template for success by other black politicians aspiring to higher office who know that an association with traditional black politics is anathema to many white voters. Ironically, then, traditional, left-of-center black politics may become a casualty of Obama's success even as the conditions that gave rise to this brand of politics persist and worsen.

A more detailed account of the current state of black politics and Obama's role in its transformation follows. Part 1 of *Barack Obama,*

Post-Racialism, and the New Politics of Triangulation focuses on the current state of traditional black politics. After providing an overview of its strengths—namely black political cohesion—and infirmities in chapter 1, part 1 then asks whether two groups, black conservatives and Latino voters, have devalued traditional black politics in the process of pursuing their own political ends and have thus helped to enable Obama's triangulation of black voters.

Only by understanding the challenges that traditional black politics had faced prior to Obama's ascent can one appreciate Obama's strategy of post-racial triangulation and the harm to black politics that it foretells. Part 2 is an exposé of these issues. It posits a derivation of post-racial triangulation from Clintonian political triangulation and then discusses the machinations of the former. In chapters 7 and 8, I address two fundamental issues posed by post-racial triangulation. Chapter 7 situates the debate about Obama's accountability to African Americans in the larger historical discussion about the problems of political accountability to black voters. The final chapter, chapter 8, asks, do African Americans need a black president for their advancement? I conclude that, symbolic importance aside, the answer is no and that a mistake of black voters is to engage in the electoral process without being guided by the framework of a self-interested political movement.

Black equality requires much more than a black president. It requires the demolishment of the root of post-racial triangulation— the recurring electoral dynamic wherein white voters insist, and politicians of all races oblige, that a price of political success must be the marginalization and closeting of black-identified issues. As I argue in the concluding chapter, black voters understand the racial constraints to which President Obama has had to respond. Consciously or unconsciously, their continued overwhelming support of a race-averse black president is an effort to repel the notion that Obama must show a certain detachment from black voters as the ransom for symbolic black political equality. Responding to electoral neglect by supporting those who practice it may seem perverse. But if disappointment with Obama were to demobilize black support, then, quite ironically, the animating cause of post-racial triangulation—white voter alienation from issues of racial equality—will have prevailed.

PART I

Before Obama

CHAPTER 1

Black Politics: Which Way Is Left?

Black politics was not thriving on the eve of Barack Obama's historic election as the first African American president of the United States. If this assertion seems at odds with the very fact of Obama's election, then a taxonomic clarification is in order. Obama was not "of" black politics, but his election depended heavily on one of its core features—black voter cohesion. The so-called new black politics represented by Obama was curiously reliant on the old notion of black solidarity for its success. Absent a near-uniform black vote for Obama in North Carolina, Virginia, Ohio, Florida, and even his home state of Illinois, Barack Obama would not have become president.

Yet the performance of black voters in the 2008 election belied a basic vulnerability of black politics that has both preceded and enabled Obama's political success. Black politics has been variously defined, and pronouncements of its demise are colored by the vantage point of each definition. This book explores black politics from a "voting rights" perspective—that is, the implicit and express political consensus around which black voters have organized their ballot-box behavior for more than four decades since the passage of the Voting Rights Act of 1965. Focusing on electoral behavior masks significant variability in African American ideology, but this variability is overwhelmingly leftist in nature; conservatism is a marginal viewpoint among blacks.[1] Thus, when voters behave as black voters do, voting in no less than the eightieth percentile for a single political party in every presidential election since 1964, certain generalizations are possible notwithstanding ideological diversity. Chance cannot explain political unity of this degree and longevity.

Unpacking the state of black politics in the early twenty-first century is essential to understanding the new politics of triangulation. As noted in the introduction, we understand Clintonian political triangulation as a three-dimensional association among Clinton, liberals, and right-of-center voters to whom Clinton would ultimately show great deference in order to survive politically. Liberals were the weaker plank of the triangle. Claire Jean Kim, associate professor of political science at the University of California, Irvine, similarly conceives of triangulation as a tripartite, hierarchical relationship. In the racial triangulation she examines, blacks and Asians are the objects of puppeteering by a dominant white triangular who valorizes Asians relative to blacks while de-Americanizing Asians vis-à-vis whites.[2] Thus, whether it is political or racial, triangulation requires a vulnerable participant. In the case of Obama and the new black politics, that vulnerable subject is traditional black politics and the black voters who enervate the traditional model.[3]

Obama's triangulation is a hybrid of the political and the racial. Its three-dimensional plane consists of Obama (in lieu of Clinton), left-of-center black voters, and right-of-center white voters. In attempting a calibration between the competing expectations of black and white voters, Obama has used the symbolism of race to cabin the expectations of blacks. This dimension of the new triangulation is intrinsically racial to the extent it must negotiate historical tensions around the race question, but, more specifically, it deploys racial symbolism to (ironically) dissuade any race-specific policy aspirations of black voters.

The political dimension of the new triangulation is at once similar to and different from the racial dimension. Black voters form the core of any national Democratic victory, but they were particularly essential to Obama's, first in the 2008 primaries, and then in the general election. It is a truism in American politics that race is partisanship and vice versa, and Obama's election is not a significant departure from this rule. But the political dimension of the new triangulation is independently significant in that the concessionary tone of Clintonian political triangulation solidified a ceiling against which black policy aspirations have continued to clash long after Clinton's departure. That is, Obama has not proven willing to alter, or otherwise capable of altering, the basic right-of-center trajectory of American public policy that preceded his election. Once the fundamental discourse in American politics is conceded by "the era of big government is over" rhetoric, the ability of government to engage the needs and aspirations of black voters is severely circumscribed, regardless of the race of the president. In such an environment, the calibration of black expectations and aspirations and the electoral imperative of satisfying the white, right-of-center mainstream will of necessity shortchange the former. The vulnerable blank of the triangle is traditional black politics and its mainstay, black voters. And, as with Kim's racial triangulation, the ultimate beneficiary of the three-dimensional exercise is the extant white power structure.

In the remainder of this chapter, I explore the corporate body of black politics that Obama and the new black politics are attempting to triangulate. More specifically, I examine both the perception and reality of its vulnerability. In subsequent chapters in part 1 of the book, I analyze specific forces that have contributed to the weakened state of traditional black politics and thus rendered it more susceptible to triangulation.

THE BLACK POLITICAL CONSENSUS

"African Americans reaffirmed the vitality of the Black Political Consensus," proclaimed the *The Black Commentator* after the 2004 reelection of George W. Bush and the postelection analysis suggesting that blacks in Ohio may have thrown the election to Bush.[4] An influential blog, *The Black Commentator* was celebrating the fact that while Bush prevailed nationally and in Ohio, his national share of the black vote was between 10 percent and 11 percent, a fairly standard showing for a Republican. From a voting-rights or voter-cohesion perspective, the black political consensus endured.

I have equated the cohesive voting behavior that characterizes African American politics to the existence of a de facto black party.[5] Cohesion is important legally and strategically.[6] The voting behavior of African Americans is not coincidental but rather has a structural explanation: historical and present-day social positions create distinct black interests.[7] The political science trio of Norman Nie, Sidney Verba, and John Petrocik traced black political liberalism to the earliest stages of systematic opinion surveys in the 1950s.[8] Even in the 1970s, as whites engaged in a backlash against the civil rights era, black opinion moved even more leftward, which Nie et al. characterized as the "extreme and homogeneous liberal opinion profile of blacks."[9]

In the latter part of the twentieth century, Robert C. Smith and Richard Seltzer observed that blacks were "near homogenously liberal when compared to whites" on economic policy.[10] In the 1990s, Smith and Seltzer continued to find large gulfs between blacks and whites regarding the role and scope of government. Tellingly, the largest chasm was on the question of whether government was spending enough to improve the living conditions of African Americans. An astonishing 85 percent of blacks felt too little was being spent, while only 26 percent of whites agreed.[11]

Social issues, however, painted a more complex picture of African Americans. Smith and Seltzer found that blacks were "somewhat more conservative than whites" on a host of social issues ranging from homosexuality to prayer in school to abortion.[12] This finding came with a significant caveat:

> [T]he data here suggest that even if conservative strategists were to…focus on lower-class mobilization around the social issues, it is unlikely they would have more than modest success. This is because socially conservative blacks, unlike whites, tend to vote their economic interests instead of their social and moral concerns. This is seen most dramatically in the liberal voting behavior of highly religious, socially conservative black voters compared to their white counterparts, in the 1984 election. For the foreseeable future, then, conservatives are likely to remain isolated on the fringes of mainstream black politics.[13]

Katherine Tate's examination of black public opinion similarly reveals that in the 1990s, blacks had become more conservative on social issues while demonstrating relative liberality on economic issues such as federally guaranteed jobs and a minimum standard of living.[14] Smith and Seltzer's prediction has come to pass in the new millennium, as they confirmed in a later work. In the 2004 Bush campaign during which same-sex marriage was used as a surrogate for moral values, blacks nevertheless ranked the economy and jobs as the number one issue; moral values was a distinct third.[15] Even among the 13 percent of blacks who regarded moral values as the most important issue, Bush claimed only 53 percent of the vote.[16] As I explore in more detail in chapter 3, blacks have not altered their liberal voting patterns, despite concerted appeals by black and white conservatives that they do so.

Moreover, race consciousness continues to be differentially salient among voting blocs. A 2010 Pew Research Center survey revealed that fully 81 percent of blacks believe that the government has not done enough to provide "equal rights" with whites. This compared to 36 percent of white respondents who shared this view and 47 percent of Latinos.[17] Forty-three percent of blacks believed that anti-black discrimination is pervasive, a figure basically unchanged from nearly a decade earlier and thus largely unaffected by Obama's election. Indeed, according to the survey, blacks were more than twice as likely as all respondents to view race as a major reason for opposition to President Obama's policies, with a majority of blacks identifying race as a major motivation. There is little wonder that one year into the Obama presidency, there was nearly a 40-point gap in Obama's favorability rating among African Americans and whites. Race—or more accurately, racial circumstance—remains a powerful source of political mobilization, a prism through which African Americans winnow a variety of political issues.

Ironically, the new black politics must rely on this consensus and cohesion even as it evades race-specific remedies to the circumstances that enervate black political solidarity and forecloses non-race-specific remedies by conceding the same policy grounds as Clintonian triangulation.

The Black Commentator's declaration that the black political consensus endures appears to remain true eight years after George W. Bush's controversial reelection, and more than 45 years after passage of the Voting Rights Act of 1965. But while consensus and black voting cohesion are sine qua nons of traditional black politics, the implementation within the broader polity of the societal vision represented by black politics is another matter. On this metric, we begin to see the fraying of traditional black politics, which in turn carries with it the potential to undercut consensus and cohesion.

Black Politics as a Vulnerable Subject

Institutions are vulnerable and can and do fail their constituents. As Martha Fineman writes in a challenge to the self-reliance precept of liberal theory, "Riddled with their own vulnerabilities, society's institutions cannot eradicate, and often operate to exacerbate, our individual vulnerability."[18] Black politics arose in response to the externally imposed vulnerability of African Americans wrought by centuries of slavery, Jim Crow, and private discrimination. But like other social institutions, it "may fail in the wake of market fluctuations, changing international policies, institutional and political compromises, or human prejudices."[19] In this section, I examine the broad causes of traditional black politics' current fragility.

Depending on the metric employed, however, it is not self-evident that black politics is failing. I have briefly discussed and will reiterate throughout this book black voters' high level of political cohesion. Importantly, this cohesion is accompanied by a similarly high level of liberal cohesion in the roll-call behavior of black elected officials. As revealed in table 1, a 20-year history of scorecard ratings by two liberal civil rights advocacy groups, the National Association for the Advancement of Colored People (NAACP) and the Leadership Conference on Civil and Human Rights (LCCHR), shows little

Table 1 NAACP/LCCHR 20-Year Roll-Call Scores for the CBC

101st Congress	(1989–91)	NAACP	93	LCCHR	92
102nd Congress	(1991–93)	NAACP	88	LCCHR	90
103rd Congress	(1993–95)	NAACP	87	LCCHR	93
104th Congress	(1995–97)	NAACP	91	LCCHR	90
105th Congress	(1997–99)	NAACP	93	LCCHR	92
106th Congress	(1999–01)	NAACP	94	LCCHR	93
107th Congress	(2001–03)	NAACP	91	LCCHR	97
108th Congress	(2003–05)	NAACP	92	LCCHR	96
109th Congress	(2005–07)	NAACP	95	LCCHR	98
110th Congress	(2007–09)	NAACP	97	LCCHR	99

variation in the average liberality score for the Congressional Black Caucus (CBC) over this period. With the exception of two sessions of Congress, the NAACP scores for the Caucus exceed the ninetieth percentile. LCCHR average scores for the Caucus were at or above the ninetieth percentile for all sessions of Congress. Tate has noted a liberal cohesion within the CBC during the 1990s that outstripped the liberality of blacks on a number of public policy issues.[20]

However, the fit between the roll-call behavior of black elected officials and the liberal consensus among black voters is a limited and misleading measurement of how well black politics is functioning. There is evidence that despite how liberal the CBC is, it could be more liberal still, even within the constrained context of roll-call votes. The *Swing State Project* set out to compare how Democratic a given congressional district is in presidential elections with how liberal the voting record of the district's representative is. Ranking all 435 congressional districts by the percentage its vote exceeded the national Democratic presidential vote, and then ranking the liberality of roll-call voting, a high partisan vote index score (PVI), and a lower liberality ranking would indicate that the representative was underperforming, and thus not fully representing, her district's interests. Comparing the 2008 presidential election returns with the *National Journal*'s liberality rankings for the 110th Congress, the *Swing State Project* found that 9 of the 20 most underperforming districts were represented by CBC members. Indeed, the top four underperformers were CBC members—Artur Davis of Alabama, Gregory Meeks of New York, Kendrick Meek of Florida, and William Jefferson of Louisiana.[21] More than a fifth of the Caucus's members underserve their districts by this metric. In the prior year, 2007, members of the CBC made up 11 of the top 20 underperforming representatives, exceeding a fourth of the Caucus's membership.[22]

Aggregate roll-call voting scores also mask significant instances of "inauthentic" voting by black representatives that betray the interests of their black constituents.[23] For instance, at the time Congress passed the Bankruptcy Abuse Prevention and Consumer Protection Act of 2005, black and Latino homeowners were 500 percent more likely to file for bankruptcy than whites. Yet nearly a fourth of the CBC supported the legislation, which made it more difficult and punitive to file for bankruptcy.[24] Many of the CBC members backing the legislation were, in turn, recipients of significant contributions from business interests. Perhaps most emblematic of inauthenticity within the CBC was former Alabama representative Artur Davis. Davis hailed from the poorest district among CBC members, yet voted for the bankruptcy bill. He would later oppose President Obama's signature overhaul of health care, prompting the Reverend Jesse Jackson to decry his actions: "You can't vote against healthcare and call yourself a black man."[25]

Political scientist Adolph Reed, Jr., however, identifies weak ideology rather than ideological inauthenticity as the cause of a fraying black politics. Reed has asserted that black politics has failed "to develop an effective language or practice of political opposition" in the postsegregation era.[26] While acknowledging that the causes of this inefficacy are multifactored, Reed trains on what he sees as the acquiescence of "black elites," including the black political gentry, to a "hegemonic national political discourse [that] has moved ever more in a conservative, victim-blaming direction."[27] Cornel West sounds a similar but more narrowly cast note in writing, "The crisis of black liberalism is the result of its failure to put forward a realistic response to the changes in the economy."[28]

What is initially striking about these critiques is their similarity to the broader critiques of the failures of liberalism—and more specifically, the Democratic Party—to create and message a coherent program to protect Americans from the ravages of a globalized economy and free-market ideology. Robert Kuttner is one of several economic writers to encapsulate the conundrum of liberalism and the Democrats:

> As government has largely ceased to offset the instability of markets, ordinary voters have given up on government making much of a difference in their lives....Republicans have been so successful at two rounds of tax cutting and deficit deepening...that many Democrats now see their main task as balancing the budget rather than restoring economic opportunity. This has the handy side effect of neutering the Democrats politically.[29]

The buffeting of traditional black politics is symptomatic of the vulnerability of larger social institutions like the Democratic Party and indeed government itself. The particularized vulnerability of black politics arises from the weaker socioeconomic baseline of African Americans, but politics is failing most Americans in some material respect. Consider the portrait of mass layoffs and underemployment scribed by Louis Uchitelle in *The Disposable American*. Nearly half of all American workers earned less than $13.25 an hour in 2004, an annual sum that barely escaped the poverty level for a family of four.[30] A 2008 analysis of the pay of individual American workers by tax analyst David Cay Johnston found that 49 percent of workers earned less than $25,000 annually.[31] A lack of skill or education cannot explain the suppressed wages of so broad a swath of the American workforce. The reason is instead a chronic paucity of skilled positions relative to the number of skilled workers.[32]

The steady decline of employment opportunity in the United States has been accompanied by a steady increase in income inequality. In 2008, the top 0.1 percent of income earners claimed more than 10 percent of all personal income in the United States, while the top 1 percent took in 20 percent of all income. In contrast, in 1975, the top 0.1 percent made only about 2.5 percent of the nation's income.[33] Despite opinion surveys showing that more than 60 percent of Americans agree or strongly agree that income inequality is too extreme, government has proven unwilling or unable to act against a malignancy that places the United States in the league of developing nations like Cameroon, Jamaica, and Uganda.

To sketch the broader failures of liberalism is to situate black liberalism as the weaker kindred it is. Steele's observation of a thin black ideology portrays a miscalculation by black leaders of the durability of the liberal welfare state.[34] Yet their very embrace of liberalism hastened its demise. It allowed the conflation of antiblack sentiment and opposition to the welfare state.[35]

One should be careful, however, not to overdetermine the shortcomings of black ideology in assessing the failure of black politics. First, liberalism's failure to redress harms from the vicissitudes of markets and a globalized economy is the mirror image of conservatism's ideological permissiveness of such harms. As Kuttner explains, it is the succumbing to conservatism, not a positivist vision of liberalism, that has alienated citizens from government.[36] Thus, the critique of black liberalism is not logically an endorsement of black conservatism. Both are deficient in different ways, and both suffer the inhibitions of the larger frames from which they derive.[37]

Overdetermination of inadequate black ideology carries another risk: the failure to examine electoral and institutional structures. That is, even if we assume a robust and unadulterated black political leadership, it must operate within the relatively confined two-party structure of American government. (This, of course, sets to one side alternatives to elective politics, such as protest.) Although not inscribed in the U.S. Constitution, the two-party system, in which virtually all candidates run and are elected as a Democrat or Republican, sharply curtails the ideological boundaries of political discourse, including discourse about race. Black nationalists rarely, if ever, inhabit the two-party sphere; the need to surpass 50 percent of the vote in what are generally bilateral elections douses the potential of such rhetoric.

The electoral structure also impedes minority access to what is arguably the most important legislative body in the world, the United States Senate. After the 2010 midterm elections, there were no African Americans serving in the Senate despite their 13 percent share of the U.S. population. The tradition of electing senators on a statewide, at-large basis rather than by district largely accounts for black invisibility.[38] I have argued that there is no constitutional requirement that this manner of electing senators be maintained, and I encapsulate that argument in chapter 8.

Lani Guinier makes a fundamental point about institutional structure that resounds in other scholars' works. Guinier contests a basic assumption of black electoral empowerment—that majority-black districts effectively represent the interests of most black voters. Principally, Guinier questions this assumption because the creation of black-majority districts does nothing to address institutional bias within a legislative body.[39] According to Guinier, black political effectiveness should be measured by "the actual ability to affect legislative decisionmaking, not simply, as now, the number of votes a representative controlled."[40]

Guinier's hypothesis has played out in the CBC. In his study of the CBC, Robert Singh observed that from 1971 to 1994, the CBC's priorities were not only unpopular among Republicans and conservative Democrats, they also lacked support among white liberals. Even during two Democratic administrations, the CBC failed to achieve its "redistributive legislative" goals.[41] Noting the similarly constraining nature of both the electoral and the institutional structure for ideological and racial minorities, Singh characterizes the institutional environment for the CBC as "inhospitable and centrifugal" and predicts very limited legislative success.[42]

If the vox populi of today's blogosphere is any indication, Singh's prediction is accurate. This medium reflects the view that political self-interest, ideological apostasy and vacuity, as well as electoral and structural impediments have all conspired to inter black politics. In a blistering critique of black leadership at all levels, including the presidency, *The Black Agenda Report* declared,

> Black politics, in the sense of elected officials that work to uplift the black community, is over. It's not over because inequalities are gone, or even lessened much. It's not over because we have achieved anything like economic or social justice. Black politics as we knew it is over because our elected leaders have given up on economic justice, and many of us have given up on them. It's been a long time coming.[43]

So in both scholarly and popular circles there is a deep sense of the decline of traditional black politics, even as the circumstances that necessitated it in the first place remain and even worsen. When people are disappointed with what they have, they will often seek a substitute—even a less adequate one. On this score, I briefly introduce the "new black politics" in the next section and connect it to the theme of triangulation before seeking a fuller understanding of the vulnerability of traditional black politics.

Enter the New Black Politics—and the New Politics of Triangulation

In *The Breakthrough*, journalist Gwen Ifill chronicles Barack Obama's rise to the presidency amidst the thorny issues of race and black intergenerational conflict. The exposé is revealing for what it does not reveal: the substantive basis of "the new black politics." But what the new black politics lacks in ideological content, it makes up for in electoral strategy. During the 2008 campaign, Obama's team was inevitably asked what his agenda was for black America. The campaign invariably responded, "It's the same as Barack Obama's agenda for all America."[44]

As a facet of psephology, this type of response is impeccable. As a matter of history and substantive governance, however, white-to-black-trickle-down theory intentionally elides the premise of the question. If black America's needs and circumstances were indistinct from white America's, then the response would be reasonable. But no rational person—and certainly not Obama or the highly talented individuals who ran his campaign—could believe this. For certain, members of the CBC do not. In the words of Congresswoman Donna Christensen, "[I]n terms of policy, there's no way that anybody in the CBC feels that a rising tide lifts all boats. There's just no way that we feel that."[45]

To use just one barometer of difference—but perhaps the most important one—since the end of World War II, the black unemployment rate has routinely been double the white unemployment rate, and blacks have been employed disproportionately in lower-echelon jobs.[46] To put a finer point on the distinctive role of race in employment opportunity even after Obama's election, blacks with a bachelor's degree or higher were 46 percent more likely to be *unemployed* than whites with a college degree or higher.[47] On the question of the Obama campaign's handling of race, Ifill steps back from her generally hagiographic tone to denude campaign rhetoric: "In narrowing the differences between Obama and the majority-white nation he was appealing to, the campaign simply set out to erase race as a negative. This was no accident. The formula counted on white voters to be comforted by this approach, and for black voters to be willing to look the other way."[48]

Would looking the other way for purposes of electing Obama also require black voters to look past their own interests during his term as president? Looking the other way certainly is not unheard of as a governing strategy. Liberals (including blacks) were successfully implored to do so during Clintonian triangulation. But Obama's triangulation would be sui generis in significant respects. First, it would be premised on African American pride in electing the first black president. That pride, in turn, would create a bond of trust that could potentially blind African Americans to the imperative of critical vigilance of performance, even in a time of catastrophic economic circumstances for blacks. Most importantly, Obama's triangulation would be performed on the corpse of traditional black politics, borrowing its vital organ— black voter cohesion—but evading any race-specific prescriptions or even rhetoric for issues that have long sustained that cohesion. To the extent white-to-black-trickle-down theory was a substitute for race specificity, Obama's likeness to Clintonian triangulation foreclosed the scale of government necessary to effectuate trickle down.

In the midst of this new triangulation, an enfeebled black politics would fail to find a way to reassert itself. A more detailed look at some of the externalities that have left black politics in this crouched position follows.

CHAPTER 2

Race and Money in Politics

For years, African-Americans have been taken for granted within the Democratic party, and at some point African-Americans should understand that their vote counts and they deserve more from the Democratic party...I'm black before I'm a Democrat.

—Missouri State Representative Jamilah Nasheed[1]

Corporations are people, my friend.

——2012 Republican presidential aspirant Mitt Romney[2]

The relationship between race and money in American politics is not obvious but is captured quite succinctly by the above quotes. Jamilah Nasheed was entangled in Missouri's 2011 race-infused redistricting in which the state lost one of its congressional seats. Republicans controlled both bodies of the state legislature and decided to eliminate the seat of Democrat Russ Carnahan, whose district was located in the St. Louis metropolitan area, as was that of William Lacy Clay, Jr., a black Democrat. Governor Jay Nixon, a Democrat, vetoed the remapping. To override, the Republicans in the assembly needed four Democrats. Four black Democrats supplied their votes for a plan designed to save two of the state's three Democratic congressional seats, both occupied by African Americans. Nasheed's statements underscore the dual role of blacks in the American political process as both the two-party system's most loyal partisans and a racial minority with interests distinct from either political party. As I demonstrate in this chapter, the United States Supreme Court has usually typecast blacks as merely a racial group and in so doing has treated them as outliers in a political process that it has heavily policed in order to ensure illusory colorblindness.

Money in politics, however, is another story. Mitt Romney was responding to a heckler who had suggested that he raise taxes on corporations since he was unwilling to hike individual income taxes. To Romney, however, corporations are people since "[e]verything corporations earn ultimately goes to people." But it doesn't. Much corporate money flows into the political process to buy influence in elections and legislation. The magnitude of this influence has been greatly expanded by the Supreme Court, whose attitude toward money in politics is so licentious that, like Romney, they accord corporations human standing. Indeed, the Court has arguably accorded money in politics greater standing than African Americans. That money, in turn, has served to debase black political ambition, fabricate a schism between the common interests of minorities and white voters, and constrain black political autonomy.

In this chapter, I aim to bring transparency to mutually reinforcing, judicially created political realities about race and money in politics. First, the Supreme Court's heightened scrutiny of race in the political process in the name of equal protection protects virtually no one except white voters. Second, when minority racial cohesion—deployed against blacks in the Court's racial gerrymandering cases—is properly understood as a political resource comparable to money, the Supreme Court's heightened regulation of race and its laissez-faire disposition toward money constitute discrimination against the black polity. Finally, to the degree that the Supreme Court's political process jurisprudence has allowed a measure of black political equality, its campaign finance rulings have in practice diminished the autonomy that is a central objective of political equality.[3]

Black Politics and the Juridical Burdens of Race

It would be difficult for today's Republican Party to become any whiter in its composition, though a small margin for complete homogenization remains. A 2011 Gallup Poll revealed that of those Americans who identify themselves as Republican or who lean Republican, 87 percent are non-Hispanic white.[4] This is not just a statistical flashpoint; this number has held steady since 2008.[5] About 68 percent of these Republicans and leaners identify themselves as ideological conservatives.[6] Although white conservative Republicans indignantly deny that race undergirds their politics—a denial belied by the 87 percent figure—all serious scholars of modern political conservatism view race as a significant factor in the rise of the conservative movement in 1964 (amidst the civil rights movement) and its success in attaining the presidency in 1980.[7] And it is not just scholars who recognize the role of race as a sorting mechanism in our party politics. Indeed, a healthy majority of Americans believe that the Civil War is "still relevant to American politics and public life today."[8]

Relatively few African Americans support the Republican Party. While the Democratic Party is disproportionately black and brown, it is far more representative of the racial composition of the general population than the Republican Party is.[9] I will discuss in more detail the depth of and reasons for black alienation from the Republican Party in the next chapter, but for now a couple of points are illuminating. In 2008, fewer than 2 percent of the delegates to the GOP presidential nominating convention were black.[10] Blacks are more than 12 percent of the country's population. In contrast, a record 24.5 percent of the Democrats' delegates were black in 2008. The GOP record for black delegates is 6.7 percent.[11] These numbers were not artifacts of Obama's historic nomination by the Democrats. Since 1936, the Republican Party has gone from a healthy share of the black vote in presidential elections that was as high as 39 percent in 1956 to a pattern of anemic black returns starting in 1964.[12] Since 1964, the Republican share of the black vote has not exceeded 15 percent, and that high-water mark was achieved more than 30 years ago by a moderate Republican, Gerald Ford.[13]

Suppose, as a juridical matter, the Supreme Court treated the Republican Party as the white party that it functionally is. Conservative white Republicans would then bear the same burdens of race in the political process that the Court has imposed on African Americans. Thus, when a state gerrymanders a district to elect a Republican—particularly when the shape of the district winds up appearing odd—that district would be subject to the highest level of constitutional scrutiny, as a comparable majority-minority district would be. The Court held in *Shaw v. Reno* and its progeny that where race predominates in the creation of an electoral district, the equal protection clause of the Fourteenth Amendment is presumptively violated unless the state can provide "compelling" reasons for its action.[14] The equal protection clause makes it illegal for a state to "deny to any person within its jurisdiction the equal protection of the laws."[15]

In contrast, if the Court treats the Republican gerrymander as a political rather than a racial gerrymander, the constitutional scrutiny accorded the state's actions is relatively lenient. In furtherance of the concept of two-party political stability, the Supreme Court allows the major parties to protect incumbents; to create proportional representation between the parties; or for one party to punish the other by drawing district lines to benefit itself.[16] If this seems out of character for a representative democracy, consider Justice Sandra Day O'Connor's defense of both the two-party system and the political gerrymander in *Davis v. Bandemer*:

> There can be little doubt that the emergence of a strong and stable two-party system in this country has contributed enormously to sound and effective government. The preservation and health of our political institutions, state and federal, depends to no small extent on the continued vitality of our two-party system, which permits both stability and measured change. The opportunity to control the drawing of electoral boundaries through the legislative process of apportionment is a critical and traditional part of politics in the United States, and one that plays no small role in fostering active participation in the political parties at every level.[17]

Although *Davis* recognized an equal protection claim for some forms of gerrymandering, a quarter century after that decision, the Supreme Court has yet to settle on a substantive standard for impermissible political gerrymandering and has yet to strike down a state's remapping on this ground.[18] There is one clear principle, though, that *Davis* announced and that state lawmakers continue to operate under: "[T]he mere fact that a particular apportionment scheme makes it more difficult for a particular group in a particular district to elect the representatives of its choice does not render that scheme constitutionally infirm."[19]

Throughout the 1990s, the Court struck down no fewer than six majority-minority congressional districts as unconstitutional racial gerrymanders, and lower courts, following the edict of *Shaw v. Reno*, struck down others.[20] Although these districts were some of the most racially integrated districts in the country, provided some states with their first black congressmen since Reconstruction, and in no way deprived white voters of proportional representation in any state, a five-justice conservative majority insisted that they bore "an uncomfortable resemblance to political apartheid."[21] Yet states continued to draw majority-white, conservative Republican districts, and to this day, the Court has not invalidated one as an unconstitutional racial gerrymander. Black politics gets refracted almost exclusively through race, while conservative white politics—despite a racial pedigree—gets refracted through ideology and partisanship. The effect of this illogical distinction is to make state action taken to enhance African American political equality suspect, while actions taken not only to benefit whites but also to promote a political ideology that is often antithetical to black interests are seen as unexceptional.

This confused race/politics symbiosis has been harmful not only to black politics but also to the Supreme Court's stated goal of color-blindness in politics. After *Shaw v. Reno,* states had a judicially gifted excuse to resist the creation of majority-minority districts. They had been resistant to begin with. The majority-minority districts in *Shaw* and in subsequent cases raising *Shaw* claims were not created out of states' racial benevolence. Rather, as the states acknowledged in defending these districts, they believed their creation was compelled by the Voting Rights Act of 1965. That act requires the creation of a majority-minority district under two circumstances. First, in states like North Carolina out of which *Shaw* arose, redistricting is done under the supervision of the United States Department of Justice (DOJ) or a federal court pursuant to §5 of the act.[22] North Carolina and several other states located principally in the South are "covered" jurisdictions whose redistricting is monitored to determine whether it retrogresses the electoral circumstances of minorities. The DOJ or a court can order the creation of a majority-minority district to prevent retrogression—that is, to prevent the implementation of a plan that renders the minority group worse off than they were under a jurisdiction's previously implemented plan.

The second circumstance in which the Voting Rights Act compels creation of a majority-minority district is where a plan dilutes the votes of a racial or language minority. A plan leads to this result under §2 of the act if (1) the minority is sufficiently large and compact to constitute a majority in a single-member district of its own; (2) the minority votes cohesively—that is, tends to prefer the same candidates; and (3) whites vote as a bloc and usually defeat the minority group's preferred candidate.[23] The defendant-states in *Shaw* and its progeny had relied preemptively on §2—that is, they sought to avoid a dilution suit. The states had also based the creation of their majority-minority districts on recommendations and objections of the DOJ during the §5 preclearance process. The Supreme Court, however, rejected these defenses, giving a narrow construction to both provisions of the Voting Rights Act.

Shaw created a needless tension between the mandates of the Voting Rights Act and the equal protection clause of the Fourteenth Amendment, making it more difficult for African Americans to secure the protections of the act and easier for states to elide its mandates. The Supreme Court subsequently further eroded the protections of the Voting Rights Act in *Bartlett v. Strickland* when it held that the statute simply does not apply if a single-race minority group cannot constitute a voting-age majority in a putative remedial district.[24] Thus, even if a minority group that is only 38 percent of a hypothetical §2 district might be able to elect the candidate of its choice with the aid of white crossover votes, these minority voters have no claim under the vote-dilution provisions of the act. Yet, given *Shaw*'s concerns with "political apartheid," it is precisely these types of cross-racial alliances that one would expect the act to encourage.[25]

Although they have made black political equality more difficult to protect, none of the Court's holdings have reduced the role of race in either redistricting or politics more generally. Barack Obama's presidential race buttresses rather than undermines this conclusion. Political scientists Michael Tesler and David Sears studied public opinion and voting during the historic 2008 presidential election and concluded that Obama's status as a black candidate led to an election that was "more polarized by racial attitudes than at any other time on record."[26] Even before 2008, in the decade following *Shaw v. Reno*, there was simply no evidence that the Court's promotion of color-blindness in the electoral process had actually reduced the role of race.[27] To the contrary, the nation continued to see highly racialized electoral contests and significant racially polarized voting at virtually all levels of government.[28]

Finally, recall Representative Nasheed's complaint that "African-Americans have been taken for granted within the Democratic party" and her remarks that "I'm black before I'm a Democrat." Far from reducing the role of race in redistricting, the totality of *Shaw*, its progeny, and *Bartlett*, increases race saliency in the redistricting process because, unable to rely on courts for protection, black voters and legislators must increasingly fend for themselves to promote black equality. Moreover, the Court's jurisprudence places a needless constraint on an already-reluctant Democratic Party's ability to reward black Democrats for their party fealty and to reduce the role of race by more thoroughly integrating blacks into the party's elected leadership. This disability in the political process obviously falls on the political party that has greater racial diversity; *Shaw* and its progeny reward a racially homogenous party—at least if it is white—by not treating actions taken to accommodate its various constituencies as racial.

Hamstringing the relationship between the Democratic Party and its core constituency is particularly perverse when one correctly apprehends the role of African Americans in the maintenance of the country's two-party system, a system that the Supreme Court equates with political stability. Were it not for Democrats' disproportionate share of the black vote, much two-party competition would be diminished. For instance, the 2010 Republican midterm landslide would have claimed far more Democrats absent overwhelming black support for that party. Tea Party-backed Republican Senate nominee Christine O'Donnell may have been the butt of national jokes for her past experimentation with witchcraft, but a majority of white voters in Delaware actually preferred her to her Democratic opponent. She lost because blacks supplied the margin of victory, giving 93 percent of their vote to Democrat Chris Coons.[29] A Tea Party-backed Republican would have also taken down Senate Majority Leader Harry Reid, who won only 42 percent of the white vote but whose combined 79 percent of the African American and 69 percent of the Latino vote was enough for victory.[30] In Obama's home state of Illinois, a Democrat who was expected to lose the governorship prevailed even though he won only 33 percent of the white vote. His margin of victory came from black voters, who turned up at the polls in a larger proportion than their population numbers and supplied the Democrat with 90 percent of their votes.[31]

There are literally thousands of election outcomes at all levels of government over the course of the last four decades that have been determined by Democrats' reliance on an outsized black—and sometimes Latino—vote while losing the white vote. Indeed, the most controversial and closest election in modern history, decided by the United States Supreme Court in *Bush v. Gore*, had racially polarized voting at its core.[32] The contest in Florida, where the national outcome hinged, was so close because black voter turnout exceeded the percentage of the black voting-age population, and blacks delivered a staggering 93 percent of their votes to Gore.[33] Examples like these go on interminably. But if American elections were decided by white voters alone, there would be far less party competition, if a two-party system could survive at all.[34] Simply put, our democracy has come to depend on black voter preferences that routinely diverge from those of the white majority.

The Supreme Court's extraordinary scrutiny of state action intended to promote black political equality is perverse in another regard: state action that harms the most basic requirement of political equality, namely the right to vote, is not subject to the same degree of scrutiny. Throughout our country today, legislatures have embarked on a variety of changes to state election laws that have a clear partisan intent and an equally clear racially disparate impact. Studies show that minorities, the elderly, and college students are significantly less likely to have state-issued photo identification than the general population.[35] Voter ID laws thus adversely affect these populations' access to the polls. Similarly, states are attempting to curtail early voting periods, to eliminate same-day registration, and to conduct purges of the voter rolls for a variety of reasons that have little to do with the integrity of the electoral process. These "reforms" adversely affect the right to vote—a right that, though not enumerated in the Constitution, has been treated as fundamental by the Supreme Court. Yet the Court has not applied its highest level of scrutiny to these "third generation" attacks on voting rights.[36] White voters' claim of a theoretic injury in *Shaw* racial gerrymandering cases is subjected to strict scrutiny and thus commensurately more likely to succeed. But unlike voters who are disproportionately affected by voter ID laws, white voters in majority-minority districts cannot demonstrate that the happenstance of their being in such a district in any way affects their access to the polls.

Given the untoward and unequal results of treating black politics atypically in the political process while according racial normalcy to conservative Republican—and a fortiori white—politics, a fairer and more intellectually honest judicial approach would recognize the multidimensionality of black voters. The Supreme Court purported to do this in *Easley v. Cromartie*, decided eight years after *Shaw*.[37] As in *Shaw*, plaintiffs in *Easley* claimed that race had predominated in the creation of one of the two congressional districts involved in *Shaw*. The district was just 47 percent black, but this did not deter plaintiffs. They maintained that the core of the new district was the same as the one struck down in *Shaw*. The state countered that it had created the district as a strong Democratic district. Because blacks in North Carolina are disproportionately Democratic, so too was the district.

The Court found for North Carolina. Writing for a five-justice majority, Justice Breyer concluded: "A legislature trying to secure a safe Democratic seat is interested in Democratic voting behavior. Hence, a legislature may, by placing reliable Democratic precincts within a district without regard to race, end up with a district containing more heavily African-American precincts, but the reasons would be political rather than racial."[38]

Both the majority and the dissent in *Easley* purported to be able to distinguish between race and partisanship. This was a pretense at judicial competence, for as we have seen in the case of white conservative Republicans, race gets comingled with partisanship in American politics. Yet the Court in *Easley* found it necessary to distinguish race from partisanship in order to extricate the Court from *Shaw*'s fiction that the black districts in *Shaw* and its progeny were racial and, as such, caused an undefined representational harm to the inhabitants of those districts. But a majority-minority district is almost always explainable on partisan or ideological grounds, as are white districts. *Easley* does not correct *Shaw*'s defect because it perpetuates the false distinction between race and partisanship, and, moreover, the false notion that courts are in any position to draw such a distinction. In the process, it perpetuates the equally false notion that white districts are ideological or partisan while majority-black districts must be specially scrutinized because they are more likely to be racial.[39]

The most accurate description of black voters is that they are a political group that coheres because of common historical and socio-economic circumstances arising from their race.[40] Indeed, race in its phenotypical sense has historically been irrelevant to these voters when they have been presented with the choice of a black conservative versus a progressive white candidate: they have preferred the white progressive.[41] This notion of race is akin to the conception that was set forth by Justice Stevens two decades before *Easley*:

> [I]t is the very political power of a racial or ethnic group that creates a danger that an entrenched majority will take action contrary to the group's political interests. The mere fact that a number of citizens share a common ethnic, racial, or religious background does not create the need for protection against gerrymandering. It is only when their common interests are strong enough to be manifested in political action that the need arises. Thus the characteristic of the group which creates the need for protection is its political character. It would be unrealistic to distinguish racial groups from other political groups on the ground that race is an irrelevant factor in the political process....Whenever identifiable groups in our society are disadvantaged, they will share common political interests and tend to vote as a "bloc." In this respect, racial groups are like other political groups.[42]

When black voters are understood as both a political and racial group, they fit neatly into Justice O'Connor's understanding in *Davis v. Bandemer* that participation in the districting process to reap its rewards is the way American two-party democracy works. This dualist notion of black electoral participation does not erase Voting Rights Act or constitutional claims for racial discrimination in the political process. First, demonstrating a violation of the Voting Rights Act does not require a showing of racial animus precisely because of the complexity of divining the intent of multiple legislative actors and voters. Second, in reference to constitutional claims where a showing of discriminatory intent is required, there have been and will continue to be circumstances where it is evident that racial animus is the driving force behind election-related decisions such as districting. The very fact that a political group coheres because of common racially discriminatory circumstances renders such a group susceptible to racial discrimination in the electoral process. But the same group's attempt to seek redress through the electoral process by claiming electoral districts for itself does not render its efforts any more racial than they are political.

Black Politics and the Juridical Burdens of Money: Black Candidate Inequality in the Money Race

If black politics is burdened by a juridical construction of race that privileges white conservative politics above black progressivism, it is no less burdened by and disadvantaged relative to money in politics. Money is not just another structural barrier to minority political equality—it lubricates the gears of a system of structural inequality. Thus, the relationship between black political inequality and money in the political process is hardly random, even if not always apparent, for money is deployed to debase black citizens, prevent cross-racial alliances, and interfere with the internal deliberations of the black polity. Indeed, as evidenced by electoral players such as Karl Rove's American Crossroads, and the billionaire Koch brothers-sponsored Americans for Prosperity, money fuels the modern conservative movement and, along with it, its attendant racial regressivism.

Consider a hypothetical black candidate, Candidate X, who is running in a congressional district that is 55 percent black, 40 percent white, and 5 percent Asian and Latino. If he typifies black candidates of the past, he is likely to be underfunded relative to his white opponent, according to studies that have examined racial differentials in the financing of campaigns.[43] Indeed, evidence of minority funding disparities for legislative offices can be found by looking at incumbent members of the Congressional Black Caucus (CBC). One study found that among major caucuses in the House of Representatives, CBC members had the lowest average net receipt of contributions—lower than even their Hispanic counterparts ($466,188 compared to $641,537).[44] Just as discrimination continues to play a role in voters' candidate preferences, it also plays a role in campaign contributions.[45]

Campaign finance inequality is a political reality about which members of the CBC are keenly aware. Congressman William Lacy Clay, Jr. has observed that progressive causes such as labor do not financially support black Democrats to a degree commensurate with their voting records, instead giving greater sums to more moderate white Democrats.[46] Clay argues that black representatives are held to a standard of ideological purity that white Democrats are not, but then are not rewarded for it.[47] In explaining why corporations are far more willing to make philanthropic contributions to the Congressional Black Caucus Foundation than they are political contributions to individual members of the CBC, Congresswoman Yvette Clarke explains, "[I]t's a lot easier to get someone to address a social issue when it comes to the African-American experience than it is to get someone to empower you politically."[48] According to Clarke, corporations see a benefit—a tax write-off, among others—in being able to boast that they have given back to the black community, which contains many of their customers. They do not see a comparable benefit in empowering blacks politically.[49] Thus, whether it is from natural allies like labor, or from labor's counterpart, corporate America, black politicians generally get shortchanged in the political money race.

Yet campaign dollars are the "mother's milk" of the electoral process, to borrow a phrase used by Congresswoman Clarke. The reasons why are not a secret to any observant American. According to the Center for Responsive Politics, in 2008, the biggest spender in House of Representatives elections won in 93 percent of the contests, while the larger spender won in 94 percent of the Senate races, continuing a trend of money prevailing in U.S. federal elections.[50] In his 2010 State of the Union address, President Obama accused the Supreme Court of "open[ing] the floodgates for special interests—including foreign corporations—to spend without limit in our elections."[51] It is rare that a sitting president criticizes the Supreme Court for one of its decisions during a State of the Union address—at which Supreme Court justices themselves are present. But then again, the Supreme Court opinion to which the president was referring, *Citizens United v. FEC*, is a rare decision.[52] To understand the import of the decision, both generally and as it relates to black political inequality, it is helpful to know a few basic terms. The funding in relation to Candidate X has to do with "hard money." Hard money is contributions given directly to candidates, party committees, or political action committees (PACs). The allowable amounts and sources of these contributions are limited by federal law.[53] In *Buckley v. Valeo*, the Supreme Court upheld limitations on hard money contributions as a valid governmental means of preventing quid pro quo corruption as well as preventing "the appearance of corruption stemming from public awareness of the opportunities for abuse inherent in a regime of large individual financial contributions."[54]

In contrast to hard money contributions, the Court in *Buckley* refused to uphold expenditure limitations. Here, it is again helpful to understand another campaign finance term, "independent expenditures." These are sums of money spent on behalf of candidates by persons or groups who are forbidden by law from coordinating their expenditures with a candidate's campaign. The *Buckley* Court saw no danger in actual corruption or the appearance of corruption in such expenditures, and, moreover, it rejected the government's purported interest in ensuring equality in the electoral process by limiting independent expenditures. As the *Buckley* majority explained: "[T]he concept that government may restrict the speech of some elements of our society in order to enhance the relative voice of others is wholly foreign to the First Amendment, which was designed to secure the widest possible dissemination of information from diverse and antagonistic sources, and to assure unfettered interchange of ideas for the bringing about of political and social changes desired by the people."[55]

Despite *Buckley's* permissiveness regarding independent expenditures, the law before and after *Buckley* prohibited corporations (and unions) from using their general treasuries to make independent expenditures. The Supreme Court had upheld this prohibition out of concern for "'the corrosive and distorting effects of immense aggregations of wealth that are accumulated with the help of the corporate form and that have little or no correlation to the public's support for the corporation's political ideas.'"[56] *Citizens United* changed this. Deciding an issue that was not even raised by the parties to the litigation, a conservative, five-justice majority of the Court concluded that, as Romney believes, corporations are people in the political process. Thus, just as it was impermissible under the First Amendment to restrict an individual's or a group's independent expenditures, so too was it unconstitutional to restrict corporate independent expenditures.[57]

Although *Citizens United* in its narrowest respect simply held that corporate independent expenditures must be treated the same as independent expenditures by a person, lower court and Federal Election Commission (FEC) interpretations of the decision have led to an evisceration of key contribution limitations. Thus, if a corporate PAC only engages in independent expenditures on behalf of candidates, it can accept unlimited individual and corporate contributions.[58] This interpretation has given rise to so-called super-PACs: large and unlimited aggregations of contributions that can be used to support a candidate so long as there is no coordination between the PAC and the candidate's campaign.[59] The notion of no coordination, however, is more mythical than real. Many of these super-PACs now undertake functions that have traditionally been performed by the candidate himself.[60]

There is now a virtual labyrinth of money flowing into elections in the United States. Already left behind in the hard money race, black candidates like Candidate X must now compete in a shadow system of campaign finance where they are no more likely to draw equal dollars than in the traditional system. The Supreme Court equates money with expression and expression with democracy. But democracy is incompatible with political inequality, and one manifestation of the inequality bred by money is the underfinancing of candidates of color. This inequity compounds *Shaw v. Reno*'s judicially fabricated inequality that makes race a liability for African Americans when they seek representation in the political process but accords legal normalcy to a virtually all-white political party that seeks the same. The Court has at once made it more difficult to justify creating majority-minority districts while at the same time making it more difficult for black candidates to succeed in non-majority-minority districts because money is a constitutionally privileged political resource of which black candidates receive less.

CITIZENS UNITED/RACES DIVIDED: HOW MONEY IS DEPLOYED AGAINST AFRICAN AMERICAN CANDIDATES AND INTERESTS

Already at a likely fundraising disadvantage, the hypothetical black Candidate X must worry about how money will be used against him. If his opponent is white, and if history is any guide, he must be concerned about racial cuing. And with the ability of outside interests to make unlimited independent expenditures, he must also concern himself with third parties' injection of race into the campaign. Racial cuing is the often subtle (but sometimes overt) priming of racial stereotypes or fears as a subliminal (or overt) prism through which to assess a candidate or an issue.[61] It is best exemplified by a controversial television ad against Democratic presidential nominee Michael Dukakis launched during the 1988 campaign. The ad focused on

Willie Horton, a black convict on furlough who assaulted a white couple, raping the woman. The ad was deployed to portray Democrat Dukakis as soft on crime, and is now widely viewed as a textbook example of racial cuing.

In Warren Beatty's *Bulworth*, Senator Jay Bulworth is a dated, erstwhile liberal attempting to dissemble himself in Clintonian, "New Democrat" clothing in order to withstand a primary challenge. Suicidally depleted by the whole charade as well as by the money chase of politics in general, Bulworth finds a political and spiritual elixir in the socially disrupted, rap-saturated ghettos of Los Angeles. It is there that he witnesses the gratuitous brutality of white cops against black youths and is lectured on the life-and-death economics of an inner-city drug trade which, on one view of it, offers the most discrimination-free employment available to black youngsters.

The abandoned inner city and its dark inhabitants are curious vehicles for the mantra of Bulworth's campaign: campaign finance reform. Or are they? Senator Bulworth, who is white and has become moderately well-off, rationalizes the linkage between the plight of black urbanites and campaign finance reform: "Rich people have always stayed on top by dividing White people from colored people. But White people got more in common with colored people than they do with rich people."

Bulworth portrays cinematically an everyday truth about money's role in politics: much political money is deployed to stoke the nation's longstanding racial divisions and to prevent poor and lower middle-class whites from recognizing what legal theorist Camille Gear Rich refers to as their "marginal whiteness." Rich argues that "once [low-status whites] become aware that calls to whiteness invariably privilege one or more subgroups of whites' interests at the expense of others, whites will learn to more skeptically evaluate claims about how existing institutional structures benefit whites, and may even come to resent whiteness overtures."[62]

Whiteness overtures purchased by the ubiquitous money in politics have long prevented many whites from recognizing their marginality as citizens. The Willie Horton ad is part of a long pedigree that has continued to the present day. When a Nixon for President commercial claimed that the country had been deluged with programs for the unemployed and the poor and that it was time to take people from welfare rolls and place them on payrolls, "[i]t would appear that Nixon meant to keep poor and black America separate from middle America, and he was signaling middle America that, if elected, he would 'protect' them from the welfare cheats, youthful hoods, and other shiftless people on the dole."[63] Is race not at work when Bernard Epton, a white candidate challenging Harold Washington, a black congressman, for mayor of Chicago ends his commercials with "Epton—Before It's Too Late"?[64] And when Peter Fitzgerald, running against Carol Moseley-Braun, the first African American woman ever elected to the United States Senate, airs television advertisements implying that his opponent misappropriated campaign funds to purchase luxury personal items despite the absence of any such determination by the relevant investigative authorities,[65] his message is one of black criminality and profligacy as much as anything else.

The 2010 midterm elections saw racial cuing recast to fit the misinformation that surrounds the first African American president, such as the myth that he is Muslim. One ad against a West Virginia Democratic congressman of Lebanese origins drew a connection between the congressman's early support of Obama's presidential bid and the congressman's affiliation with Arab American organizations.[66] Other variations of cuing focused on the Latino community, but in so doing, they made certain to portray Latinos as visibly "swarthy" or brown-skinned. Nevada Tea Party–backed Senate candidate Sharron Angle produced multiple spots of this nature.[67]

Each election cycle, ads of varying degrees of race potency hit the airwaves and radio waves and invite white voters to consider matters that have little to do with the issues that most affect their well-being. In addition to television and radio ads, broadcast and print media segments that focus on race also have the potential to prime racial stereotypes.[68] No consensus exists regarding the effectiveness of political commercials generally.[69] But race-cuing ads are sui generis in that their effectiveness is measured in large part by what they do not say. Explicit racial appeals violate our widely embraced norms of equality, and thus are unlikely to be successful.[70] An implicit appeal such as the Willie Horton ad has greater potency precisely because it invites a white viewer to make an association between race and crime that does not alert him to the possibility that he is violating equality norms.[71] Priming summons preexisting but often subconscious biases, for as Tali Mendelberg reminds us in her groundbreaking book *Race Card*, "Campaigns…rarely alter racial predispositions, but they do activate or deactivate racial predispositions in the mind, leading citizens to give greater or lesser weight to them."[72]

Racial cuing will be of particular concern to the hypothetical black Candidate X in a biracial contest in which 40 percent of the electorate is white. The percentage of whites in an electorate is highly determinative of a race-cuing ad's effectiveness.[73] The fewer majority-minority districts there are, the more vulnerable black candidates and voters become to white susceptibility to be distracted by race (and racism). We will return to the subject of racial cuing in chapter 6 both in relation to Barack Obama and black candidates generally, but it is important to appreciate this phenomenon as a byproduct of the Supreme Court's solicitous view of money in politics and as an integral feature of modern black political inequality.

OTHER PEOPLE'S MONEY: RACE AS EXPRESSION

"But money is speech!" some will say. The Supreme Court agrees. But citizens have different speech resources. Money is just one. There is no good reason to privilege it. Recall the discussion of black political cohesion from chapter 1 and the expansion upon that concept in this chapter. This political cohesion is also a form of expression in the political process. The right of citizens to aggregate their votes with like-minded fellow citizens in order to acquire power in government is as fundamental to the First Amendment as the right to spend unlimited sums of money on behalf of a candidate in order to gain power in government.[74] Vote aggregation meets at the nexus of free speech and free association. Government action that burdens the ability of citizens to exercise this fundamental right should be subject to the same protections the Supreme Court has afforded the expenditure of money. The Supreme Court has determined that restrictions on independent expenditures—the type of money at issue in *Citizens United*—"reduces the quantity of expression by restricting the number of issues discussed, the depth of their exploration, and the size of the audience reached."[75] But if this is true of money, is it not also true where a state restricts consideration of racial diversity in its legislative apportionment? Why should our democracy depend on wealth alone to determine which issues of the day will receive attention?[76]

Under the Supreme Court's jurisprudence, a state voter photo identification law that would make it more difficult for minorities to vote is constitutionally permissible even though the state lacks a shred of evidence that voter fraud has ever been a problem. This is precisely what occurred in a recent Supreme Court case arising out of Indiana, and is precisely what is occurring throughout the country presently. Yet the money that pours into the political system to support candidates who vote for laws that suppress minority access to the polls is virtually unregulated because groups can raise and expend unlimited sums on behalf of such candidates as long as they do not coordinate with the candidates' campaigns. If minority voters in Indiana wish to offset the influence of money by collectively petitioning the legislature for more minority-controlled districts that will elect representatives more sympathetic to their plight, they are met with the strictures of *Shaw v. Reno* and its progeny. Indeed the very act of blacks lobbying the legislature as a racially identifiable group can be used as evidence of an equal protection violation.[77] If minorities can demonstrate that they can effectively control a district as a plurality with the support of white crossover voters, under *Bartlett v. Strickland*, even if the minority lacks an equal opportunity to elect its preferred candidate in the absence of such a district, they are not entitled to a crossover district. Simply put, the Court has constitutionally hamstrung citizens of color from protecting their interests in the political process while allowing money to directly and indirectly damage those same interests in the name of free speech.[78]

Equality versus Autonomy: Black Votes, White Dollars

Let us assume that Candidate X prevails in his congressional race. This is a victory for political equality. But political equality is illusory unless it is accompanied by a measure of autonomy. Suppose, for instance, that Candidate X, though black, is not the preferred candidate of the majority of black voters. Instead, he is elected by gaining a preponderance of the white vote and some black votes. (This would be a likely scenario in a Democratic primary.) The election of Candidate X promotes the perception of equality, but that perception belies the reality that a majority of black voters have not been able to elect the candidate of their choice in a majority-black district. Quite simply, equality is distinct from autonomy, and the history of the movement for black political equality reflects an equal concern with the achievement of some measure of subgroup autonomy.[79]

But what if Candidate X prevailed with a majority of the black vote but was funded by campaign contributions from whites or white-led organizations? In this regard, Candidate X would be a prototype of the average black candidate. But is it possible to have black political autonomy if whites finance black politics? Black political dependence on white campaign contributions affects black political power in at least two distinct but interrelated ways. First, white dollars have the potential to influence the votes and issue stances taken by black representatives, and even if they do not in fact exert such influence, they still give rise to the appearance of undue influence by white interests.

Second, white dollars may interfere with black political choice by empowering candidates who may be black but who are not the black-preferred candidate.

The extent of minority voters' campaign giving is under-studied, yet there is substantial evidence of minority underrepresentation.[80] During the 2000 election cycle, a mere thirty zip codes gave twenty or more contributions to black candidates. Of those thirty zip codes, only six had majority-black populations.[81] In the 2004 election cycle, predominantly black zip codes contributed only 2.7 percent of the federal campaign contributions of $200 or more.[82] Predominantly Latino zip codes contributed only 2.2 percent of the federal campaign contributions of $200 or more. Non-Latino white zip codes provided 89.1 percent of federal campaign contributions of $200 or more during the 2004 election cycle despite the fact that nonwhites constitute 24.8 percent of the United States population. Federal campains thus appear to be disproportionately financed by white Americans.

All major 2004 presidential candidates raised the bulk of their individual contributions of more than $200 from majority non-Latino, white neighborhoods.[83] This means the two African American candidates, Carol Moseley Braun and Reverend Al Sharpton, both raised most of their campaign funds from white neighborhoods.[84] Although the 2004 presidential contest marked a watershed in the rate of giving by small donors (those contributing $100 or less),[85] there is no evidence that voters of color participated in this uptick in small-donor participation. Indeed, the Institute for Politics, Democracy & the Internet, which reported on the increase in contributions by small donors during the 2004 presidential election, provided demographic data on income, education, age, gender and religious faith—but not race.[86] Nevertheless, the data presented suggests voters of color were not participants in this phenomenon, for "[t]he small donors stand somewhere between large donors and the general public in many respects. Small donors were neither as wealthy nor as highly educated as large donors, although they were more so than the general population."[87] Given the socioeconomic indicators that portray blacks and Latinos as lagging the general public, it is a fair inference that the new small-donor class is disproportionately white.

The only published analysis that suggests black candidates raised most of their funds from black constituents focused on local elections in North Carolina. The study examined elections in Charlotte and

Mecklenburg County from 1975 to 1980, finding black Democrats constituted 89 percent of the contributors to black Democratic candidates.[88] However, the study did not indicate that the majority of those candidates' campaign funds came from black contributors.[89]

Thus, the likelihood is that the victorious campaign of Candidate X has been financed largely by white dollars. But if the voting scorecards of the National Association for the Advancement of Colored People (NAACP) and the Leadership Conference on Civil and Human Rights (LCCHR) reviewed in chapter 1 are indicative of the progressive record of most CBC members, perhaps the receipt of white money simply has no effect on black legislators' performance in office. A principal schism in the campaign finance reform debate has been over whether money buys influence. On the one hand, there are former Federal Election Commission Chairman Bradley Smith's repeated assertions that "[t]he plain and simple fact is that research shows, over and over, that campaign contributions just aren't that important."[90] On the other hand, there is the Supreme Court's thorough refutation of Smith's academic perspective in *McConnell v. FEC*,[91] which relied on the experience of legislators themselves in upholding key provisions of the McCain-Feingold campaign finance reform bill against constitutional attack.[92] But if we accept *McConnell*'s premise that money purchases access to candidates and influence,[93] what then is the relationship among black candidates and elected representatives, and the primarily white dollars that fund their campaigns?

Lani Guinier suggests that we can no more assume the authenticity of black representatives under these circumstances than we could if those representatives were elected from a majority-white district.[94] While Guinier's focus was the color of the votes cast for black candidates, the critical question is whether there is equal reason to suspect less authentic minority representation when the minority candidate must substantially depend on whites to finance his campaign.

We are handicapped in this inquiry by the lack of scholarly attention afforded the effects of campaign finance laws on minority candidates, representatives, and voters.[95] Nevertheless, Congress's passage of the Bankruptcy Abuse Prevention and Consumer Protection Act of 2005[96] and other legislation thought to be inimical to minority interests may offer some cautionary insights. According to the Leadership Conference on Civil and Human Rights, black and Latino homeowners are 500 percent more likely to file bankruptcy than whites.[97] That venerable civil rights organization opposed the bankruptcy bill, which, among other punitive changes, created a presumption of abuse of bankruptcy if the debtor's income exceeds a specified threshold.[98] However, ten members of the then forty-one member CBC voted in favor of the legislation.[99] Several of the ten defectors had been heavily funded by and otherwise connected with business interests.[100] For instance, Representative Artur Davis of Alabama, who hailed from the poorest district among Caucus members, collected 75 percent of the monies he spent in his 2004 primary from business interests.[101] Similarly, Representative David Scott of Georgia received 66 percent of his 2005–2006 funding from PACs; 80 percent of the PAC money came from business PACs.[102]

Scott is one of four Caucus members who not only voted in favor of the bankruptcy legislation but also for two other issues—repeal of the estate tax and energy legislation—that were either antithetical to black interests or almost exclusively beneficial to wealthy white interests.[103] Davis voted for two of the three.[104] Only a fraction of one percent of blacks stood to benefit from repeal of the estate tax, and the energy legislation provided massive subsidies to the oil industry.[105] Davis and the CBC members who aligned on bankruptcy, the estate tax, and the energy bill shared a similar fundraising profile: a significant source of their campaign funds came from business interests.[106]

The concern over the influence of money in politics has not been limited to quid pro quo corruption,[107] nor should concerns be so limited in examining the relationship of politicians of color to white money. If the appearance of corruption can serve as a constitutional basis for regulating contributions and banning "soft money,"[108] the "inauthentic" behavior by politicians of color who receive significant campaign funds from white interests is a legitimate basis for at least questioning whether white largesse can finance minority political autonomy.[109] In 2010, the conduct of CBC members vis-à-vis corporate donations came into sharp relief in a *New York Times* exposé. In addition to its political action committee, the CBC operates a nonprofit organization, the CBC Foundation. From 2004 to 2008, the Foundation collected over $55 million in corporate and union donations. The ostensible purpose of these contributions is to provide scholarships and internships for disadvantaged African Americans, conduct seminars on topics relevant to African Americans, and generate policy papers.[110] Given the fund-raising imbalances that black candidates ordinarily face, it is puzzling that the CBC would use its instrumentalities to fund endeavors unrelated to the political growth of its own Caucus. Only about a million of the $55 million went to the CBC's PAC.[111]

But even the charitable purposes of the CBC were not met. According to the *New York Times*, the bulk of the $55 million was spent on "elaborate conventions." More disturbing, however, was the array of corporate interests that made substantial contributions: cigarette companies, internet poker operators, alcoholic beverage companies, and rent-to-own businesses.[112] These are industries whose products are regarded by many as being harmful to African Americans. The CBC Foundation's director candidly admits that these companies are seeking access and influence: "They are trying to get the attention of the C.B.C. members. And I don't think there is anything wrong with that. They're in business, and they want to deal with people who have influence and power....Black people gamble. Black people smoke. Black people drink," she said in an interview. "And so if these companies want to take some of the money they've earned off of our people and give it to us to support good causes, then we take it."[113]

There is absolutely nothing unusual about the fact that corporate interests seek to influence CBC members through available legal channels. But politics-as-usual is problematic for the CBC. The CBC, according to Representative Barbara Lee of California, is supposed to be "the conscience of the Congress."[114] Lee declares that CBC members are "unbossed and unbought," as does every other congressman who receives corporate largesse. But if *McConnell* is correct that money buys access and influence, black voters can no more assume the probity of their representatives than can white voters. Moreover, if *Buckley v. Valeo* is correct in its assumption that the appearance of undue influence can be as troubling as its actual existence, black politicos are placed in the awkward position of appearing compromised by the American political money chase but receiving few of the benefits that inure to their white counterparts.

Let us examine Candidate X in one final iteration to explore the second way in which white political money threatens black political autonomy. Suppose that Candidate X, who is now Congressman X, is consistently progressive in his voting, and, moreover, is consistently outspoken on a number of black-related and non-race-related national and foreign policy issues. That is, suppose Congressman X's style is closer to former representative Cynthia McKinney than to former representative Artur Davis. Like McKinney in 2002 and again in 2006, Candidate X seeks reelection in his marginally black district, secures a majority of the black vote in the Democratic primary, but is defeated by a black opponent who carries the white vote by a substantial margin.[115]

Money played a key role in McKinney's 2002 primary defeat as well as the defeat of another black incumbent, Earl Hilliard. McKinney and Hilliard were both outspent by opponents who were heavily financed by outside corporate and other white contributors. In his 2002 defeat, Hilliard raised $812,164.[116] In contrast, his opponent, Artur Davis, raised $1,567,429.[117] In the same election cycle, McKinney raised $953,621 compared to $1,935,723 for her successful opponent, Denise Majette.[118]

The comparison of Congressman X to McKinney and Hilliard might encourage a discursion on the part of some who will note that McKinney in particular was "controversial," advocating on behalf of Palestinians in the Middle East and floating conspiracy theories about the U.S. government's role in the 9/11 attacks. These responses are understandable, but they are ultimately beside the point. First, there have been and remain plenty of "extreme," right-leaning white representatives in Congress—for example, Tom Tancredo, Michele Bachmann, Steve King, and so forth. Any notion of political equality that entitles whites to elect nonmainstream white candidates but restricts the ideological spectrum from which black voters may choose black representatives is the very essence of equality without autonomy. More importantly, §2 of the Voting Rights Act of 1965 explicitly ensures minority voters an equal opportunity "to elect representatives of their choice," unqualified by reference to whether those candidates are too controversial for white voters.[119] To be sure, in the words of the Supreme Court, "minority voters are not immune from the obligation to pull, haul, and trade to find common political ground[.]"[120] But if whites are afforded a disproportionately greater opportunity to elect nonmainstream candidates than blacks, neither the letter nor the theory of the Voting Rights Act is satisfied. Moreover, if the money that the Supreme Court has permitted to become so essential to elections in our democracy is more likely to go to "mainstream" black candidates than outliers who may be preferred by black voters, then political money abets an artificial moderation of black politics and a curtailment of black subgroup autonomy.

Law, Race, Money, and Triangulation

Let us return to the construct of post-racial triangulation introduced in chapter 1 and recall a common premise of both political and post-racial triangulation: it is the weaker plank of the triangle that suffers. Triangulation is not an equal-opportunity form of manipulation. Supreme Court jurisprudence on race and money in politics, and the

Court's failure to recognize the imbricate relationship between the two, have made traditional black politics considerably less robust than it would be under a less race-averse juridical framework. The Court has, in short, helped to render blacks susceptible to triangulation in the political process, indeed far more susceptible than white voters are under most circumstances.

If disadvantageous jurisprudence existed in a vacuum, then black politics would perhaps still be able to maintain its robustness. But law does not exist in a vacuum. It interacts with other institutions and political phenomena that also deplete black politics of its effectiveness. The combination of these factors helps us to understand how and why black voters have become the object of triangulation. In the two chapters that follow, I explore two parasitic political phenomena, black conservatism and Latino swing-vote rhetoric, that interact on the judicial landscape sketched in this chapter and further soften traditional black politics for post-racial triangulation.

CHAPTER 3

Black Tea: Black Conservatives and the Rhetoric of Social Conservatism

Moderator: Um, anything else?

Blogger: Yes, thank you. Um, I wanted to ask you regarding your inclusion of diverse populations of the Republican Party, what is your plan moving forward?

Michael Steele: My plan is to say, "Y'all come" (laughter) because a lot of you are already here.

Unknown commentator: I'll bring the collard greens!

MS: There ya go! I got the fried chicken and potato salad ok. (laughter) No, the goal of this party has been from its inception about inclusion. How do I know that? Well damn, it's a pretty inclusive idea to say black people are human beings and should not be slaves.[1]

There was a period before Obama's election when former national GOP chairman Michael Steele could be taken more seriously than the mainstream media now does and when the Republican Party appeared to be slowly progressing in a strategy to whipsaw traditional progressive black politics between the currents of race solidarity on the one hand and a supposed untapped affinity to conservative principles on the other. This is no longer the case. Consider this stark irony: 2010 produced the largest bumper crop of black Republican candidates since Reconstruction, many of them inspired by Obama's election as the first African American president.[2] Yet the election of Obama, a Democrat, as the first black president presages the consolidation of black support for the Democratic Party for years to come. Black Republicans are largely to blame.

Why? Ask Michael Steele. Steele came to DePaul University on a sun-drenched but chilly Chicago day in April 2010 at the invitation of DePaul's Department of Political Science and its chapter of the

College Republicans. The canned format, in which Steele would not take questions directly from the audience, did not prevent a moment of recoiling candor when the moderator asked Steele, why should an African American support the Republican Party? Steele's response would reverberate through the media: "You really don't have a reason to, to be honest—we haven't done a very good job of really giving you one. True? True."[3]

One need look no further than Steele's statement for an explanation of why black conservatives have been complicit in the Democratic capture of black voters: they (and the Republican Party) have failed to provide a viable alternative. Electoral capture is a condition under which neither of the two major parties in the United States has an incentive to address the concerns of African Americans. Republicans do not because they derive greater electoral benefit from racializing politics than addressing black concerns. Democrats can therefore soft-pedal black interests and take black votes for granted.[4] The election of a black Democrat as president adds a fresh dynamic to this historical pattern. Democrats could become more responsive, or they could exploit the symbolism of having elected a black man and triangulate black voters by distancing Obama from the substantive concerns of traditional left-of-center, race-conscious black politics. In this way, Obama could insulate himself from the ire of white voters. As will be explained more fully in part 2 of this book, Obama has opted for the latter. This chapter explains the enabling, if counterintuitive, role of black conservatives in the new politics of triangulation.

In his provocatively titled work *The Emerging Black GOP Majority*, political commentator Earl Ofari Hutchinson explores the challenges facing the GOP in attracting black voters. According to Hutchinson, the GOP had to forge a marriage between the party's political conservatism and blacks' "inherent social conservatism," appear colorblind while making racial appeals, and make the GOP a more moderate, racially inclusive party.[5] Hutchinson was writing in 2006, two years after George W. Bush had secured reelection in part by emphasizing to black voters the GOP's support for anti-gay marriage propositions on many states' ballots. In 2006, three credible statewide black Republicans—Ken Blackwell of Ohio, Lynn Swann of Pennsylvania, and Michael Steele himself—demonstrated how the party's running black candidates could siphon off greater numbers of black votes from the Democratic column. But it was also two years prior to the rise of Obama, not to mention the advent of the racially tinged Tea Party movement. What was a daunting task before Obama's election suddenly became a distinct impossibility for the foreseeable future. Black voters would be no better off for having been courted by the GOP.

Racial symbolism is often a crude proxy for substantive positions in American politics. The famous "white-hands" commercial telegraphed Senator Jesse Helms' opposition to affirmative action and racial progressivism generally to white voters in North Carolina.[6] Conversely, the GOP's appointment of its first black chairman 20 years after the Democrats elected Ron Brown as their first was a response to the election of Obama as the first black president. Some proxies, however, are cruder than others. The GOP's use of black candidates and appointed officials has rarely telegraphed racial liberalism because neither those individuals nor the GOP have typically embraced it. Instead, the GOP's invitation to African American voters is one in which these voters are invited to discover long-overlooked political commonalities with conservative white voters.

It is, in short, an invitation to the funeral of traditional black politics even as the socioeconomic conditions enervating that movement remain alive and unaddressed by the invitation. To appreciate the absence of hyperbole in this assertion, it is helpful to first reexamine a basic tenet of black politics: voter cohesion. This will help in making a cost-benefit assessment of the GOP invitation. Second, let us examine the relative racial progressivism of the two major parties, both in modern and historical terms. This will allow us to probe both the earnestness and feasibility of the GOP invitation. Then let us examine the ways, if any, in which black conservatives diverge from GOP conservative orthodoxy. This will tell us whether the GOP and black conservatives merely traffic in symbolism or whether the presence of black candidates on the frontline has some substantive effect on Republican policy relevant to African Americans.

LESS IS MORE?

Black voter cohesion is perhaps the most visible permutation of racial essentialism in modern American culture. It is an inconvenient fact for proponents of uncategorical American individualism. Justice Clarence Thomas has criticized longstanding jurisprudence that recognizes the right of minority voters to elect their preferred candidate in some instances. To Thomas, judicial recognition of the reality that minorities often prefer a different candidate to the white majority succumbs to the stereotype that minorities "must all think alike on matters of important public policy."[7] Yet Thomas has never been able to reconcile his concerns with the facts of American political life: since

1964, blacks have consistently delivered at least 80 percent of their votes to Democratic presidential candidates.[8] Obama's 95 percent showing among black voters marked the pinnacle of this trend. At the same time, only once in the past 48 years—in 1964—has a majority of white voters preferred the Democratic presidential candidate. In the past 20 years, white voters nationally have never delivered a majority of their votes to congressional Democrats. In contrast, the lowest percentage that black voters have supplied is 82 percent.[9] If these numbers do not suggest racially distinct partisan and candidate preferences, it is hard to imagine what evidence would. Dismissing the judicial protection of minorities' candidate preferences as stereotyping confuses Steele's "fried chicken" invitation with the law's concern for an inclusive democracy.

Like Thomas's jurisprudence, black political conservatives have premised their movement on undermining a basic precondition for the protection of minority voting rights: minority voter cohesion. There are several organizations laboring to disaggregate the black vote. Their scope is both local and national. The African American Republican Leadership Council, for instance, has a target of 25 percent black support for GOP candidates who support the Reagan Republican agenda. The Black Republican Council of Texas is a regional group that has set a target of 35 percent black support for Republicans. A more recent entrant, the National Black Republican Association, formed in 2005, seeks to "[return] Black America to its Republican roots."[10] These, along with numerous other black conservative organizations and the proliferating number of black conservative commentators on the radio and elsewhere, could pose a credible threat to black voter cohesion. While the analysis of their goals is usually tactical and political, a more fundamental critique has been missing from the discussion. To understand the fallacy of the "don't put all of your eggs in one basket" colloquialism that black conservatives—and other swing-vote proponents—invoke, it is necessary to understand a basic way in which minority voting preferences are protected.

Assume you are a black voter who lives in a state legislative district that is 40 percent black and 60 percent white. For the past several elections, a black candidate has run for and lost the state legislative seat. Although the candidate received more than 80 percent of the black vote each time, blacks do not constitute a proportionate share of the vote because their overall population is younger than that of whites, and socioeconomic factors such as less flexibility to show up at the polls on a Tuesday workday yield them a lower turnout rate. Moreover, the black candidate received less than 20 percent of the white vote each election while her white opponent, who is a Republican, received the remainder. If it is difficult to imagine this kind of racial polarization, one need look no further than Obama's performance in the South in 2008. Obama won only 14 percent of the white vote in Louisiana, 11 percent in Mississippi, and 10 percent in Alabama.[11]

So the hypothetical is certainly realistic. In this example, black voters have a preferred candidate. Even if the race of the black candidate is changed, there would still be an identifiably black-supported candidate as long as blacks continue to give a preponderance of their votes to one candidate of a particular party. Assuming that blacks were underrepresented in the state legislature relative to the state population, and assuming further it was possible to reconfigure this legislative district so as to give it a majority of voting-age black citizens in a compact design, the Voting Rights Act of 1965 provides a remedy to black voters. That remedy is usually a single-member district in which blacks constitute a voting-age majority of the population.

Now envision the type of electorate desired by black conservatives. Rather than blacks supporting the Democratic candidate over the past several elections in the eightieth percentile or better, they split their vote, giving roughly 55 percent of it to the black (or Democratic) candidate and 45 percent to the white Republican. It is possible under these circumstances to identify a candidate who received a greater share of the black vote. Yet a court's ability to identify a black-preferred candidate for purposes of fashioning a legal remedy is far less because it is not as clear that blacks have a consensus candidate as it is when they are giving 80 percent of their vote to the same candidate. The more evenly divided the black vote, the more likely it is that the black-preferred candidate has lost because of the discursive preferences of blacks themselves rather than because of the design of the district.

If we set the vote totals at equipoise, giving 50 percent of the black vote to the black candidate and 50 percent of the black vote to the white Republican, then it becomes impossible for a court to determine who the minority-preferred candidate is. The response to this scenario may well be that under a situation of equipoise in black voter preferences, there is no need for a legal remedy because blacks are participating as expected in normal, deracialized politics. Yet the inability of half of a significant minority population to elect the candidate of its choice is certainly less than a democratic ideal and merits a remedy that the Voting Rights Act may be unable to afford under its current jurisprudence. When blacks disaggregate their votes, they defeat their legal remedies.

They also limit their political effectiveness. Blacks are only 13.6 percent of the U.S. population. To appreciate the constraints and advantages of this number, visualize yourself as one of the 131.1 million voters who participated in the historic 2008 presidential contest. Doing so should not make you feel very efficacious: your chances of actually affecting the outcome were one in several million. Now envision yourself as a member of a like-minded political group numbering 16.1 million voters of the 131.1 million participating in the election. It takes no mathematical genius to conclude that your chances of determining the outcome of the election just increased dramatically. But wait. Divide that 16.1 million in half, as black conservatives would have it, and you are backsliding to inefficacy.

Of course, we do not have national elections per se in the United States. Instead, the presidential contest is really a state-by-state contest in which the popular vote in each state determines the distribution of electoral votes. Thus, in states like Virginia and North Carolina, with heavy concentrations of blacks in which Obama's 2008 margin of victory turned on overwhelming support from minorities, the disaggregation of the black vote would have meant the difference between victory and defeat. Yet this is the prescription of black conservatives who speak against a so-called monolithic black vote. From a tactical standpoint, self-dilution of one's vote is an insupportable position.

Invitation to a Tea Party?

Insupportable—unless the benefits outweigh the costs. Maybe the invitation by the GOP and their black conservative stalwarts is not an invitation to a funeral after all. Perhaps instead it is an invitation to a party. In evaluating the costs and benefits of attending, it pays to know your host.

Chairman Steele's remarks at DePaul about the Republican Party's failure to give blacks a reason to support it may have been just another in a series of blunders that led the national media to portray him as a "clown."[12] But the remark actually built on other observations Steele had made about his party's suspect past with African American voters, namely the Republicans' use of a "southern strategy" to racialize American politics.[13] Steele's remarks were no blunder. They were, instead, an awkward invitation for reconciliation.

But who else did Steele invite to the party? During his visit to DePaul, Steele also professed an affinity for the Tea Party movement, seemingly oblivious to the incongruity between his critique of the

Republican Party's appeal to African Americans and his embrace of these white conservatives. Steele told his DePaul audience, "I have advised our state chairs: don't turn your nose up or turn away from those who are active in the tea party movement. Embrace them. Welcome them. Talk to them. Those activists have now become a large part of our voting bloc. They represent a third or more of the voting-age population and so they're going to have a profound impact on elections and in some cases in the primaries this November and the spring. Both parties had better pay attention."[14] In proposing a coalition between the Tea Party and African Americans, however, Steele was attempting to alloy racially disparate elements. This is not a new conundrum for the GOP, but the emergence of the Tea Party as a major force brings into sharp relief the inherent incompatibility between blacks and the modern Republican Party.

A 2010 multistate University of Washington study of white voters is illuminating. An overwhelming majority of Tea Party adherents (60 percent) believe that the country has gone too far to ensure equal rights. When asked if some Americans are denied equal opportunity, only 23 percent of devout Tea Party adherents agreed, compared to 55 percent of all respondents. When asked if greater equality would alleviate some of the country's troubles, only 31 percent of devout Tea Party members agreed, compared to 54 percent of all respondents. Tea Party purists were far more likely to believe that the government can racially profile its citizens, with only 33 percent opposing such actions, compared to 57 percent of all respondents. They were nearly 20 points more likely to compare blacks to white immigrant groups and to believe that like those groups, blacks should advance "without special favors." And Tea Partiers were significantly more likely to dismiss the significance of race in explaining black inequality, with 72 percent disagreeing that "slavery and discrimination have created conditions making it difficult for blacks to work their way out of the lower class." In comparison, only 58 percent of all white respondents disagreed. Unsurprisingly, then, Tea Partiers were much keener on the proposition that blacks could do as well as whites "if they just tried harder" (73 percent v. 56 percent).[15]

A *New York Times* poll found similar results. Fully 25 percent of Tea Party supporters believed that the Obama administration favors blacks over whites, compared to only 11 percent of the general public. The *Times* poll found that Tea Party supporters were more likely than the general public to believe that the problems of African Americans have been overemphasized and that blacks and whites have an equal opportunity of advancing in today's society.[16]

Survey data are matched by compelling anecdotes. Tea Party Express organizer Mark Williams—who is white—infamously wrote a public letter to President Abraham Lincoln, purporting to speak in the voice of African Americans. Williams mockingly stated, "We Coloreds have taken a vote and decided that we don't cotton to that whole emancipation thing."[17] Tea Party Congressional Caucus founder Congresswoman Michele Bachmann rewrote American history in arguing that the founding fathers had fought against slavery, notwithstanding that many owned slaves and that blacks were counted as only three-fifths of a human being in the original Constitution.[18] Bachmann might be forgiven in light of revelations that her rival for the GOP presidential nomination and another Tea Party favorite, Governor Rick Perry of Texas, leased and frequented a hunting camp, the name of which was prominently displayed as "Niggerhead."[19] To Glenn Beck, formerly of Fox News, Obama's handling of Harvard University professor Henry Louis Gates's arrest qualified him as a "racist," a charge so ludicrous that Beck retracted it in the face of a revolt by his show's advertisers.[20] Tea Party Republican Hank Williams, Jr.'s likening of Obama to Adolph Hitler was so beyond the pale that ESPN pulled him off the air.[21] So racially tinged has the Tea Party movement's rhetoric been that even the moderate National Association for the Advancement of Colored People (NAACP) has condemned its constant invocation of race and racial stereotype.[22]

The Tea Party movement and the Republican Party share important characteristics. In May 2009, the Pew Research Center reported on partisan attitudes about race and toward African Americans. Although both major parties and independents have become less empathetic to racial issues, Republicans were 11 percent more likely than Democrats to believe that discrimination against blacks is rare today. Democrats were more than twice as likely as Republicans to believe that there has been scant improvement in the position of blacks in recent years. Sixty percent of Republicans believe that the country has overextended its quest for equal rights, compared to just 35 percent of Democrats.[23] A separate 2009 poll found that a scant 18 percent of Republicans favor continued affirmative action programs that give preferences to minorities in higher education and employment. Fifty-seven percent of Democrats favor continuing such programs.[24]

This is the party that African Americans have been invited to join. This is today's GOP. If one sought a rough historical parallel, the uneasy alliance of southern Dixiecrats with liberal northerners and blacks in the New Deal Coalition would come to mind. But that coalition dissolved in large part because of the dissonance between black voters and the attitudes of conservative white voters. In signing the Civil Rights Act of 1964 and the Voting Rights Act of 1965, President Lyndon Johnson forsook white southern Democrats (who even today represent the largest geographic segment of white conservatives) because it was apparent that racially regressive whites were not willing to be part of a coalition with African Americans. Kevin Phillips, who would go from being one of the principal architects of the "southern strategy" to a perceptive critic of the GOP, has estimated racial policy accounted for one-third to one-half of southern white flight from the Democratic New Deal Coalition.[25]

The rise of the Tea Party may render the past as prologue for the GOP's relationship with African Americans. Before there was the Tea Party, there was the Republican Party of Barry Goldwater, Richard Nixon, and Ronald Reagan. These standard-bearers racialized American politics based on a simple premise that is diametrically inconsistent with efforts to enfold blacks within the GOP: many whites are reluctant to be members of a political coalition with blacks.[26]

Goldwater staked his 1964 campaign on opposition to the Civil Rights Act of 1964, a fundamental protection against discrimination on the basis of race, gender, religion, or national origin in the workplace. Newly elected U.S. Senator Rand Paul, a 2010 Republican candidate who boastfully embraced the Tea Party movement, helped to reinvest the GOP in Goldwater's legacy by publicly questioning the validity of the '64 act. Goldwater's opposition to federally enforced civil rights was anathema to African Americans. Martin Luther King, Jr. famously characterized Goldwater's campaign as "Hitlerism."[27]

In contrast to Goldwater's caricaturability on race, it is easy to misapprehend Nixon's racial politics. Nixon was an economic neo-populist who ran to the right of Democrats on race, culture, and crime.[28] But for Nixon, race and economics were part of the same strategy to racialize American politics. Nixon sought to assure white middle-class voters that Republicans would maintain the social safety net of the New Deal while rejecting what Nixon advertised as the narrowly targeted programs of the Great Society disproportionately benefiting minorities.[29] Signs of Nixonian racialization are apparent in the Tea Party's effort to pick and choose which government programs are more government-like than others, attempting, for instance, to draw unprincipled distinctions between Medicare and "Obamacare." Indeed, the Tea Party's paroxysm of fiscal rectitude only when a black ascends to the presidency fuels suspicions of racialism. The national debt grew by $4.1 trillion under Obama's predecessor, George W. Bush.[30] Yet there was no Tea Party then, and to the extent those of the Tea Party's ilk objected to Bush's spending, their opposition was not nearly as virulent as it is toward Obama. Florida representative Frederica Wilson, a member of the Congressional Black Caucus (CBC), expresses her skepticism of the Tea Party in no uncertain terms:

> [A]ll of a sudden when we elect a black president of the United States, the Tea Party emerges out of—I don't know from where, but they emerge. And they're stronger than parties or as strong as parties that have been around for generations—the Republican Party, the Democratic Party. And I think that that party was prompted by race.... President Bush had a deficit. He had wars. He put us in this position. It took him eight years to do it. I never heard of the Tea Party. Did you?[31]

The GOP has recently embarked on an effort to amend the Constitution to prevent automatic citizenship for children born in the United States to illegal immigrants. Aimed squarely at Latinos, the rhetoric is hardly novel and indeed regresses to an era of more primitive racial politics. During the economic contraction of the early 1980s, Reagan perfected the language of political code to blame the nation's woes on "welfare queens" (read blacks). Invoking the most violent memories of domestic terrorism against civil rights activists, Reagan began his 1980 campaign in Philadelphia, Mississippi, the site of some of the most heinous anti-civil rights violence. Early in his political career, Reagan had explicitly opposed the Civil Rights Act of 1964 and had berated the Voting Rights Act of 1965 as "humiliating to the South."[32]

By the time he ran for president in 1980, rather than oppose civil rights laws outright as Goldwater did and some in the Tea Party movement now do, Reagan spoke more subtly against "preferential treatment" and appointed a conservative judiciary that would provide a legal veneer for scaling back rights. Reagan's racial regression was executed with an adroit symbolism that elided Goldwater—and even elides the modern Tea Party movement. Obama has said that Reagan "changed the trajectory of America in a way that Richard Nixon did not and in a way that Bill Clinton did not. He put us on a fundamentally different path because the country was ready for it."[33] Although avoiding mention of race, Obama was referring to the country's backlash against the 1960s and 1970s. Race, however, was arguably the most visible part of the backlash on which Reagan seized. Even as most whites believed his policies hurt African Americans, they overwhelmingly supported Reagan. Conversely, most blacks viewed Reagan as a "racist."[34]

The Republican Party that African Americans are being encouraged to attend has a "back-to-the-future" theme, finding itself in the past while attempting to return to the twenty-first century. But perhaps the black agents of the GOP are present in the party to redirect rather than mimic its positions. In that case, the cost-benefit analysis of attending the party, of voluntarily disaggregating the black vote, may not skew so heavily against the invitation.

QUEERS AND QUOTAS

Atlanta, Georgia, is known as "the gay capital" of America. It is a curious location for such a moniker. It is the South. It is teeming with churches and religiosity. It is (still) a black city. Yet it is a place of palpable cultural contestation among African Americans. It is this breach that black conservatives have sought to exploit nationally.

Black conservatives have learned to vary their arguments for disaggregation of the black vote. Instead of splitting the black vote in a given election, some advance the theory of simply not always voting for the same party in each election. The arguments presuppose that African Americans prefer the Democrats to the Republicans out of habit rather than self-interest. Or that Republicans' hostility to African American concerns is born of a lack of African American support rather than a political calculus that such hostility nets more votes than it forfeits. In short, they presuppose a commonality between blacks and the conservative whites who constitute the GOP. After more than four decades of African American bloc voting in favor of Democrats, black conservatives suggest that African Americans have been missing something about themselves and the Republican agenda. That something appears to be the shared social values of blacks and white conservatives.

The 2004 presidential election remains a flashpoint in the debate over black social conservatism and the threat it poses to black voter cohesion. George W. Bush's reelection was decided in Ohio, and many such as black politics commentator Hutchinson ascribe his victory to black votes, of which Bush received 16 percent, a figure appreciably higher than his national black vote totals. Hutchinson and others attribute Bush's showing in Ohio to the state gay marriage ban initiative that revved up black evangelicals, bringing them to the polls to vote not just for the initiative but for Bush and Republicans who had attempted to make their own elections referenda on gay marriage.[35]

Others dispute the significance of Ohio. The *Black Commentator* declared in a post-2004 election analysis that the "Black consensus remains intact" because Bush's black numbers nationally fell well short of hyperbolized media projections that speculated Bush could win as much as 18 percent of the black vote.[36] He won 10 percent to 11 percent of the black vote, a fairly typical showing for a Republican. Moreover, even in light of Bush's 2004 Ohio showing, religion appeared a long way from trumping race among blacks. One political scientist, Eric McDaniel, concluded from his analysis of the election that very religious whites were more than two-and-a-half times more likely to vote for Bush than very religious blacks.[37]

The ultimate significance of Ohio, however, is less whether blacks threw the election to Bush or even the role of religiosity in black voting behavior. Rather, the significance of Ohio 2004 is the disturbing way in which the debate over black conservatism would henceforth be framed. It would not be about strengthening the black family by strengthening its economic foundations. It would not be about stemming the tide of teenage pregnancy by offering a brighter alternative to young girls. Nor would it be about using religion to stamp out gun violence in the black community. Indeed, what Angela Onwuachi-Willig has identified as the core principles of black conservatism—nonvictimology and self-reliance[38]—scarcely define the current political debate over black conservatism. Instead, the metric and parameters for the debate now simply mimic white conservatives' obsessive fixation with gay rights. Far from offering an alternative to neglectful Democrats, black political conservatives have shown themselves to be unimaginative captives of the Republican Right.

From the pulpit to the radio to the national political arena, black conservative condemnation of homosexuality and gay marriage has grown in inverse proportion to the dismal socioeconomic indicators for African Americans. Atlanta megachurch preacher Bishop Eddie Long, ironically the defendant in sexual misconduct lawsuits filed by young males, marches to the tomb of Martin Luther King, Jr. to protest same-sex marriage.[39] (King's daughter, Bernice King, marched alongside Long, belying the little-known history that Dr. King was taught nonviolence theology by a gay black man, Bayard Rustin.)[40] Black churches perform exorcisms of gay black teenagers.[41] Black civil rights organizations are accused by black ministers and white conservatives of being co-opted by the gay movement.[42] Radio talk show hosts, such as Chicago's Charles Butler, are quick to rattle off the mantra, "We're conservative on values…[L]ook at California [Proposition 8]."[43] And in a novel argument from a black politico that ironically makes the case against all marriage, Chairman Steele opposed gay marriage on grounds that it would add to the costs of small businesses, which would have to pay benefits like health insurance to gay spouses.[44]

Within the black community, the dominant fault lines in this debate have focused on whether the discussion is diversionary—that is, whether it concerns African Americans at all—and whether gay marriage is a "civil rights" issue. From the standpoint of progressive black politics, however, both themes miss more fundamental concerns. To be sure, black political conservatives—including conservative religious leaders—risk "Kansasizing" black politics by obsessively focusing on this and other social issues. In his 2004 bestseller *What's the Matter with Kansas: How Conservatives Won the Heart of America*, Thomas Frank convincingly argues that poor and middle-class white voters have forsaken their economic interests in pursuit of conservative social policy by supporting Republicans.[45] More vulnerable than their white counterparts on every socioeconomic indicator, African Americans can ill-afford a similar diversion. Thus, it is understandable when progressive black religious leaders such as Reverend C. T. Vivian, a lieutenant to Martin Luther King, Jr., dismiss the role of social issues in black voters' political calculus. Said Vivian: "[I]t's not that important. It's not even that important for poor white folk."[46]

His response, however, is inadequate to combat the real harm of black conservatives' attempt to entice African Americans into the nation's antigay culture war. David Malebranche, an Emory University medical researcher who specializes in acquired immune deficiency syndrome (AIDS) in the black community, unearths a core racial premise in stoking homophobia among blacks (thereby encouraging covertness among black gays). According to Malebranche, many black gay men go to great lengths to hide their sexual identity because they are already burdened by the trauma of blackness and maleness.[47] Malebranche's observation can readily be extended to the broader debate among African Americans about gay marriage and gay rights. Arguably, what drives black resistance is not what drives white resistance. What drives the former is a fear of identifying with an unpopular cause or group when blacks are already burdened by their own historical circumstances. In this regard, the appeal by black conservatives to African Americans to enlist in the fight against gay marriage is racist because it exploits black social vulnerability while doing nothing to eliminate it.

None of this is to suggest that gay marriage is or is not a civil rights issue. The characterization is irrelevant. The use of a populist ritual—the referendum and initiative—to define the rights of any unpopular minority is a far greater threat to black interests than drawing histori-cal parallels to the civil rights movement. Let us return momentarily to the ways in which the Voting Rights Act of 1965 protects the candidate preferences of minority voters. Black voters in the hypothetical state legislative district are simply unable to exercise their will in elections without legal intervention to redraw districts that give them a controlling majority. But even after a legal remedy is granted, there remains the possibility of racial exclusion in the legislature itself. That is, the same racial polarization that characterizes voting in legislative elections may also characterize legislators' votes once elected. Lani Guinier, among others, has suggested that the Voting Rights Act has a role in preventing this type of conduct, perhaps by imposing on the legislature a supermajority requirement when an issue is one of especial importance to African Americans.[48] Her suggestion reflects a countermajoritarian tradition that is fundamental to the American political process but is completely antithetical to black and white conservatives' efforts to deploy gay marriage as a cultural schism.

We protect minority interests against majority encroachment every day in this country. The filibuster, under which a minority party is able to impede passage of legislation unless some of its members can be persuaded to vote with the majority, exemplifies how second nature this protection is. The minority need not be defined by race, religion, or any other characteristic that has been invoked in the culture wars in America. Contrary to this tradition, the participation of African Americans in initiatives and referenda in a manner that gives approbation to majoritarian absolutism sets African Americans up for a similar dismissal of their interests by populist frenzy.

That the dismissals have come at the hands of black conservatives using the same vehicles—initiatives and referenda—as gay marriage opponents is a difficult fact to ignore. Ward Connerly, a black conservative, has spearheaded several successful state initiatives banning affirmative action. Although black conservatives have arguments—some say principled ones—against affirmative action, the merits of those arguments are unimportant from the standpoints of democratic process and coalition-building. Blacks overwhelmingly support affirmative action, including the type that gives minorities special preferences in education and hiring. A 2009 Pew Research Center survey of black self-described Democrats and Democratic-leaning independents placed the level of support at 60 percent.[49] A 2009 Quinnipiac University national poll of voters placed the black support level at 78 percent.[50] Black conservatives have not relied on the power of persuasion to sway the opinion of black voters, as one would logically expect a group courting this demographic to do. Instead, their actions portray only an interest in appealing to the very racial backlash of white voters, so often expressed as opposition to "racial preferences," that continues to estrange blacks from the Republican Party. That is no way to treat guests.

Black conservatives consistently demean the 90 percent of black voters who support the Democratic Party by charging, as Republican congressman Allen West has, that these voters live on a "21st century plantation."[51] Black GOP presidential candidate Herman Cain considers these voters to be "brainwashed" because, according to Cain, they refuse to consider a conservative point of view.[52] Quite apart from the wisdom of insulting voters whom one is allegedly attempting to convert, these sorts of arguments contain an assumption that exposes the degree to which black conservatives rely on their race in lieu of substantive ingenuity. Black conservatives cannot seriously believe that blacks have not already evaluated the conservative perspective on both social and economic issues. Modern African American conservatives are virtually indistinguishable from their white brethren, except that black neocons attempt to apply white conservative and neoconservative axioms to race.[53] The black Right seems to suggest that conservative doctrine should be heard differently if an African American is speaking it even if nothing different is being said. In other words, identity politics are fine, so long as they redound to the benefit of the Right.

These and other inconsistencies have opened black conservatives up to charges of economic and political opportunism. By his own acknowledgment, Clarence Thomas had no background in civil rights when he was appointed by Ronald Reagan as Assistant Secretary for Civil Rights in the Department of Education.[54] Thomas wrote in 1997, "I always found it curious that, even though my background was in energy, taxation, and general corporate regulatory matters, I was not seriously sought after to move into one of those areas."[55] As an opponent of quotas and affirmative action, Thomas's decision to accept the position was a curious one.

Janice Rogers Brown, a black jurist appointed to the D.C. Circuit Court of Appeals by President George W. Bush, was a cause célèbre in conservative circles before her appointment. As an associate justice on the California Supreme Court, she authored the opinion upholding that state's ban on race-based affirmative action.[56] Yet Brown was appointed to the state high court over the negative recommendation of California's Commission on Judicial Nominees Evaluation. That commission, which was part of the formal process for appointment to judgeships in California, overwhelmingly rated Brown unqualified to sit on the state high court.[57] At the time, Brown was the only nominee to receive such a rating and still be appointed to the state Supreme Court.[58] Like Thomas, there is clash between Brown's opposition to quotas and affirmative action and the story of her own career.

Connerly's crusade against affirmative action evinces both contradictions and pecuniary motives. Although Connerly has successfully promoted Proposition 209 in California and initiatives in other states to ban affirmative action in employment, education, and contracting, Connerly himself received more than $1 million in state business through a minority contractor program that released him from the competitive bidding process.[59] Moreover, an erstwhile ally of Connerly who was the plaintiff in the Supreme Court case that challenged the University of Michigan's affirmative action program has accused Connerly of profiteering from his antiaffirmative action crusade, paying himself between $1.2 and $1.5 million annually from the charitable donations received by his nonprofit, the American Civil Rights Institute.[60] Thus, it is simply untrue when Connerly protests, "I don't wear my race on my sleeve. I don't try to benefit from it. I have never, ever in my life tried to take advantage of my race to get a benefit."[61] Indeed, for whites, the effectiveness of Connerly's crusade against affirmative action rests in part on the fact that he is a *black* man opposing affirmative action.[62]

As long as modern black conservatism offers up the likes of West, Cain, Thomas, Brown, and Connerly, African Americans are unlikely to perceive it as anything other than a racial Trojan horse for a party and philosophy that remain antagonistic to their aspirations.

SHORTCOMINGS BEGET TRIANGULATION

So how crude is the symbolism of the Republican Party in running and electing (all in white, Republican districts) black conservative Republicans? Extremely. It tells us nothing about the party's racial liberalism, as the candidates elected reflect white, conservative values, not those of traditional, progressive black politics. As black Tea Party favorite West readily admits, "I registered myself as a Republican because my views and perspectives were more in line with that party."[63] Cain similarly reveals himself as a conformist to modern Republican orthodoxy rather than a change agent within that party when he states, "I don't believe racism in this country today holds anybody back in a big way."[64] Indeed, the minorities elected as Republicans are often more conservative than white conservatives.[65]

As columnist Frank Rich points out, the only evidence of racial liberalism under these circumstances is that very conservative whites did not allow lingering racial antagonism to override their other convictions.[66] But even this charitable construction suffers from circularity because those other convictions are not entirely disconnected from racial antagonism.[67]

In a contest about symbolism, however, nothing can trump the election of the first black president, which has refortified black allegiance to the Democrats, possibly for several years to come. The failure of black conservatism to leave the ideological confines of white Republicans has left Republicans unable to compete for African American loyalties on policy grounds. Absent such a contest, Obama's Democratic Party has little incentive to entertain the left-of-center agenda of traditional black politics. Instead, Obama's postpartisan approach to governing amounts to a post-racial approach, for who are the nation's most loyal partisans? African American voters. To this group, Obama is able to say, "I cannot pass laws that say I'm just helping Black folks. I'm president of the entire United States."[68] At the same time, Obama and the Democratic Party must count on outsized black vote margins for their survival.

Blacks, in turn, are expected to revel in the symbolism of having a black president and tacitly to accept that their substantive policy ambitions must be relegated to the president's political survival. Progressives were held at similar bay by President Bill Clinton, as Clinton adopted the language and policies of the Right to survive politically. That was political triangulation, though even political triangulation by a Democrat disproportionately harms minority voters.[69] But the political imperative for the first black president to show he is not beholden to black voters casts triangulation in a distinctly racial vein.

In the post-racial triangulation of Obama, politics are neither black nor white. In the post-racial conservatism of black conservatives, blacks are neither Democrats nor Republicans but rather are unconsciously conservative. Post-racial triangulation meets postpartisan conservatism at an important nexus: both depart from traditional left-of-center black politics. Black conservatives seek to destroy the cohesion that undergirds traditional black politics. Obama's post-racialism must maintain this relic in order to survive politically while not appearing to white voters to embrace the politics that animate black voter cohesion. White voters are the beneficiaries of this racial conundrum. But so too are Obama and other moderate black politicians like him.

CHAPTER 4

Contradictions in a Latino Moment: Latinos as Less Black?

Latinos in the United States are black. Not necessarily in the phenotype sense of the term, but rather in the British sense. That is, whether or not they perceive themselves as black, they are involuntarily racialized.[1] Indeed, Americans now narrowly perceive Latinos as being more victimized by discrimination than African Americans.[2] Moreover, a 2009 survey revealed that substantially more Americans believe that there are strong conflicts between immigrants and native-born Americans than between blacks and whites.[3] Thus the British idiomatic use of "black" seems particularly apt. Similar to that idiom, in American politics, "black" is less a color than a category of treatment; it is less a race than an ideological shorthand reflecting a basket of issues that intersect with racial and ethnic inequality. This frame is important to understanding the relationship of Latino politics to the triangulated state of African American politics.

In chapter 3, I argued that Obama could successfully triangulate black voters in part because Republicans, especially black conservatives, have alienated this bloc, notwithstanding their purported interest in black support. Obama is thus all the more able to exploit the electoral capture of black voters, for as shabbily as they may be treated by the Democrats, where else are they going to go?

The notion of electoral capture permeates the story of the relationship of Latino voters to black politics. In their purported desire to avoid electoral capture, Latino voters have engaged in a triangulation of their own. In portraying themselves as neither a traditional Democratic bloc vote as blacks are, nor an atomistic collection of voters as whites are, the Latino moment—the arrival of political might by Latino voters—plays these two constructs off each other.

If this manipulation seems reminiscent of Obama's false equanimity between black and white voters, and even black conservatives' false common ground between blacks and white conservatives, it is especially similar when we consider who is ultimately harmed by the triangulation. For the Latino moment celebrates its individuality in a preexisting rather than a prepolitical social context. That context is one of black subordination and white political hegemony. Thus, Latino disassociation from black politics is more harmful to blacks than their purported disassociation from white political norms is to whites. It may even be harmful to Latinos themselves.

The Creation of Latino Voter Mystique

Latino voters are frequently portrayed as politically unmoored and "up-for-grabs." These descriptors are not neologisms but rather are borrowed from the discourse on the incessantly polled, media-romanticized "independent" voter. Demographic generalizations about such a dynamic and morphing voting bloc as independents are difficult to make. What is clear as of 2010, however, is that 71 percent of independents are white compared to 62 percent of Democrats and 88 percent of Republicans.[4] So the Latino swing vote discourse unfolds in a context in which there are appreciable demographic differences among the three major partisan voting blocs in the United States. This is not without racial implications—in particular for black politics.

Prominent Latino thinkers reject the deployment of the African American experience as a proxy for that of other racial and linguistic minorities such as Latinos. The basic objection of these theorists is that a predominant or exclusive focus on black oppression marginalizes the subordination of other minorities.[5] As I discuss shortly, this seemingly simple proposition is fraught with internal inconsistencies, if not outright contradictions. In the context of voting behavior, however, callers for the end to the black-white binary must decamp from their ivory tower and meet politics on the ground.

This encounter of theory and praxis creates interpretive problems in which a white political establishment hears the message "we are not like them (blacks)" differently than it may be intended. Another audience, blacks themselves, may translate such a message as the product of social distancing from blacks, rendering alliances between blacks and Latinos more difficult to form and further weakening traditional black politics.

The objection to a black-white binary in voting also elides an important structural reality about voting in the United States: voting itself is defined in binary terms because in practice there is a two-party system that is racially polarized. This has little to do with a neglect of Latinos and everything to do with the now 46-year-old disproportionate reliance of the Democratic Party on African American votes for its base. Quite literally, there would not be a competitive two-party system in the United States without the outsized allegiance of blacks to the Democratic Party. Even the most conservative of Democrats recognize this, as Senator Mary Landrieu of Louisiana did after a close 2002 reelection secured by an overwhelming share of the black vote. Landrieu declared: "The African-American community, which is the soul of the Democratic Party, rallied. I just can't thank the community enough. There were prayers and shouts of joy."[6]

The emergence of the so-called swing or independent voter does not significantly modify the racialized two-party structure in which Latinos must make voting decisions. First, the allure of the label "independent," with its allusion to the Declaration of Independence, probably increases voters' tendencies to ascribe to this moniker even when they are already predisposed to one of the two major parties.[7] Second, independents are overwhelmingly white. Latinos' ascription to one partisan label versus another is thus an ascription to political groups with clear racial identities. Third, the call for the end to the black-white binary ignores those Latinos who fit that binary in its most literal sense—Latinos who are phenotypically and culturally black, not just idiomatically black.

Despite the uniqueness of voting, scholars continue to insist on a rejection of the black-white binary. Sylvia R. Lazos, a leading voting rights expert, is an example of this rhetorical move. According to Lazos, "The Black-White paradigm is no longer statistically accurate. The results of the 2000 Census revealed that Latinas/os now numerically surpass African Americans and Asian Americans."[8]

Without clearly indicating the inapplicability of the black-white paradigm—or for that matter even explaining exactly what that paradigm means in voting—Lazos continues:

> In embarking on creating a meaningful scholarship in the electoral context, LatCrit must construct a concept of race that avoids the pitfalls of falling into Black-White bipolar analyses. Mainstream descriptions of APIA [Asian and Pacific Islander American] and Latina/o voters—generalizations about their characteristics as voter groups—often fall into the bipolar logic of the Black-White paradigm. These ascriptions and simplistic generalizations parallel the "model minority" pigeon-holing that Asian Americans have experienced in the context of the affirmative action debate.[9]

Finally, Lazos slips into the valorized language of the independent voter in describing a supposed postpartisan Latino voter: "Rather than being party affiliated, the Latina/o and APIA vote is increasingly tied to issues. The Pew Hispanic Trust's poll data shows what was already common knowledge within the Latina/o community that Latinas/os base their votes on substantive policy, and that the most important issues to Latinas/os are immigration, education, the economy, and health care."[10]

Lazos's analysis contains several of the (inconsistent) elements of Latino voter mystique that perpetuate the notion that these voters are sui generis and, moreover, are above the current bipolar state of play in U.S. politics. On the one hand, Lazos objects to categorizing Latinos as merely an ethnic group because it "waves off the history of Jim Crow practices that Latinas/os...suffered."[11] Although Jim Crow itself is an analogy to black subordination, Lazos insists that Latino voters merit a new "concept of race that avoids the pitfalls of falling into Black-White bipolar analyses."[12] This is at once a flight from traditional black politics and a reliance on the very history that engendered its creation.

It is difficult to determine what this new concept of race would look like either in the abstract or on the ground. This is due in part to the nebulous status of Latino voters in the law. As a juridical matter, Latinos have sometimes been treated like a racial group and sometimes treated as a linguistic or an ethnic minority. In one of the few successful racial vote dilution cases brought under the Equal Protection Clause of the Fourteenth Amendment, the United States Supreme Court drew no analytic distinction between black plaintiffs in Dallas County, Texas, and Mexican-American plaintiffs in Bexar County. Instead, the Court agreed with the finding that Mexican Americans had been denied access to the political process of Texas "even longer than the Blacks were formally denied access by the white primary."[13] Importantly, in making this comparison to African Americans, the Court did not designate Latinos as a race but instead found them to be "an identifiable class for Fourteenth Amendment purposes."[14]

In *Hernandez v. New York*, the Court shunned analogy to African Americans.[15] Faced with a prosecutor's use of preemptory challenges to remove potential Latino jurors, the Court, not unlike the black-white binary abolitionists, saw a complexity to categorizing Latinos. Because "the breadth with which the concept of race should be defined for equal protection purposes" was not fixed, language was not always a proxy for race, and thus distinctions drawn on the basis of bilingualism were not always subject to the highest level of constitutional review, strict scrutiny. In *Hernandez*, the very murkiness of Latino racial categorization—that is, the departure from the black-white binary—redounded to the detriment of Latino litigants, as the prosecutor's preemptory removal of Latinos ultimately received less constitutional scrutiny.

A consistent application of *Hernandez*, however, may have benefited Latino voters in *Bush v. Vera*.[16] In that case, white plaintiffs attacked a Latino-majority congressional district created pursuant to the Voting Rights Act of 1965 as an unconstitutional racial gerrymander. The Court assumed without discussion that Latinos were a racial group. Consequently, the Court applied strict scrutiny to the district, striking it down. Had the district been treated as a language-minority rather than as a minority district, a lesser constitutional standard of review would have applied, and the district likely would have survived constitutional challenge.[17] In this regard, Lazos's objection to ascribing "ethnicity" as opposed to "race" to Latinos may appear somewhat puzzling to some.

Bush v. Vera, however, is not an example of the attributes of discarding the black-white binary. Rather, it is what Darren Hutchinson has referred to as the inversion of minorities' rights—their commandeering by white plaintiffs in the name of colorblindness.[18] White plaintiffs prevailed in *Vera* not because white congressional representation was diluted in relation to Texas's white population or because the plaintiffs suffered any other tangible harm. Instead, they prevailed because a narrow conservative majority embraced a judicial policy of colorblindness that slighted the imperative and original intent of race consciousness under the Reconstruction amendments.

The juridical treatment of Latino voters is further complicated by the basis for their inclusion in the protections of the Voting Rights Act. The legislative history of the 1975 amendments to the act reveals the black-white binary as being a rights-protective paradigm rather than an underinclusive construct. In arguing for the inclusion of Latinos under the act, persuasive comparisons were made to the disenfranchisement of southern blacks. At the same time, the debate reflected an appreciation for the distinctions between racial and language minorities. One of the amendments' cosponsors, Representative Herman Badillo of New York, recognized that "Spanish-speaking groups may be of one racial group or another. They might be white; they might be black; they might be Indian; or they might be a mixture of two or three different groups."[19]

The displacement of the black-white binary would add no clarity, let alone benefit, to the juridical treatment of Latino voters. Even if the displacement expanded Latinos' political possibilities by, for instance, treating Latino districts as language-based rather than racial, it would also contract Latino protections where their litigation posture is offensive rather than defensive. Thus, Latinos might prevail in *Bush v. Vera* because strict scrutiny would not be triggered, but lose cases like *Hernandez v. New York* because, again, strict scrutiny would not be triggered.

Setting to one side issues of clarity, the displacement of the black-white binary would not make voting rights jurisprudence more inclusive, either rhetorically or as a practical matter. In the larger debate about the utility of the black-white binary, Juan F. Perea, among others, has made the curious charge that the iconic status of the black civil rights movement "suggests that the African-American Civil Rights Movement is the only civil rights movement, or the only important civil rights struggle."[20] It is unclear against whom Perea and others are leveling this criticism. Against blacks for claiming their own history? Against black scholars? Against the courts? Against lawmakers? Against civil rights laws?

The rhetoric of the underinclusiveness of the black-white binary often assumes an accusatory tone in which scholars suggest the disadvantages of Latinos and Asian Americans are underappreciated. Roy Brooks, however, has demonstrated that these charges are exaggerated. Brooks notes that all civil rights laws, and the Reconstruction amendments, apply to races and ethnic groups outside the black-white binary.[21] To the extent Latino theorists are attempting to direct the scholarship of African American scholars away from the black experience, they are merely substituting the black-white binary with an insider-outsider binary, an overbroad construct that would have the effect of trivializing the unique black experience in the United States, informed by slavery, Jim Crow, and lynching, among other exceptional circumstances.[22]

Moreover, the claim that the black-white binary is underinclusive ignores the manner in which the binary often operates. In practice, the binary often works as a racial continuum in which nonblack minority groups strategically exploit their distinctions from African Americans to assume the post of "honorary whites."[23] As Brooks notes, "[T]here are moments in American history when certain Asian Americans and Latinas/os have attempted to achieve equality by asserting that they are not Black or like Blacks, and/or that they are White. There are costs as well as advantages associated with occupying both ends of the polarity...and non-black racial groups have often been able to avoid the costs and exploit the advantages."[24] Brooks's observation dovetails with Eduardo Bonilla-Silva's prediction that America is slouching toward a Latin American style "triracial" caste system, in which white Latinos are treated as "honorary whites" and light-skinned Latinos occupy an intermediate position between whites and blacks.[25]

Brooks's and Bonilla-Silva's latter point leads us back to the voting context specifically. In this context, claims of underinclusion are particularly puzzling because no voter demographic—not Latinos, not Asians and certainly not whites—is trying to assume the marginalized mantle of African American voters. To the contrary, the rhetoric of the independent or swing Latino voter is directly in contradistinction to the Democrat-captured black voter, the electorate's most loyal partisan. Thus, whatever the merits of the argument for abolishing the black-white paradigm as an academic proposition, in voting, such a proposition does little more than contribute to the discursion of the role of the Latino voter.

Discursion characterizes the Latino voters' role not only as a juridical matter but also as an internal reality. As political scientist Cristina Beltrán observes in her illuminating work, *The Trouble with Unity*, despite the variegated national origins and cultures of American Latinos, "Latino elites have found it useful to present themselves as a politically cohesive national minority group equivalent to African Americans."[26] This concept of pan-ethnic civic *Latinidad* embodies the collective political and cultural identity of American Latinos of various national origins.[27] It is decidedly a construct rather than a state of nature. The sheer diversity of races, nationalities, cultures, and political ideologies among Latino Americans renders the concept of civic *Latinidad* internally conflicted. Yet, driven in no small part by both the success of and envy for the black civil rights movement, Latino intellectuals have been forced to propagate the notion of pan-ethnicity among Latino voters in order to augment their power as a voting bloc.[28] Beltrán observes:

> Because high levels of group cohesion and political unity are characteristic of black politics, Latino civic elites have put enormous political energy into developing a recognizable set of "Latino political interests" and stressing the necessity of a united Latino political community to achieve these goals. Portraying Latino voters as a potential bloc or swing vote in highly contested elections is a crucial element of echoing the African American paradigm.[29]

Thus, in voting, it turns out that the black-white binary is quite a useful paradigm for Latinos. Useful, that is, until it insinuates too close a relationship to black voters. While deploying the construct of Latino pan-ethnicity to bolster Latinos' numerical presence as a political force, Latino intelligentsia have gone to great lengths to promote the Latino vote as a new swing vote that defies partisan labels and ideological pigeonholing.[30] As discussed in chapter 3, black voters are the ultimate Democratic partisan. What is especially remarkable about Latino swing-vote rhetoric is that it fails to capture these voters' actual voting behavior, at least in national elections. Since 1988, roughly 65 percent to 70 percent of Latinos have supported the Democratic presidential candidate, while 30 percent to 35 percent have supported the Republican.[31] Although not as monolithic as the black vote, these numbers hardly justify the mystery in which the Latino vote seems to be shrouded election after election. Yet the rhetoric continues.

THE RACIAL AESTHETICS OF SWING-VOTE RHETORIC

Political scientists will correctly note that I have up to this point used "swing vote" interchangeably with "independent voter" when actually the two terms are not always the same. Before discussing the harm of Latino swing-vote rhetoric to traditional black politics, let us unpack these terms in order to place the distinction in a relevant context.

In academic parlance, one definition of swing voters describes them as late-deciding voters who move between parties from election to election.[32] This definition would clearly exclude African Americans, who are consistent Democratic partisans. Another definition excludes historical voting patterns and examines only "how many members of [a demographic group] were undecided or weakly committed during the general election campaign."[33] Under this overly capacious definition of swing voter, "blacks are not dramatically less likely to be swing voters than whites are" because the concept simply "does not measure how lopsided or equally divided a group's eventual vote totals turn out to be."[34]

The latter definition is simply incongruent with reality. Blacks cannot be both a "captured interest" and a swing vote. For a voter to be a swing vote means both major parties are actively pursuing his vote.[35] On the other hand, a voter is captured when the opposing party does not want his vote for fear that courting it may alienate its base, leaving the voter with no choice other than the neglectful party in which he currently finds himself.[36] This is the plight of the African American voter. They are a captured interest of the Democrats. As

Donna Brazile, Al Gore's 2000 presidential campaign manager, has emphasized, Democrats do not treat blacks as swing voters. Rather, they are treated as "mobilization voters," on whom resources are usually spent late in the campaign cycle on get-out-the-vote rather than issue-persuasion efforts.[37] Brazile's views as a campaign professional dovetail with the media narrative of swing voters as demographically skewed.[38]

Thus, just as independent voters are disproportionately white, so too are swing voters. Although I have used the terms interchangeably in describing Latino voter mystique, independents (particularly of the pure sort) are often a subset of swing voters. That is, swing voters can also have declared party affiliations.[39] Once again, being strictly bounded by the nomenclature of political science is not analytically helpful since it is the rhetoric of Latino voter mystique we are focused on, and that rhetoric is propagated using common, rather than technical, meanings. In common parlance, it is not unusual to equate swing voters with political independents.[40]

If, as I have shown, Latino swing-vote rhetoric is an identification with a disproportionately white voter demographic, does that mean it is also a deliberate flight from traditional black politics, even as the Latino intelligentsia emulates the latter model to portray Latinos as a voting bloc? Stated differently, is Latino swing-vote rhetoric an effort to make Latinos less black (in the British idiomatic sense as well as literally)? Finally, can any observed flight from traditional black politics be explained in strategic rather than racial terms? If the answer to the latter question is yes, then perhaps whatever harm to black politics there may be is simply an unavoidable cost of Latino self-interest. But perhaps not.

During the 1990s and early 2000s, Republicans pursued the Latino vote in a manner without parallel to its minimal courtship of the black vote.[41] Although the location of Latinos in key electoral states helps to explain Republican interest, Republicans' perceptual distinction between Latinos and African Americans is at least as important. Republicans believed they could pursue the Latino vote at the national level without alienating their base.[42] To Republicans, Latinos were less black. Latino swing-vote rhetoric exploited this perception and continues to do so—even as Latinos, in an idiomatic sense, become more black, and even as they rely on the black exemplar to construct a pan-ethnic notion of Latinos as a cohesive voting bloc.

As discussed in chapter 3, despite their deployment of racial symbolism by electing black conservatives and their stoking of homophobia among blacks with the gay marriage issue, Republicans do not see the black vote as malleable as the Latino vote. Moreover, the core beliefs of the Tea Party-infused Republican Party place the party's base at substantial odds with black voters' beliefs and priorities. Compounding black disability, despite their proven role as the lifeline of the Democratic Party, black voters have not exerted a directional influence on the party commensurate with the party's reliance on black votes. Yet Democrats, like Republicans, showed no reluctance to actively and overtly court the Latino vote during the 1990s and early 2000s. Indeed, despite the pivotal role they played in the minute closeness of the controversial 2000 presidential election, black voters during the campaign felt that Democrats expended most of their time courting suburban women and Latinos.[43]

The relationship between the major parties' perception of Latinos as swing voters and Latinos' promotion of themselves as such is a dialogic one and has been informed by the communicants' contradistinctions between blacks and Latinos. Political scientist Paul Frymer has convincingly argued that the major parties have made a racial calculus that overt pursuit of the black vote would be electoral suicide. It is difficult to dismiss the possibility, however, that Latino voters have made a similar racial calculus, reflecting not merely a strategic concern but also antiblack sentiment.

For instance, Lazos notes that recent Latino immigrants are less reliable partisans than more established ones, are more conservative, and are more likely to identify as independent or Republican.[44] These nascent political tendencies can be viewed as race-neutral only if they are abstracted from the racially polarized two-party context of U.S. politics in which modern conservatism and Republicanism are not free of racist ideological content. Moreover, these developing political tendencies can be viewed as race-neutral only by decontextualizing the larger relationship of the Latino community to African Americans.

In her probing work on color and nationality discrimination among Latinos, Tanya Hernández discusses the "social distance" between Latinos and blacks.[45] Social distance measures the social discomfort that different ethnic or racial groups have with each other. Hernández notes that while the greatest social distance exists between more recent Latin American immigrants and blacks, more established communities of Latinos also feel significantly estranged from African Americans while embracing whites. Examining survey data from the 1990s through 2003, Hernández concludes:

It is somewhat ironic that African Americans, who are publicly depicted as being averse to coalition building with Latinos, provide

> survey responses that are actually more in accord with all the socioeconomic data that demonstrates the commonality of African American and Latino communities. Meanwhile, Latinos in contradistinction provide survey responses that fly in the face of all the socioeconomic data demonstrating African American and Latino parallels....The Latino affinity for White-Anglos over African Americans is part and parcel of the Latino identification with whiteness.[46]

Given the social distance of many Latinos from African Americans, it is difficult to conclude that Latino swing-vote rhetoric is merely a strategic imperative. Electoral capture could be just as easily avoided by expressly affiliating with African Americans as a political force and exerting greater pressure on Democrats to be responsive to the many shared interests of blacks and Latinos. In this scenario, neither blacks nor Latinos must marginalize the other in order to enhance their own political fortunes.

It is no answer to label such an approach impractical because of inevitable conflicts. Conflicts exist among African American voters, but this has not prevented them from functioning as the most cohesive voting bloc in the nation. And compromise has already been evident. For instance, the job-loss effect of Latino immigration on African Americans is, at a minimum, a contested issue.[47] Because African Americans have traditionally occupied the lower-rung jobs that recent immigrants are more likely to qualify for and seek, there is at least theoretic potential for conflict. Yet it is noteworthy from a coalitional standpoint that in the 1990s, when even a majority of white Democrats in the House were supporting draconian constraints on illegal immigration, the Congressional Black Caucus (CBC) overwhelmingly rejected such measures.[48] Compromise is possible.

Compromise is also evident in important coalitional victories. After receiving only 20 percent of the black vote in his initial failed bid to become Los Angeles's first Latino mayor, Antonio Villaraigosa received approximately 48 percent of that vote in successfully unseating a white incumbent four years later.[49] Blacks also preferred Fernando Ferrer to white progressive Mark Green in Ferrer's first-place finish in a 2001 New York City Democratic primary.[50] Latinos had delivered 64 percent of their vote to help make David Dinkins the first black mayor of Gotham City by a narrow margin.[51] Similarly, Latino voters were an important part of the coalition that elected Harold Washington the first black mayor of Chicago.[52] If coalitions are possible in these melting pots where ethnic and racial rivalries have historically been acute, it is not plausible to dismiss the coalitional claim.[53]

Moreover, the coalitional approach is more consistent with the current legal protections of Latino voters than is swing-vote rhetoric. If, by definition, swing voters decide many elections, they cannot be consistent losers in the electoral process. Indeed, they are often winners. However, the Voting Rights Act of 1965 is simply not intended to protect groups who suffer the normal vicissitudes of the electoral process. It instead protects groups who are shut out of that process because they are on a fairly consistent basis unable to elect the candidate of their choice. That is the basis under which Latinos and other language minorities were brought under the protections of the Voting Rights Act. Under a swing-vote conception of Latino politics, however, the act would become inapplicable to Latinos.

Latinos, however, are becoming more black, idiomatically speaking. Even as Latino swing-vote rhetoric continues, Arizona and other states have passed draconian legislation effectively authorizing the racial profiling of Latinos in order to determine their legal status.[54] It is the second time in as many decades that Latinos as a group have been vilified in the name of curtailing illegal immigration. California governor Pete Wilson's embrace of Proposition 187, which sought to prevent delivery of social services to illegal immigrants by requiring verification and reporting of all individuals' immigration status, was the first infamous foray by Republicans in the 1990s.[55]

Today, a Tea Party-infiltrated GOP has embraced nativist legislation at the national level that would amend the Fourteenth Amendment to the Constitution to deny automatic citizenship to the children of illegal immigrants.[56] To be sure, there are ways of viewing this and other illegal immigration legislation in nonracial terms, but that prism requires an erasure of historical context. The present-day discourse is not merely a discussion about illegal immigration; it also reflects a bias against Latino "otherness."

For all the talk of Latinos being the new swing voter, they could just as well be called the new black voter. But this moniker lacks a desired racial aesthetic—whiteness.

REINFORCING TRIANGULATION

President Barack Obama has consistently been asked how he plans to address the outsized, disproportionate economic woes of African Americans. He has routinely framed his response in colorblind terms: "I think it's a mistake to start thinking in terms of particular ethnic segments of the United States rather than to think that we are all in this together and we are all going to get out of this together."[57] Yet Obama has courted various other segments of the

voting population—identifiable by their gender, sexual orientation, or ethnicity—on issues that these groups have championed and with which they have become identified in the public's eye. One of Obama's first actions as president was to sign the Lilly Ledbetter Fair Pay Restoration Act, courting women voters in the process.[58] Likewise, in demonstrating his support for the gay community, Obama repealed "don't ask, don't tell"; has supported amending federal workplace discrimination laws to protect against sexual orientation discrimination; has supported full civil unions with full federal rights for gay, lesbian, and transgendered couples; and has supported the Respect for Marriage Act, which would require the federal government to accord the same rights to gay and straight couples.[59] To many, these are sensible, progressive policies that are long overdue. *But they are also policies that address the concerns of a particular constituency.*

Let us return to the subject of human vulnerability introduced in chapter 1. Martha Fineman's rebuke to liberal theory's myth of the self-reliant citizen posits that vulnerability is a universal human condition, yet humans are vulnerable for different reasons and in different ways.[60] In addressing the vulnerabilities of gay Americans, it would make little sense to ignore their sexuality if their vulnerabilities arise from their sexual orientation. A sexual-orientation-neutral or universalist approach would not adequately address their concerns. Human vulnerability does not work differently for African Americans. Where race is a distinguishing feature in their plight, as it is in employment, education, health care, criminal justice, and voting rights, the political process should not shrink from addressing their concerns, regardless of how white voters might perceive such action.

Arguably no group has been courted by Obama as assiduously as Latinos, who are an "ethnic segment" of America, to borrow Obama's term. Obama appointed the first Latino Supreme Court justice. Meanwhile, African Americans have merely descriptive representation on the high court. Justice Clarence Thomas is ideologically estranged from the civil rights tradition that underpins African Americans' relationship to the law.[61]

Latino leaders have been fairly explicit in using immigration reform as a litmus test for Obama, even though it has been a perennial issue throughout both Democratic and Republican administrations. Congressman Luis Gutierrez has been harshly critical of what he views as Obama's backtracking on creating a path to citizenship for the country's twelve million undocumented immigrants.[62] President Obama did not seek to minimize Gutierrez's concerns as ethnic or tribal. Instead, he endorsed the reform that Gutierrez had been pushing.[63]

What is particularly striking—and triangulating—about Obama's courtship of Latinos and his embrace of comprehensive immigration reform is how little attention is given to how African Americans would be impacted by immigration reform. Black support seems to be either assumed or disregarded as a factor. Indeed, notwithstanding the findings of Hernández that the social distance between blacks and Latinos is largely a function of Latino efforts to separate themselves from blacks, Obama has suggested that African American suspicions of immigrants renders them guilty of racism.[64] But African Americans largely do not fit the celebrated American aphorism that "we are all immigrants." Rather, most are the descendents of slaves forcibly brought to the Americas.[65] Setting to one side whether Obama would ever accuse Latinos of antiblack racism, Obama's attempt to win Latino votes simply ignores the complex historical relationship between blacks and immigration. Since colonial times, occupational displacement by immigrants has been a concern among blacks.[66] The decades following the Revolution bore out this concern. In the early 1800s, black artisans in New York City saw their economic position eroded by European immigrants fleeing the Napoleonic Wars.[67] The 1830s brought a marked increase in immigration due to the Irish famine. Although these immigrants were largely uneducated and unskilled, they nevertheless displaced northern free black workers. In the 1830s, most domestic servants in New York City were black; by the 1850s, most were Irish.[68]

Between 1850 and 1882, in excess of 320,000 unskilled laborers came from China to work on railroads, ranches, and plantations, work for which blacks were as qualified. What is particularly illuminating about this period is that after the Civil War, some of these laborers were brought to the South by plantation owners in order to obviate the hiring of newly freed blacks.[69] The great wave of immigration from southern and eastern Europe between 1880 and 1920 was devastating to the occupational security of northern blacks. Much like the immigration conflict today, employers strategically pitted blacks against immigrants, bidding down wages and weakening unions.[70] By 1910, black males in Cleveland, Ohio, held just 11 percent of the skilled trade jobs, down from 32 percent in 1870.[71] Although the economically undeveloped South was not a magnet for most immigrants, this did not stop experimentation to displace blacks in that region with white immigrant workers. In the 1890s, the recruitment of Italians to the South was a major controversy among black southerners.[72]

The Great Migration of African Americans to the North followed by the influx of Latino immigrants, who situated themselves in the

same large cities as blacks, brought the question of black displacement into sharper relief. Ironically, the national tenor set by the civil rights movement of the 1960s eased the way for the passage of legislation, the Hart-Celler Act, which would facilitate the influx of Latino (and Asian) immigrants.[73] Today, the impact of immigration on black job displacement is inconclusive.[74] Vanderbilt University political scientist Carol Swain has concluded that "[t]he best research on the impact of immigration on native workers has found that immigrant competition for jobs hurts natives by holding down wages and reducing employment opportunities for native workers at different occupational levels."[75] According to Swain, a disproportionate number of the black unemployed are high school dropouts and high school graduates. These workers must compete with an oversupply of low-skilled immigrants who since 1990 have increased the labor supply by 25 percent for the kinds of jobs traditionally performed by high school dropouts and graduates.[76] Of course, Swain's findings have been contested. Although some economists concur that immigrants displace low-skilled black workers, they also believe that this is a net positive on the assumption that these black workers move on to better jobs.[77]

It is precisely the inclusiveness of the issue that justifies black concern. But when Obama was asked a question about black job displacement by illegal immigrants during a 2008 debate with Senator Hillary Clinton, this was his response:

> Well, let me first of all say that I have worked on the streets of Chicago as an organizer with people who have been laid off from steel plants, black, white, Hispanic, Asian, and, you know, all of them are feeling economically insecure right now, and they have been for many years. Before the latest round of immigrants showed up, you had huge unemployment rates among African-American youth....
>
> And, so, I think to suggest somehow that the problem that we're seeing in inner-city unemployment, for example, is attributable to immigrants, I think, is a case of scapegoating that I do not believe in, I do not subscribe to.[78]

Latinos supported Hillary Clinton in the Democratic primaries by a margin of nearly two-to-one.[79] Yet this was Senator Clinton's answer to the same question on black job displacement:

> Well, let me start with the original question from Kim, because I think it deserves an answer. I believe that in many parts of our country, because of employers who exploit undocumented workers and drive

down wages, there are job losses. And I think we should be honest about that.

There are people who have been pushed out of jobs and factories and meatprocessing plants, and all kinds of settings. And I meet them. You know, I was in Atlanta last night, and an African-American man said to me, "I used to have a lot of construction jobs, and now it just seems like the only people who get them anymore are people who are here without documentation." So, I know that what we have to do is to bring our country together to have a comprehensive immigration reform solution.[80]

Obama was not willing to acknowledge the reality that Clinton confronted directly and that is apparent to anyone passing a construction site or staying at a hotel with maid service: that African Americans have virtually disappeared from various industries in certain cities and have been replaced by Latino immigrants.[81] Latinos have propagated an electoral mystique around swing-vote rhetoric, and Obama has been prepared to pursue it notwithstanding its clear "ethnic" identity and notwithstanding its potential to harm African Americans. Blacks are being triangulated not only vis-à-vis whites but vis-à-vis Latinos, whose signature issue of immigration can be openly discussed and embraced by Obama because Latino voter mystique has made Latinos something other than black.

Traditional black politics—a progressive, race-conscious, voter-cohesive movement—has been buffeted over the past two decades, and one of its vitiating detractors has been Latino swing-vote rhetoric. As long as the relationship between black politics and Latino politics remains strained, neither will achieve its full potential. But Latino swing-vote rhetoric plays a unique role in reinforcing the captured state of black voters and in facilitating the new post-racial triangulation by an otherwise well-intentioned black president.

The history of black voters in the United States is one of their being abandoned by "natural allies," such as poor and working-class whites. This in turn contributes to a perception of African American voters as electoral untouchables to be courted at arm's length. Latino swing-vote rhetoric reinforces this perception.

Latino distancing from black voters can only encourage Obama's strategy of post-racial triangulation. But accessing whiteness has not been and will not be easy for Latinos, for in American politics, triangulation is almost always a process undertaken to gain the support of the median voter—in the United States, the right-of-center white voter. A triangulation that pits Latinos and blacks against one another is one in which both sides stand to lose because—aspirations to honorary whiteness notwithstanding—neither plank of the triangle is really white. Thus, even as it embraced the "ethnic" issue of comprehensive immigration reform, in 2010, the Obama administration deported record numbers of illegal immigrants, most of whom were without criminal records and thus were lower priority deportees.[82] Participating as the beneficiary in the triangulation of blacks did not—and will not—insulate Latinos from being triangulated.

The new triangulation presupposes that the first black president must placate white voters for electoral survival by distancing himself from traditional black politics, particularly its express race consciousness. At the same time, black voters are expected to ignore any apostasy because their political options are limited and, perhaps as importantly, because the symbolic importance of the first black president overrides any political neglect. This strategy would be far more difficult to deploy if Latinos did not seek to be less black. Part 2 turns to the new triangulation.

PART II

Barack Obama and the New Politics of Triangulation

CHAPTER 5

Triangulation 101: The Old Conceives the New

Black politics has been demonized by the United States Supreme Court, which has scrutinized accommodations to black interests, including the creation of majority-black districts, in a manner that has no parallel to government's routine acquiescence to white-identified interests. Moreover, black politics has endured an attack from within by black conservatives seeking to fracture black voter cohesion, which, as a practical matter, would only deliver black votes to a party, the Republicans, that has shown no willingness to retreat from its march to the political and racial Right, where hardly any black voters reside. Add to these formidable burdens on black politics an inability to forge an enduring alliance with Latinos as well as the creeping influence of white money on the candidate selection process in black districts, and the state of black politics becomes clear: it was not thriving on the eve of Barack Obama's historic election as the first black president.

Nor is it now. Nor will it again without a visionary self-reassertion. And what is the fallout from the supine state of black politics? The triangulation of black voters. But to appreciate Obama's relationship to black voters in this new triangle, it is helpful to get a fuller comprehension of Clintonian-style triangulation and Obama's embrace of it. As it turns out, the "small-government" concessions of Clintonian triangulation compel the concessions of Obama's post-racial triangulation that in some measure disserve the interests of black voters. Yet where government is scaled back or "starved" to a point of zero-sum scarcity, the historical claims of African Americans for socioeconomic justice should be more, not less. Race, in other words, should be saved as part of our national dialogue and agenda. Since government can no longer attack problems on their largest—and hence most race-neutral—scale, race consciousness is justified, both as a political and legal matter.

This common-sense proposition is an inconvenient one for Obama and the new black politics. While needing and desiring black voter cohesion, the drape of race specificity in policy or rhetoric would threaten the electoral success that commends the new black politics as a substitute for the old. The solution to this conundrum is to feed black voters, already starved of a vibrant political movement, a hefty dose of the next best thing—and perhaps the least offensive thing to white voters whose sentiments on race have historically proved conservative—symbolism. This time, however, the cycle of trust and symbolism that had last been rehearsed under Obama's Democratic predecessor, Bill Clinton, would pose a special threat to the black body politic. For if Obama stood on the shoulders of his black political and civic forebears, he also stood on the corpse of a black politics that needed no additional muzzles of its last gasping breaths of race consciousness. A successful triangulation of black voters—a successful political compromise of their race consciousness to white voters' aversion to racial remediation—required precisely such a muzzle.

The Reemergence of Political Triangulation

Political jargon comes and goes, but sixteen years after its naming by Republican political consultant Dick Morris, the term "triangulation" resurfaced in relation to President Obama's governing strategy. Having campaigned for repealing the 2001 George W. Bush tax cuts for wealthy income earners, Obama allowed a two-year extension of the cuts after Democrats hemorrhaged more than 60 House seats in the 2010 midterm election. Obama then chided the Left for criticizing his compromise. For many, Obama's situation was reminiscent of President Clinton's predicament after outsized midterm election losses by the Democrats in 1994, and so was his response.[1]

Clinton's resuscitation after the 1994 rout was considered an act of political legerdemain, yet a betrayal of principle. Engineered by Morris, a Republican who had advised candidates as conservative as Senator Jesse Helms of North Carolina, Clinton sought a third position that accommodated Republican demands for smaller government while not entirely fleeing progressive ideas.[2] Morris's simplest definition of triangulation is that it is a "moderate alternative, a third way."[3] In other iterations, however, Morris elevates triangulation to the philosophical: "It's not merely splitting the difference between left and right. Clinton's objective was to combine the best theme from each side: 'opportunity' from the left and 'responsibility' from the right."[4]

Despite Morris's more laudatory descriptions of his creation, progressives had a decidedly less sanguine view of triangulation. To liberals, through triangulation, Clinton "deliberately sought to embarrass and undercut Democratic liberals to gain personal political advantage."[5] Under triangulation, Clinton signed the Defense of Marriage Act, allowing states to deny full faith and credit to a same-sex marriage consummated in a sister state. He reneged on a promise to end the ban on gays in the military and instead created the now discredited policy of "don't ask, don't tell." And perhaps most emblematic of triangulation, Clinton signed into law a draconian welfare reform bill, the Personal Responsibility and Work Opportunity Act, so punitive that it stripped *legal* immigrants of disability and health benefits.[6] These and a host of other center-right maneuvers by the "new" Democrat Clinton created great mistrust in progressive circles and fostered the perception that "it is the Left which swallows the soft promises of Clinton and the Right that demands, and gets, hard guarantees."[7]

Aware that the progressives felt shortchanged by triangulation, the Obama White House issued a denial more convincing in its description of the term than its disavowal: "Triangulation…is an intentional political strategy to win favor with swing voters by pushing off the left. That's not what the president is doing, and that's not our strategy."[8]

Yet whatever Obama's intentions, triangulation was within the realm of his instincts. Of Clinton's "third way," Obama had written: "It was Bill Clinton's singular contribution that he tried to transcend…ideological deadlock, recognizing not only that what had come to be meant by the labels of 'conservative' and 'liberal' played to Republican advantage, but that the categories were inadequate to address the problems we faced."[9] Obama recognized, however, that Clinton's third-way policies were "modest in their goals." Which begs the questions: Can modestly progressive economic and social policies close the yawning racial gaps between black and white Americans? Or would Obama be significantly more ambitious than Clinton?

To fulfill his vision of race-neutral remedies to racialized economic and social disparity, Obama would have to be. For it is not merely Clinton's third way on politics with which Obama identified, but also Clinton's third way on race. Before his ascendancy to the presidency, Obama wrote: "An emphasis on universal, as opposed to race-specific, programs isn't just good policy; it's also good politics."[10] In this regard, African Americans were not getting much more on the race question by electing the first black president than they achieved in electing Bill Clinton. Obama would appoint to the United States Supreme Court Elena Kagan, and to his administration Bruce Reed as the vice president's chief of staff. Kagan and Reed were the architects of Clinton's "race neutral opportunity agenda."[11] Despite the opposition of black advisors, such as Harvard Law School's Chris Edley, Kagan and Reed carried the day.[12] Their mantra was strikingly similar to Obama's: "[T]he best hope for improving race relations and reducing racial disparities over the long term is a set of policies that expand opportunity across race lines and, in doing so, force the recognition of shared interests."[13]

Like Kagan and Reed, Obama acknowledged the need for some race-specific remedies—at least prior to his election.[14] But make no mistake: according to Obama, "[T]he most important tool to close the gap between minority and white workers may have little to do with race at all. . . . [W]hat ails working-class and middle-class blacks and Latinos is not fundamentally different from what ails their white counterparts. . . ."[15]

We should recognize that this residual approach, which I referred to as white-to-black trickle down in chapter 1, is hardly ingenious. Given black disadvantages in most socioeconomic categories, almost any government intervention that does not disadvantage African Americans stands a good chance of helping them disproportionately. Yet as Edley points out, relying on race-neutral social welfare programs to close racial gaps is largely what has been done in the past, and it simply has not worked.[16]

Putting to one side the merits of race neutrality, nearly three-quarters of the way through his first term, Obama's apparent embrace of Clintonian political triangulation had significantly hampered his ability to fulfill his vision of race neutrality. Yes, Obama had succeeded in passing universal health coverage.[17] But on jobs, education, income security, income inequality, Medicare, Medicaid, and Social Security, Obama found himself debating the scope of government on conservative Republican terms, which meant that the scope of any intervention could not possibly be large enough to address racial disparity in broad, nonracial terms.

It was not merely Obama's reneging on his promise to discontinue the Bush upper-class tax cuts that signaled his concessionary posture. A recurring nemesis of Democratic progressivism once again precluded race-neutral advancement of African Americans (if it were possible to begin with): budget deficits born largely of conservative Republican tax and spending policies. As one *Washington Post* opinion writer observed, the renewed and heightened focus on reduction of the nation's federal debt "indicates how thoroughly Republicans are dominating the political discussion."[18]

It was political déjà vu. Faced with the budget deficits of the Reagan and Bush I eras, President Clinton shelved his plans for social investments early in his presidency and placed the greatest priority on deficit reduction.[19] As the political science duo Paul Pierson and Jacob S. Hacker observe in their illuminating book *Winner-Take-All Politics*, pressured by Wall Street allies Robert Rubin and Alan Greenspan, Clinton "replaced his social investment strategy with an 'interest rate' strategy," in which fiscal rectitude would be the engine for growth. In the process, however, Democrats forfeited the opportunity to provide substantial direct support to the middle class (to say nothing of the poor).[20] Moreover, "the more Democrats committed themselves to austerity, the more they allowed Republicans to play Santa Claus." Thus, Republicans could increase defense spending and cut taxes for the upper class while leaving Democrats with the bill.[21]

Three-quarters of the way into his first term, Obama was becoming Clinton: a cleanup act. This stage was largely set by George W. Bush's deficits born of massive tax cuts, an unfunded expansion of Medicare, and two wars funded by debt. But according to former Federal Deposit Insurance Corporation (FDIC) Chairwoman Sheila Bair, between 2008 and the spring of 2009, the federal government had also committed almost $14 trillion in assistance to financial institutions to stabilize markets in the face of a recession induced at least in part by their own conduct.[22] These subsidies further constrained Obama's ability to assist the middle class and the poor, let alone minority communities, who were the least well-off among these groups. On this austere terrain, there could be little hope of closing racial gaps through broad, non-race-specific remedies in any enduring fashion. Political triangulation became a necessity, and a new post-racial triangulation would be practiced in tandem.

Obama's budget proposals bespoke this reality. Shortly after he extended the Bush tax breaks, Obama proposed a 2012 fiscal budget that would freeze discretionary spending for five years and reduce deficits by $1.1 trillion over the next decade by making such cuts as heating assistance for the poor, employment and labor training, and community block grants.[23] Under Obama's proposed budget, nonsecurity discretionary spending as a percentage of gross domestic product (GDP) would drop to a level lower than that seen under Presidents Reagan and Clinton, and one not seen since 1962.[24] Domestic discretionary spending encompasses a number of categories vital to any vision of the race-neutral elimination of racial disparities, such as education, health services, and housing assistance.[25] A dispirited Representative Jesse Jackson, Jr. quipped, "How can we stop the Republican cuts when the President has one-upped them?"[26]

Although Obama proposed modest increases in education funding, such as support for Pell Grants, the increases did not come close to the scale of spending needed to begin erasing racial inequality without some focus on race. For one thing, even as Obama was proposing his increases, state and local governments were drastically scaling back their investments in education.[27] For another, the black-white achievement gap in education is simply too yawning and complex to be bridged by incremental funding increases in education. Former Education Secretary Roderick Paige observes in his recent work in this area that blacks lag whites by large margins in virtually every measurement of educational achievement.[28] Among others, Columbia University education professor Michael Rebell has persuasively argued that money matters—and not merely the money needed to make up the per-pupil expenditure difference between poor and wealthier school districts. Instead, Rebell argues that poverty itself is an impediment to closing the racial achievement gap and that government (and private agencies) must make substantial investments in the "out-of-school" conditions from which poor students hail.[29]

Pushed further rightward by congressional Tea Party Republicans threatening to cause the nation to default its debt obligations by voting against an increase in the national debt ceiling, Obama began to concede even broader cuts, this time as part of a commitment to reduce deficits by $4 trillion over 12 years.[30] To achieve this, the president agreed to reduce Medicare and Medicaid—health insurance programs for the elderly and poor—by tens of billions of dollars over ten years.[31] The figure of $4 trillion was not coincidental. It was the figure that U.S. credit rating companies such as Standard & Poors had insisted the federal government cut from its spending in order to avert a downgrade of U.S. treasury bonds.[32] (These same credit rating companies had contributed to the 2008 Great Recession by misjudging the soundness of the mortgage-backed securities that became the loci of the financial markets' unraveling.[33])

As debt-reduction/debt-ceiling negotiations dragged on during the summer of 2011, whispers of triangulation became echoes. Continuing reports of Obama's willingness to allow deep cuts to federal agency budgets and entitlement programs prompted several congressional Democrats to question whether Obama shared the core values of the Democratic Party.[34] The White House once again denied the charge it was emulating Clintonian triangulation, arguing that it was instead seeking a "grand bargain" to reduce the deficit that would include taxes on the rich.[35] But during the negotiations, Obama had proposed far more in spending cuts to entitlement and other programs than he had revenue increases from taxing the wealthy and corporations.[36] Indeed, at one point during the negotiations, Obama had agreed to a plan that was further to the political right than at least two major bipartisan competing proposals.[37] Obama was willing to raise the Medicare eligibility age from 65 to 67 and to adjust the Social Security cost-of-living formula to one less generous to seniors.[38]

Obama's tilt to the right drew sharp criticism from progressive commentators such as economist Paul Krugman, who opined "It's getting harder and harder to trust Mr. Obama's motives in the budget fight, given the way his economic rhetoric has veered to the right. In fact, if all you did was listen to his speeches, you might conclude that he basically shares the G.O.P.'s diagnosis of what ails our economy and what should be done to fix it."[39] Others believed that Obama's accommodation to Republicans was less tactical and more a reflection of weak leadership. Jonathan Chait of *The New Republic* inveighed, "There's a limit to how much faith one can place in a man who has so badly misjudged his political opponents time and time again."[40]

The deal that was ultimately struck was almost completely on Republicans' terms. It contained no tax increases. But it sliced more than $2.1 trillion in government spending over ten years through a combination of designated cuts and cuts to be proposed by a joint congressional committee.[41] Although the bipartisan commission, consisting of equal numbers of Democrats and Republicans, could in theory recommend tax increases, Republicans had successfully resisted such increases during the debt-ceiling negotiations and Speaker John Boehner declared them off the table for the future.[42] The plan divided Obama's party in the House, where Democrats split 95 to 95 on the plan. Yet Obama praised the plan because it resulted in "the lowest level of annual domestic spending since Dwight Eisenhower was president."[43] This was a curious encomium from a president who claimed not to be triangulating his base. It was also an ironic disposition for a president who touted race-neutral remedies to black socio-economic disparities.

After the 2010 midterm elections and the debt-ceiling negotiations, there was no need for Obama to expressly channel Clinton's triangulating aphorism—"The era of big government is over."[44] Obama's concessionary behavior spoke louder than slogans. Indeed, by the eve of the commencement of Obama's reelection campaign, his economic team looked strikingly similar to Clinton's.[45] Moreover, like Clinton, Obama's concessions to the Republicans assumed that Republicans were actually interested in deficit reduction. They were not. They were interested in smaller government, something altogether different.[46] Deficits resulting from tax cuts were acceptable to Republicans because they would "starve the beast"—that is, they would force shrinkage of government social programs.[47] This, in turn, meant that there was simply no possibility of broad-based, race-neutral social expenditures that would speed the closure of racial disparities. Instead, like Clinton, Obama would have to wait out a recession and hope that the black boats at the bottom would be lifted by a rising economy. This, however, is simply the ephemeral equality of boom and bust.

Boom and Retrenchment

In *The Audacity of Hope*, then-Senator Barack Obama praised the concept of "a rising tide lifting minority boats." Citing the reduction in black unemployment in the 1990s to record lows and the record high growth in black income, Obama wrote, "If you want to know the secret of Bill Clinton's popularity among African Americans, you need look no further than these statistics."[48]

To continue with the sailing metaphor, one problem with Obama's fondness for macroeconomics as a palliative for African Americans is that in a rising tide, there are boats, yachts, and cruise ships. Black boats get lifted, but a boat is still just a boat. Equally troubling with Obama's rising-tides philosophy is that many African Americans experience a relative ripple rather than a wave but fail to distinguish the two.

And so it was with Clinton. Despite the economic milestones reached among blacks during the Clinton years—that is, record rates of employment, reductions in the rate of poverty, and greater educational proficiency—a nagging inequality persisted between blacks and whites that would render blacks first-line victims to the savagery of the Great Recession that ushered in the Obama presidency. By the mid-1990s, while the poverty rate among blacks had declined significantly, more than a quarter of black families continued to live in poverty while only one in ten white families did.[49] In 1997, the median per capita income for whites stood at $20,425; for blacks, $12,351. Indeed, more than midway through the booming 1990s, the very poorest blacks—those at the bottom quintile—experienced a net loss in their average income compared to a net gain by the very poorest whites.[50] While the poorest blacks were the worst off, black inequality existed at all income strata. Thus, even in white-collar professions, black incomes trailed white comparators by substantial margins.[51]

Income differs from accumulative wealth. On this metric, the 1990s were likely less kind, if not unkind, to African Americans. In 1997, the median net worth for white households was $43,800 compared to $3,700 for blacks.[52]

These disparities did not prevent many African Americans from misperceiving their own economic circumstances relative to whites—a phenomenon that may partly explain the latitude blacks have afforded Obama to triangulate them. In the mid-1990s only 10 percent of blacks believed that African Americans were economically better off than whites. By 2000, however, that number exceeded a quarter of African American respondents. Concomitantly, the number of blacks who believed that blacks were worse off than whites fell from nearly 65 percent in 1984 to 43 percent in 2000.[53] Contrary to Obama's belief that economic progress accounted for Clinton's popularity among blacks, political scientists Melissa Harris-Lacewell and Bethany Albertson have concluded that blacks' strong identification with the Democratic Party colored their perceptions of how well-off they were economically and, in the case of many, of how well-off they were relative to whites.[54]

Those false perceptions were crushed by the brutal realities of the Great Recession of 2008, which perhaps once and for all demonstrated that the equality of boom and bust is insufficient to address the needs of black America. The Kirwan Institute for the Study of Race and Ethnicity at Ohio State University published a series of reports on the differing impacts of the recession and the divergent paths of recovery. One year into the recession, black men had a staggering official unemployment rate of 17.6 percent compared to 9.1 percent for white men.[55] The unemployment rate for black women was nearly double that of white women.[56] Black unemployment rates have historically come down faster than white unemployment during an economic upswing.[57] But the grinding recovery from the Great Recession tested this pattern. Although the recession officially ended in June 2009, from October 2009 to October 2010, the black unemployment rate continued to climb while the white unemployment rate declined.[58] Two years after the official end of the recession, black unemployment continued to rise, and black men recorded the lowest level of employment since the government began maintaining records in 1972—only 56.1 percent compared to 68.3 percent for white men.[59]

Other economic indicators vividly illustrate the perils of boom and bust equality. In 2004, the median net worth of white households was $134,280 compared to $13,450 for black households. By 2009, while the median net worth for whites had fallen 24 percent, the median black net worth had fallen a staggering 83 percent to $2,170.[60] Meanwhile, 2009 saw an increase in the black poverty rate to 25.8 percent, or more than one in four persons.[61]

As the Obama White House trained its attention on the Republican-driven issue of deficit reduction, the driving force of so much of black America's misery—unemployment, or more accurately, disemployment—appeared to be forgotten.[62] But not by African Americans. Two years after the official end of the Great Recession, unemployment remained the top concern among blacks.[63]

Obama's adherence to Clintonian triangulation left him bereft of the ability to deploy dwindling government resources toward race-neutral remedies, a disability to which he seemed resigned after the 2010 midterm election if not before. And while he had previously celebrated the ability of the boom in economic cycles to close racial gaps, racial gaps clearly persist during economic upturns and retrench during subsequent busts, in some cases leaving African Americans worse off than they were at their starting point. Markets alone cannot ensure enduring racial equality. Under these circumstances, a concerted focus on race is not only logical but principled. Race, however, appeared to have a stultifying effect on Obama. Even when it was logical and principled to address race head-on, Obama dodged, auguring his triangulation of black voters.

THE CALL OF RACE

Obama was a constitutional law scholar prior to winning a U.S. Senate seat and then the presidency. His talent for pedagogy followed him to the Oval Office, as evidenced by this response to a question regarding the disemployment crisis in black America:

> The only thing I cannot do is, by law I can't pass laws that say I'm just helping black folks. I'm the president of the entire United States. What I can do is make sure that I am passing laws that help all people, particularly those who are most vulnerable and most in need. That, in turn, is going to help lift up the African-American community.[64]

By law? With mounting and irrefutable evidence that unemployment in African American communities had reached epidemic proportions and that ordinary market forces were incapable of curing this recurring malaise, the president pointed the finger to the United States Supreme Court—to which he would soon appoint a proponent of race-neutral affirmative action, Elena Kagan.[65] But it is really a triangulation tailored to a black president and his African American voters much more than the law that explains Obama's response.

Imagine a federally administered jobs program in which dollars were directed to the zip codes with the highest and most persistent unemployment rates over a period of five years.[66] The concept is similar to proposals by the Congressional Black Caucus (CBC) that would send grants to the areas most deprived of jobs.[67] There would be nothing race-based about this program on the face of it, though it is reasonably clear that its beneficiaries would be those who are disproportionately afflicted by unemployment—blacks and Latinos. Such a program would be Obama's analog to President Johnson's War on Poverty, a program of non-race-specific application but aimed at those disproportionately affected by poverty—blacks.[68]

What might be the Supreme Court's objection to this program? It's difficult to see any reasoned equal protection basis to declare the program unconstitutional, though, as we learned in chapter 2, the conservative majority on the Court has overdetermined race when doing so has suited its purposes. Put differently, if there were a drought in Iowa, the Supreme Court could not declare special aid to that state unconstitutional because it is overwhelmingly white. And so goes unemployment: special assistance for the economic catastrophe in areas primarily inhabited by blacks and Latinos cannot be any less constitutional than disaster relief to Iowa—or New Orleans and Mississippi after Hurricane Katrina. The Supreme Court ordinarily applies its strictest level of constitutional scrutiny only to racial *classifications*, not to government action that merely has a racial impact.[69] The putative jobs program would not deploy the kinds of race-based presumptions that rendered the federal government's minority subcontracting program vulnerable to attack in *Adarand v. Pena*. There, the federal law defined its targeted beneficiaries—subcontractors controlled by socially and economically disadvantaged individuals—in racial terms by presuming that racial minorities fit this category.[70]

But use of a zip code is neither a racial presumption nor category. It is simply the government's means of determining where its dollars can have the greatest impact. And in this instance, there is a politically—if not legally—conservative justification for limiting the government's intervention to the highest and most persistent areas of unemployment: scarce government resources.[71] Conservatives cannot have it both ways. They cannot make the use of broad-based, race-neutral social programs to close racial gaps fiscally infeasible by starving the government of revenue and at the same time protest narrowly cast remedies that avoid racial categorization but redound disproportionately to the benefit of racial minorities.[72] The compounding of these two positions is simply a prescription for the ossification of black socioeconomic inequality.

Nor can Obama have it both ways. He cannot celebrate race neutrality in government policies that advance racial equality but agree to shrink the size of government to the point that the scale of any such policies pales in comparison to the racial inequality they are intended to indirectly address. Nor can he plausibly portray himself as the captive of a race-averse Supreme Court as opposed to a politician averse to the risks of addressing race. As the heuristic above shows, there is judicial latitude to address racial disadvantage without running afoul of the Constitution. Obama's legalistic response ignored this latitude and substituted a straw man, that is, "I can't pass laws that say I'm just helping black folks," for the essential question: to what degree was the Obama administration prepared to advocate and implement legally permissible programs targeted at the economic woes of black Americans?

After the midterm election debacle, Obama conceded that fiscal constraints, or at least his willingness to negotiate the scale of government based on Republicans' views of fiscal constraints, made broader jobs programs such as a large infrastructure bank impossible.[73] Even aside from this, however, Obama's vision of white-to-black trickle down had far less application in the unemployment context than in other policy areas. Most serious legal scholars and other observers who have examined the issue of black unemployment agree that discrimination plays a major role.[74] In other words, black unemployment is an issue that calls out for some consideration of race.

The historical and sustained rates of disproportionate black unemployment belie the ability of nonracial factors to explain this phenomenon. Educational achievement differences cannot independently explain unemployment differentials when, according to the Bureau of Labor Statistics, blacks with a bachelor's degree or higher were 43 percent to 46 percent more likely to be unemployed than similarly educated whites.[75] In the nation's all-too-important retail sector, where lower educational attainment is a given, African Americans face systemic discrimination in both attaining and maintaining jobs. Analyzing personnel data from a large U.S. national retail firm, a 2009 *Journal of Labor Economics* study found that the race of a hiring manager was a significant determinant in the job prospects of black applicants. Specifically, all nonblack managers—whites, Latinos, and Asians—were more likely to hire more whites and fewer blacks than were black managers.[76] When a nonblack manager replaced a black manager, the rate of black employment decreased by 15 percent if the store was located outside the South and 28 percent if it was located in the South.[77]

The retail-firm study also found that, once hired, black employees fare worse under nonblack managers than black managers, incurring more dismissals and receiving fewer promotions.[78] These findings are consistent with statistics from the U.S. Equal Employment Opportunity Commission (EEOC). Of the approximately 100,000 charges (complaints) the EEOC receives annually, a disproportionate 35.9 percent are race-discrimination charges, largely by African Americans claiming discrimination in being terminated from their jobs.[79]

Obama sought not only to deracialize the unemployment crisis with stock responses—"[T]he most important thing I can do for the African-American community is the same thing I can do for the American community, period, and that is get the economy going again and get people hiring again"—but also to portray the crisis as white.[80] Shortly after the debt-ceiling drama in the summer of 2011, Obama realized that congressional Republicans had succeeded in diverting his attention from the most pressing issue among voters—unemployment. Obama embarked on a jobs tour through the Midwest at which he stopped only in white communities. A *Wall Street Journal* headline reporting on the tour blared, "Obama Aims to Keep White Voters on Board."[81] The slight to communities of color was puzzling. Although blacks and Latinos constituted 25 percent of the labor force, they were 35 percent of all unemployed Americans at the time of Obama's bus tour.[82] Obama's strategy of ignoring this disproportionate suffering was so transparent to members of the CBC that these ordinarily stalwart supporters of the president lashed out. Representative Maxine Waters of California protested, "We're getting tired. The unemployment is unconscionable. We don't know what the strategy is. We don't know why on this trip that he's in the United States now, he's not in any black community."[83] This was one of several instances in which the first black president's attempt to flee race wound up highlighting it in unconstructive ways.[84]

Obama's attempt to erase race from a social ill possessing a significant—indeed, obvious—racial component is part of his and the nation's propensity to resist the call of race. That this pattern on the part of Obama is not an unbroken one does not defeat the claim.

(Similarly, triangulation marked much but certainly not all of Clinton's term in office.) Obama's resistance to race is still quite strong, even if, as discussed in the next chapter, it is explainable as strategic. For all of his studied resistance, however, even in the limited instances where Obama appeared to achieve his vision of race neutrality that redounded disproportionately to the benefit of minorities, he was powerless to keep race at bay. This point is better understood if we think of racism as a marketplace in which the words and actions of African Americans, as perceived by white Americans, are much more susceptible to racialization than the conduct of other market actors. I have defined racialization as a type of racial profiling that assigns to its object the cultural stereotypes associated with the object's racial group and leads to assessments based on these stereotypes.[85] In this market, racial subordination is meted out commensurately to the perceived infraction of white cultural and political norms.

If empirically accurate, this conceptualization of racism poses an immediate problem for Obama's vision of race-neutral governance and his tactical avoidance of race: because he is black, Obama's actions are susceptible to racialization regardless of their race-neural intent or content. Obama's landmark health-care legislation, the Patient Protection and Affordable Care Act, provides a useful example. Obama rightly boasts of this measure as being of especial importance to African Americans. According to the U.S. Department of Health and Human Services, as of 2007, 19.5 percent of blacks were uninsured compared to 10.4 percent of whites.[86]

On Obama's view of it, a universal health-care plan should command broad, cross-racial support since "[a]n emphasis on universal, as opposed to race-specific, programs isn't just good policy; it's also good politics." Every Democratic president since Franklin Delano Roosevelt, and several Republican presidents—including Richard Nixon—had sought to expand health coverage or provide universal coverage.[87] Nevertheless, because of the strong association many Americans make between African Americans and governmental services, support for government-mandated universal health care was racially divided prior to Obama's election.[88] It was even more so after Obama was elected and became chief spokesperson for the issue. Comparing survey data on Bill Clinton's government-mandated health insurance proposal to the same proposal in the Obama plan revealed a drop-off in white support and an increase in black support of the Obama plan.[89]

Michael Tesler and David Sears describe this schism as the "spillover of racialization." Employing a concept of racialization similar but not identical to my own, Tesler and Sears examined the role of racial resentment (and liberality) in Obama's 2008 election contest. Noting that most white Americans fall on the racially conservative side of a continuum of racial empathy developed by Sears, Tesler and Sears examined the role that individual racial predispositions had on vote choice in 2008. Using a series of regression analyses to control for the effects of partisanship and other variables, Tesler and Sears concluded that the general election contest between Obama and Republican John McCain was one in which the racial resentment of racially conservative whites had "an unusual salience," making it more important than in previous all-white presidential contests.[90] This was not because either candidate invoked race either explicitly or implicitly, or because the issues context of the election was race related. To the contrary, Obama's campaign assiduously avoided racial issues. Rather, "The historic racial significance that was unmistakably associated with Barack Obama's candidacy meant that voters' racial predispositions were in most cases highly accessible to them…allowing racial attitudes to play a major role in forming their evaluations of him."[91]

Overwhelming support among racial liberals, an economy teetering on the brink of depression, and a hugely unpopular Republican incumbent allowed Obama to overcome the major impact of racial resentment and secure a historic victory. Racial resentment, however, would continue to play a role in the public's evaluation of Obama's policies. Tesler and Sears conclude: "Barack Obama racialized evaluations of other objects via transfer of affect—racial predispositions were transferred from opinion about Obama to related political evaluations when there was a strong association between the two."[92]

That transfer of racialization was in full view in remarks by Senator Tom Coburn of Oklahoma. When the conservative Republican was asked at a town hall meeting whether Obama wanted to destroy America, Coburn linked Obama's support of government programs to Obama's race:

[T]hink about his life. And think about what he was exposed to and what he saw in America. He's only relating what his experience in life was.…

His intent isn't to destroy. It's to create dependency because it worked so well for him. I don't say that critically. Look at people for what they are. Don't assume ulterior motives. I don't think he doesn't love our country. I think he does.…As an African American male, coming through the progress of everything he experienced, he got tremendous benefit through a lot of these programs. So he believes in them. I just don't believe they work overall and in the long run they don't help our country. But he doesn't know that because his life experience is something different.[93]

That a president who had gone to extraordinary lengths to take race off the table in national policy dialogue could nonetheless have his race used by a member of the U.S. Senate to explain his policy agenda suggested the entrenched limitations of Obama's race-neutral approach to governing. Members of the CBC were percipient witnesses to Obama's racialization on Capitol Hill and, unlike Obama, they have inveighed against what they saw and heard. In discussing health care, Representative Eleanor Holmes Norton of the District of Columbia reaches anecdotally the same conclusion that Tesler and Sears arrived at in their research:

> I think I figured that [opposition to Obama's health-care legislation] out. I said what is this about? Now I think I know, and blacks should understand this if I am correct. And the reason is, hey, most people had health insurance; therefore, they think this is for black people and for poor people.... I do not now have as much amazement as to why it was not embraced. And when you load onto that that it's an African-American who will be seen as doing it because African-Americans need healthcare, well, that's all you need. But, remember, this started with the stimulus [bill] as well.[94]

Speaking in the context of the debt-ceiling debate in which Republicans insisted on a balanced budget amendment to the Constitution, Jesse Jackson, Jr. is perhaps the most pointed in his critique of the Republicans' racialization of Obama:

> Treating President Obama differently than all past Presidents reflects an institutional bias against the South Side of Chicago. Rep. Joe Wilson reflected the same institutional bias when in an unprecedented manner he called the President a liar in the middle of his State of the Union Address. Speaker John Boehner reflected a similar institutional bias when he said he and the President had the same responsibility, equating his job as Speaker, a legislative function, with the job of the President of the United States, an executive function. Doubting the birth place of Barack Obama, doubting his Christian faith and experience, calling him a Muslim and a Socialist reflects the same institutional bias. The Republicans' proposed balanced budget amendment reflects a similar institutional bias. The only other place where there is a BBA, a balanced budget amendment, is in the Constitution of the Confederate states of America.[95]

Congressman William Lacy Clay, Jr. of Missouri also cites the occasion of Congressman Joe Wilson's interrupting Obama's State of the Union address to call Obama a liar as evidence of the exceptional treatment to which the first black president has been subjected. Of Obama and the opposition to his legislative agenda, Clay opines: "He didn't think they would resort to racial politics, which in effect they have.... He still is a black man in America."[96]

Given the great potential for racialization of social welfare initiatives supported by an African American president, Obama's vision of race neutrality in public policy is more precatory than real. The question for Obama was not whether he could avoid the call of race—he could not. Instead, the question was how he would broker racial divisions that in some instances would become greater because he was the nation's first black commander-in-chief. Obama's gradual adoption of Clintonian political triangulation would largely deprive him of his ability to mediate race through white-to-black trickle down—and any meaningful attempt to realize that vision would likely have been racialized anyway. Even before the midterm election and debt-ceiling negotiations cemented his embrace of Clintonian triangulation, however, Obama demonstrated he would deal with race the same way almost any white Democrat would—by ignoring it and paying homage to racial symbolism. Except that Obama was not white.

With Obama in office, the new politics of triangulation were the old politics of race avoidance accompanied by a heightened political imperative for the enforcement of this avoidance given the president's race. Coming as it did in the post-civil-rights-era nadir of black politics, the new triangulation threatened to supplant racial inequality as a national issue more effectively than if Obama had never been elected.

CHAPTER 6

The New Politics of Triangulation: Obama and Post-Racialism

In order to get beyond racism, we must first take account of race. There is no other way. And in order to treat some persons equally, we must treat them differently. We cannot—we dare not—let the Equal Protection Clause perpetuate racial supremacy.

—Justice Harry Blackmun, *Regents of the University of California v. Bakke* (1978)[1]

A black man *can't be president of America. However, an extraordinary, gifted, and talented young man who happens to be black can be president.*

—Cornell Belcher, Obama Pollster (circa 2008)[2]

Separated by thirty years are two contrasting visions of how the nation must address racial inequality. The first is that of Justice Harry Blackmun, a moderate white Republican jurist appointed to the United States Supreme Court by President Richard Nixon. The second is that of Cornell Belcher, Obama's pollster and another embodiment of the new black politics. To better understand this juxtaposition, we should appreciate the meaning of Belcher's emphasis on "black man": a black candidate running with a strong identification with "black" issues is unelectable. That a middle-aged white Republican in 1978 was more inclined to engage the question of racial inequality than a disciple of the new black politics in 2008 underscores the bind of African American voters. But why should the equality that blacks sought more than 30 years ago through the courts—but have not yet fully obtained—be a verboten subject in the political process today? The reason, which is this chapter's principal exploration, is that white voters often insist on the triangulation of black voters as the price of white support for a black candidate.

The American two-party system's relationship to issues of race is best characterized in a word: avoidance. Race may erupt in the form of a crisis or as a calculated appeal—usually by the racially conservative party—to win political advantage, but the norm in American politics is to suppress discussion of racial equality for fear of losing broad support.[3] Until 2008 and the election of Barack Obama as president, this norm was sustained under white political leadership. One of the great ironies of Obama's political ascendancy has been his determination to reinforce this norm, and indeed to fortify it. But doing so has proved a more complicated slalom than even someone as politically astute as Obama could have imagined. Yes, Obama would avail himself of the same racial symbolism as Bill Clinton—speeches before the Congressional Black Caucus (CBC) gala, honoring black artists with lifetime achievement awards, and a genuine affinity with black audiences and voters that no Republican could boast. But for a black president, avoidance of race meant that when race inevitably arose, its significance increased for both Obama's most ardent supporters (black voters) and his most skeptical (white voters). The outcome would not be racial avoidance at all, but rather racial deferral accompanied by intermittent implosions of the logjam. The new triangulation triangulated not just black voters but its practitioner-in-chief, the first black president.

The Quadruple Handicap of the Post-Racial Black Politician

Fairly or unfairly, Barack Obama has faced a unique liability as the first black president. The hopes of 41 million blacks were transposed onto his election, while the suspicions of even the moderately progressive whites who supported him would be instantly aroused were he to overtly indulge the substantive aspirations of his black and brown benefactors. Obama understood—perhaps intuitively, but certainly from his professional advisers—what political scientists have documented as a fact of American political life: a racial milieu harms a minority politician in a white-majority electorate.

Keith Reeves has proven this proposition through an inventive "social experiment." Reeves manipulated the race of a fictional mayoral candidate using news articles issued to a probability-screened group of voting-age white adults. Participants were given one article in which the candidates disagreed on either an environmental issue or affirmative action. In each article, the description of the candidate was the same, except the race of one candidate, Gregory Hammond, was sometimes varied. There was no other differentiation between the candidates. Reeves sought to measure the participants' support for Hammond in his black incarnation versus his white incarnation. Of particular significance are Reeves's conclusions regarding the preferences of the experimental group that was given the article describing Hammond as black and as favoring affirmative action as a remedy to "an identifiable history of discrimination by an employer." The combination of the mention of Hammond's race and his position on affirmative action stimulated racial stereotypes and accompanying resistance among whites to Hammond's candidacy. When participants were asked for whom would they vote if the election were held today,

> [W]hites were unwilling to say that they would cast a ballot for either the white Christopher candidate or his black challenger [Hammond]. . . . [T]he findings reveal a striking tendency on the part of whites simply to "vacate the field," that is, stampede toward the undecided category, as evidenced by the 49 percent who declared themselves "undecided." Observe that among those who read the biracial contest story, *the percentage of undecideds more than doubled.*[4]

Reeves concludes from a study of the racial attitudes of the undecided participants that they were unlikely to support the black Hammond once inside the voting booth. The experiment has broad implications for the post-racial African American politician:

> [B]ecause our study participants were randomly assigned to the experimental condition of reading one news story, as compared to another, the resistance to supporting the black Hammond candidate in the affirmative action story experiment can be attributed to only a single causal explanation: the subtle appeal of race. Second, because great care was taken "to anticipate and defend against" the weaknesses generally associated with experiments, the results here "can be safely generalized to populations of real interest."[5]

From Reeves's work, we discern the first handicap of the post-racial black politician, which is really a descendant of the centuries-old American taboo: post-racialism entails a norm against discussing race, especially racial inequality. Note the context in which race arises in Reeves's social experiment. It is not the race-baiting context of, say, Senator Jesse Helms and his infamous commercial depicting a white man being turned down for a job because of affirmative action. Instead, Reeves is portraying a more subtle cognitive processing of race in which the color of the speaker disadvantages him because the subject of the speech—affirmative action—activates the latent stereotypes associated with the speaker's racial group.[6] This is the sociolinguistic dimension of racialization.

If the mere discussion of race as a substantive issue can disadvantage a black politician, then racial cuing by political opponents and the media can certainly compound his disadvantage. Cuing introduces three additional post-racial handicaps to a quadrant of disabilities that besets black candidates today. A racial cue is a latent message about an ostensibly nonracial issue that encourages the viewer to subliminally deploy racial stereotypes in interpreting the communication.[7] The infamous 1988 Willie Horton ad, featuring a black convict who assaulted a white couple while on furlough, is often discussed as the paradigm of racial cuing. Crime is the issue in the ad, but the association between criminality and blacks imbued the ad with racist potentiality. Such a dated example risks being swept aside in a post-racial world in which the nation has elected its first black president. However, Charlton McIlwain and Stephen Caliendo examined hundreds of political ads for U.S. House and Senate races produced between 1970 and 2006. In *Race Appeal,* they conclude that the use of ads with racial cuing actually increased during the 1990s and into the twenty-first century.[8] They predict that as more minority candidates compete against whites in electoral contests, the increasing trend of white candidates deploying campaign ads with high racist potentiality will continue.

At seeming variance with their prediction, McIlwain and Caliendo conducted an experiment involving the use of a racially cued ad by a white candidate in a hypothetical biracial contest in which they found that the use of racial cuing did not benefit its white proponent.[9] The researchers note, however, that their findings were "contrary to historical trends," and add that variances in results of models intended to predict voting choice are "not particularly surprising."[10] Thus, they do not attempt to contradict the findings of social scientists such as Reeves but instead supplement those findings with empirical evidence that corroborates the first disability of the post-racial black politician and dovetails with the others. Although the black candidate in McIlwain and Caliendo's experiment did not use an implicit racial appeal in his ad, the researchers found that 41 percent of the white respondents believed the black candidate was injecting race into the contest. It appears that the black candidate's mere presence in a biracial contest was sufficient to racialize the contest in the minds of these white respondents.[11] Yet, just as the (mis)perception that the black candidate had invoked race gained votes for the white candidate, the accurate perception that the white candidate had invoked race gained support for the black candidate.[12]

Consistent with the norm of race avoidance, McIlwain and Caliendo conclude that voters seek to enforce an "acute colorblindness," in which the discussion of race is simply not tolerated.[13] This reinforces the first disability under which the post-racial black politician must function. The difficulty with acute colorblindness is that it "invalidates the possibility of any racial response—that is, the possibility that candidates may still need to point out, respond to, or otherwise resist the very real fact that prejudice and stereotypical thinking, often at the subconscious level, consistently have been, and still very much are part of America's collective racial psyche."[14]

And thus the quadrant is complete. Post-racialism entails a norm against discussing race, especially racial inequality. Yet racial cuing by white candidates may prove effective; therefore, the black candidate must respond. But responding at all fortifies a white predisposition to see the black candidate as racializing the contest, while responding too vigorously plays into white predispositions that the black candidate is a "race man."[15]

In an environment such as this, what was Obama do to? The most obvious choices were that he could engage race at his own political peril, or he could triangulate black voters, keeping matters of racial inequality at bay while making it appear that he was seeking equanimity between black aspirations and white suspicions. But in apparently choosing the more conventional route of triangulation, Obama would find a twist that did not await Clinton: black voters could be triangulated, yet the implicit demand by white voters that blacks be triangulated meant that a black triangulator could not himself transcend race. Quite perversely, racial "accidents" or implosions would mark Obama's ascent to the White House and his first term in ways that, at least in hindsight, made it prudent to defy race avoidance as a political tactic from the very beginning.

REVEREND WRIGHT, OBAMA, AND SPLITTING THE DIFFERENCE UNEVENLY

The American prohibition on race talk is far from egalitarian. The contours for acceptable discourse vary according to the race of the speaker and the race and social positions of those about whom the speech is made and those evaluating the speech.[16] Senator Trent Lott of Mississippi was forced to step down as U.S. Senate Majority Leader after remarking that if segregationist Strom Thurmond had been elected president in 1948, America "would not have had all these problems." Four years later, however, he was elected Minority Whip for the Senate GOP. Senator George Allen's anti-Indian slur, "macaca," did not prevent him from carrying a majority of the white vote in his reelection campaign in Virginia. Likewise, Congressman Joe Wilson was comfortably returned to office after a historic breach of decorum in which he yelled during Obama's State of the Union address, "You lie!" Another congressman likened Obama to a "Tar Baby."

The treatment for African Americans who utter racialized statements that are considered beyond the pale is decidedly different. Louis Farrakhan's remarks concerning Jews earned him a motion of censure in the United States Senate—the same body that permitted Lott to reascend to its leadership ranks.[17] A white law professor at the University of California, Los Angeles, was fêted as a national intellectual for suggesting that blacks would be better off attending lower-ranked law schools, while Leonard Jeffries was ousted from his chairmanship at City University of New York for accusing various white ethnic groups of discriminating against blacks. The meta-principle should be apparent: the national prohibition on race talk—what McIlwain and Caliendo call acute colorblindness—is really a speech restraint on racial protest because whites are chronically "exhausted" by issues of race.[18] Whites, however, remain abundantly free to engage in offensive racial utterances and hide behind an intent defense—"I didn't mean to offend"—or the hypersensitivity accusation, "Why are they always trying to make something into a racial issue?!" And of course, the ever-imbricated line between what is racial versus what is simply conservative ideology further insulates white speech.

This is the cultural backdrop for the Reverend Jeremiah Wright's introduction to the nation during the 2008 presidential primaries. Obama had attended Wright's church on the South Side of Chicago, Trinity United Church of Christ, for twenty years. By Obama's own acknowledgment, their association was a close one: Wright had counseled Obama on scripture, officiated his wedding, and baptized his children. But at a critical juncture during the primary season, the media unearthed video of some of Wright's sermons. Both broadcast and print media tended to condense the sermons to their most controversial elements, which created potentially irreparable political harm to Obama's presidential candidacy. For example, the *New York*

Times described Wright's comments as incendiary and went on to quote the following passage from one of Wright's sermons following the 9/11 terrorist attacks on the United States: "We bombed Hiroshima, we bombed Nagasaki and we nuked far more than the thousands in New York and the Pentagon, and we never batted an eye…America's chickens are coming home to roost."[19]

One would not know from the *Times'* early reporting on the story that Wright had throughout the sermon condemned the 9/11 attacks on the United States as an act of "hatred." Nor would a reader be able to discern that Wright was expanding on the comments of a white U.S. ambassador who, according to Wright, had also observed that U.S. militarism begets terrorism against the United States.[20] Indeed, the substance of Wright's remarks is quite similar to that of Congressman Ron Paul, a candidate for the Republican presidential nomination in 2008 who remarked:

> Have you ever read the reasons they attacked us? They attacked us because we've been over there; we've been bombing Iraq for 10 years.….I'm suggesting that we listen to the people who attacked us and the reason they did it, and they are delighted that we're over there because Osama bin Laden has said, I'm glad you're over there on our sand because we can target you so much easier.[21]

Paul was celebrated in some conservative circles for his remarks, was twice reelected to his congressional seat since making them, and reentered the presidential contest for 2012, running more successfully than in his first bid. Meanwhile, Wright was simultaneously radicalized and racialized, for as you may recall from the previous chapter, even in the absence of express racial content, a black speaker's words can be interpreted through a racial prism, particularly where they activate dormant stereotypes about the speaker's identity group. In Wright's case, the association between blackness and lack of patriotism made his speech fodder for racialization.[22]

Parts of Wright's other sermons were specifically about race, abridging the rules of engagement on race talk for a black speaker. Of Hillary Clinton, Obama's chief rival for the Democratic nomination in 2008, Wright said: "Hillary never had a cab whiz past and not pick her up because her skin was the wrong color. Hillary was not a black boy raised in a single-parent home. Barack was. Barack knows what it means to be a black man living in a country and a culture that is controlled by rich white people. Hillary can never know that. Hillary ain't never been called a (EXPLETIVE DELETED)."[23]

Wright condemned America for its racism in a videotaped sermon that was perhaps the most frequently played excerpt during the news flare-up in the 2008 primaries:

> When it came to treating citizens of African descent fairly, America failed. She put them in chains. The government put them on slave quarters, put them on auction blocks, put them in cotton fields, put them in inferior schools, put them in substandard housing, put them in scientific experiments, put them in the lowest paying jobs, put them outside the equal protection of the law, kept them out of their racist bastions of higher education and locked them into position [sic] of hopelessness and helplessness. The government gives them the drugs, builds bigger prisons, passes a three-strike law, and then wants us to sing God bless America? No, no, no. Not God bless America; God damn America![24]

In short, Wright decided to discard the memo on race-talk etiquette in the United States for an African American. Obama, however, had no such luxury. He was bound by both the quadruple disabilities of the post-racial black politician and the rules for race speech by African Americans. In a brilliant and eloquent speech in Philadelphia in March 2008, Obama attempted to lift himself from this bind. On first impression, it was a signal that Obama just might eschew triangulating black voters in favor of a more honest and substantive relationship with this core constituency. On closer inspection, it fore-shadowed post-racial triangulation by Obama.

The speech was intended to put the Wright controversy behind Obama, but its breadth went well beyond Wright to discuss race in America generally. This was promising. That Obama condemned Wright's remarks was hardly remarkable, and indeed was obligatory to Obama's political survival. Wright understood this: "He's a politician, I'm a pastor. We speak to two different audiences. And he says what he has to say as a politician."[25] But much of what Obama had to say as a politician was fundamentally at odds with the African American experience and could reasonably be viewed as a signal to white voters. The speech was not intended for African American voters.

Obama reinforced the restraints on black protest speech when he alleged that Wright's remarks expressed a "profoundly distorted view of this country—a view that sees white racism as endemic...."[26] But for most blacks, it is endemic. Just three months after Obama gave his Philadelphia speech, a CBS News/*New York Times* Poll asked blacks if they thought race relations in the United States were "generally good" or "generally bad." Fifty-nine percent of the respondents said generally bad.[27] At the time of his speech, 43 percent of African Americans identified racial discrimination against blacks as a "very serious" problem, while only 11 percent of whites felt the same.[28] An earlier Gallup Poll found that 81 percent of African Americans believed racial minorities in the United States did not have the same opportunity as whites for a job, a view consistently borne out by black and brown unemployment statistics.[29] A 2010 ABC News/*Washington Post* poll found that only 11 percent of African Americans believed they had achieved racial equality.[30] For whom was Obama speaking? Not for blacks. To whom was he speaking? To white Americans who insisted that he speak this way as the price of his electoral success.

Obama, however, did appear genuinely empathetic to the plight of African Americans in a portion of the speech in which he detailed the history of discrimination against blacks and sought to situate the tenor of Wright's remarks in the generational confines of those who came of age in the '50s and '60s. There were at least two problems with this approach, though. First, Obama reduced Wright's expression to "anger and bitterness"—terms ordinarily used to elide the substance and factual predicates of black protest speech. Most problematically, Obama appeared equally empathetic to what he saw as "a similar anger" in segments of white America:

> Most working- and middle-class white Americans don't feel that they have been particularly privileged by their race. Their experience is the immigrant experience—as far as they're concerned, no one handed them anything. They built it from scratch. They've worked hard all their lives, many times only to see their jobs shipped overseas or their pensions dumped after a lifetime of labor. They are anxious about their futures, and they feel their dreams slipping away. And in an era of stagnant wages and global competition, opportunity comes to be seen as a zero sum game, in which your dreams come at my expense. So when they are told to bus their children to a school across town; when they hear an African-American is getting an advantage in landing a good job or a spot in a good college because of an injustice that they themselves never committed; when they're told that their fears about crime in urban neighborhoods are somehow prejudiced, resentment builds over time.[31]

Obama artfully attempted to deploy a theme of economic populism to bridge the black-white divide—it was a subspecies of his "rising tides" philosophy. But the risk of conflation was high and borne on the backs of African Americans. Most white people do not believe they have been the victim of any discrimination; most black people do.[32] The very definition of racial privilege is the license to live free of discrimination because of one's race. Racial privilege is merely the inverse of discrimination.[33] To allay white voters' fears in this manner—to seduce them into thinking that whiteness is a hardship comparable to blackness—is misleading, even if perceived as politically necessary. White hardship exists. But when a controlling majority in a liberal democracy experiences hardship at the hands of its own *chosen* government, the inequality it suffers is different in kind than that imposed on a racial minority whose electoral choices are often different. In short, to couch it in terms of Thomas Frank's *What's the Matter with Kansas*, white Americans have often gotten what they voted for even when it has not been good for them. Obama's equating of black anger over material conditions in America with white anger over the same was simply a false equivalence.

And it was the first of many turns to triangulation.

FATHER'S DAY WITHOUT PAY

Obama's March 2008 Philadelphia speech was followed soon after by a visit to a black church in Chicago on Father's Day. He used the occasion to criticize absent fathers—black fathers in particular—stating, "We need fathers to realize that responsibility does not end at conception."[34] The *New York Times* observed that "Mr. Obama laid out his case in stark terms that would be difficult for a white candidate to make...."[35]

Obama's remarks prompted a stern (and profane) rebuke from the Reverend Jesse Jackson, who believed Obama was "talking down to black people."[36] Jackson was not alone in impugning Obama's remarks. Within academic circles, commentators found that, "It's hard not to believe that such statements were meant to distance Obama from the Bad Black Man image."[37]

On the face of it, however, Obama had simply deployed his in-group racial familiarity to chastise a segment of the black community. Jackson himself had in the past done the same, once frankly commenting that, "I hate to admit it, but I have reached a stage in my life that if I am walking down a dark street late at night and I see that the person behind me is white, I subconsciously feel relieved."[38] Both Obama's and Jackson's remarks are superficially distinguishable from Bill Clinton's invocation of an obscure black rapper, Sister Souljah, in the wake of the 1992 Los Angeles riots. Clinton condemned Souljah for allegedly advocating black-on-white violence, but, in context, he appeared to be attempting to distance himself and the Democratic

Party from blacks—a racial dimension of Clintonian triangulation.[39] In any case, Clinton is white, depriving him of any traditional claim to in-group racial familiarity. Why, then, were Jackson and others so miffed by Obama's calling out of derelict black dads?

Because, as with Clinton, context matters. There was no racially transformative policy context that accompanied Obama's remarks in 2008, and even less of such a context during his first term as president when he made similar remarks. Transformative politics are policies that are both remedial and forward-looking in nature, that transcend ordinary political discourse, and that offer the promise of fundamental life alteration to those toward whom such policies are directed.[40] Among other legislation, the Civil Rights Act of 1964, the Voting Rights Act of 1965, and the Social Security Act of 1935 fit this hallowed category. The crisis within black families concerning absent fathers is part of a larger American exigency concerning black men generally. As recently as 2004, more than one in ten black males between the ages of 25 and 29 were incarcerated.[41] African Americans as a whole are eight times more likely to be incarcerated than whites.[42] Add to these figures gaping health disparities—including a black male life expectancy six years shorter than that of white men—and a black male unemployment rate that is consistently double that of white men, and you have the makings of an epidemic.[43] The crisis requires nothing less than transformative politics.

Even a white billionaire Republican-turned-independent, Mayor Michael Bloomberg of New York, recognized this crisis and has been unafraid to address it with race-specific remedies. Using a portion of his own personal fortune as well as city and other private funds, Bloomberg proposed a $130 million program to address the high rate of incarceration, undereducation, and unemployment among New York City's black and Hispanic males.[44] Bloomberg placed the weight of New York City's government behind the program even though, "by focusing so heavily on a subset of city residents, he risks angering those unlikely to be helped by the new resources."[45]

In contrast, when Obama was called upon to exercise his racial familiarity to forge a transformative solution to the joblessness epidemic among black men—surely a major contributor to paternal absenteeism—his racial familiarity became selective. He reverted to his "a rising tide lifts all boats" philosophy or to legal arguments about not being permitted to single out blacks for help.[46] This is triangulation. It is a reliance on the symbolism of a Father's Day speech about parental responsibility in lieu of transformative policy. The speech, like Clinton's invocation of Sister Souljah, communicated to whites a no-favorites disposition toward African Americans but did African Americans themselves little practical good.

Although Jesse Jackson was forced to apologize for the intemperate character of his criticism of Obama—as with Wright, the media obsessed over semantics rather than meaning—he ultimately articulated a critique to which the Obama administration could only demur: "My appeal was for the moral content of his message to not only deal with the personal and moral responsibility of black males, but to deal with the collective moral responsibility of government and the public policy which would be a corrective action for the lack of good choices that often led to their irresponsibility."[47]

OBAMA, GATES, AND THE WHITE COP: CHEERS TO WHITE AMERICA?

The facts are by now familiar to most Americans. In July 2009, Henry Louis Gates, Jr., the chairman of Harvard University's African American Studies Department, was returning home to Cambridge, Massachusetts, from travels abroad. His house door stuck shut, Gates and his cab driver, also black, pried the door open. A neighbor called the police and reported that two black men were attempting a burglary. Cambridge police dispatched Sergeant James Crowley, a white man. In a disputed account, Gates claimed that after showing his identification to Crowley, the officer still disbelieved that he lived in the upscale neighborhood in which his house was located. A contretemps ensued, in which Gates accused the officer of discrimination and asked for his name and badge number. Crowley arrested Gates for disorderly conduct. Charges were quickly dropped.[48]

President Obama injected himself into the controversy not so much because it involved a black man arrested in connection with entering his home, but rather because Gates was a friend from Harvard, Obama's law school alma mater. Yet Obama was unusually declarative on an issue infused with race: "I don't know—not having been there and not seeing all the facts—what role race played in that, but I think it's fair to say, number one, any of us would be pretty angry; number two that the Cambridge police acted stupidly in arresting somebody when there was already proof that they were in their own home."[49]

Obama continued his impromptu comments to a reporter's question: "Separate and apart from this incident is that there's a long history in this country of African-American [sic] and Latinos being stopped by law enforcement disproportionately."[50] Unlike his Philadelphia speech, here, Obama was actually representing the sentiments of black Americans. Fifty-nine percent of African Americans believed that Crowley acted stupidly, while only 29 percent of whites agreed.[51] Undoubtedly, the perspective of black respondents was impacted by their own individual experience with police. Asked if they had felt personally mistreated by a police officer because of their race, 56 percent of blacks responded yes, compared to a mere 6 percent of whites.[52] Obama's words had captured the frustration of black America on an issue that had long possessed a racial dimension—police misconduct.

But Obama blinked. Pressured by demands of Massachusetts police unions that he apologize, Obama stated at a later press conference that he "could have calibrated" his words better. Obama then personally telephoned Crowley, who suggested to Obama—the leader of the free world—that they have a beer together. The White House subsequently arranged the famous brew summit among Obama, Crowley, and Gates.[53] Polling revealed that most blacks and whites thought the meeting was a "good idea."[54] But even the relatively conservative *Wall Street Journal* observed that, "To many African-Americans—including Mr. Obama—his comments stated the obvious: that a man should not be arrested in his own home after proving he belongs there, regardless of any anger he expresses toward police."[55] Once again, however, Obama succumbed to the speech restraints on blacks who dare address race—as common-sense as the remarks might be, the race of the speaker and the object of his criticism delegitimated the speech. Moreover, Obama was once again squeezed by the quadrant of disabilities under which the post-racial black politician labors. Surely the victors in this vignette were not African Americans. Having initially affirmed their point of view, the president retracted his support. Blacks were being triangulated while white political primacy was affirmed by the first black president.

It did not have to be this way. The media fixated on the controversy because Obama had largely steered clear of race issues in his initial months in office.[56] *Politico.com* deemed Obama's comments about Crowley "an iconic moment in American race relations."[57] The editorial pages of the *New York Times* cogitated whether Obama was "taking a risk politically by wading into a fraught racial issue."[58] All of this tumult was not over race-specific policy—which Obama would adamantly refuse to pursue during his first term—but over mere comments mentioning race. But if the rarity of race as a national topic made it politically risky, perhaps a greater race salience—the normalization of race as a national issue—was one way to decrease its risk. This was one alternative to post-racial triangulation of black voters. Moreover, the political capital that Obama expended on the symbolism of making comments about Gates's arrest was surely better used pushing policies targeted at African Americans. Since Obama had to pay a political price for racial symbolism, as he would for racially transformative policy, why not choose the latter?

To be sure, like in the case of Clinton, some Obama symbolism was innocuous. Whites clearly do not pay the same heed to the mere fact that a president is addressing the National Association for the Advancement of Colored People (NAACP), as they would when a president suggests, as Obama did, that race may have played an operative role in a black man's arrest. But this continuum of triangulatory symbolism with its coordinate points of white acceptability threatens to reduce the post-racial black politician to a racial figurehead. Whites are simply predisposed to be "exhausted" with race as an issue. They are discomforted by the discussion of race. And there is a national white sensitivity and resistance to the charge of racism. To abide white American sensibilities on questions of race meant not only that Obama would triangulate black voters, but that, quite ironically, he could not lead on an issue that had plagued the country for more than two centuries. This created at least two other problems for Obama. First, race is rarely a stand-alone issue. It infiltrates multiple important national policy questions. Hence, an inability to address race signified broader incapacities to govern. Relatedly, even taking as a given that whites might reward a black politician for distancing himself from race in its transformative sense—an inherent assumption of post-racial triangulation—they nevertheless will punish him for failing to lead. Sometimes the process of distancing spawned and accentuated backlash even from the nominal beneficiaries of post-racial triangulation.

Shirley Sherrod and Obama's Fear of Shadows

The Shirley Sherrod incident revealed that Obama's studied detachment from race issues had crescendoed into a fear of even the shadow of race. Sherrod, an African American, was a career employee in the U.S. Department of Agriculture in Georgia. A conservative blogger and activist, Andrew Breitbart, acquired a video of a speech Sherrod had given in which she recounted her successful effort to overcome internalized reactions to white racism in order to help a white farmer. The video posted by Breitbart, however, was edited and made it appear that Sherrod had withheld assistance from the white farmer.[59] Sherrod was immediately fired by Agriculture Secretary Tom Vilsack and denounced by the White House. There was no investigation. When the full video of Sherrod's speech was released by the local NAACP that hosted her engagement, a chastened Obama phoned Sherrod to apologize. She was offered her job back.[60] But, as the *Washington Post* observed, the incident became "the ubiquitous face of the Obama administration's misstep on race."[61]

Claims of reverse-discrimination by whites are an important part of a rhetorical arsenal intended to control and blunt black racial protest. Given how few whites claim to have ever personally been victims of discrimination based on their race, reverse-discrimination is best understood tactically rather than substantively. Breitbart posted the edited video of Sherrod's speech as retaliation against the NAACP for its denouncement of Tea Party racism.[62] Sociolinguists such as Teun Van Dijk note that denials of charges of racism against whites are often accompanied by the tactic of "reversal" in which the accuser of racism is painted as the racist.[63] Racial hierarchy facilitates the effectiveness of reversal.[64] The premise of the tactic is simple: minorities' claims of racial discrimination lose their moral legitimacy if the accusers themselves can be portrayed as racist.[65] In reversal, the minority complainant becomes marginalized in a way that an accusation of racism against a white person rarely achieves, because the minority already labors under a social inequality that is compounded by reversal.[66] Sherrod and the NAACP were the victims of an attempted reversal.

Obama and post-racial triangulation were accomplices. The dispatch with which Sherrod was dismissed was one indication of how intent the Obama White House had become on inoculating the president against racialization. But the fact that the source of the accusation was a right-wing Tea Party sympathizer and that the administration had given credence to Breibart over Sherrod's own protestations of innocence demonstrated that Obama's inoculation strategy had become warped. The strategy was triangulating not just the Reverend Wrights of black America, but also far less controversial African Americans like Sherrod.

THE TRIANGULATOR SUFFOCATES HIMSELF

Neither the Reverend Wright, the Father's Day, the Gates, nor the Sherrod incidents would have had nearly the importance they assumed if Obama, both as candidate and president, had made the decision to pursue racially transformative policy rather than trafficking in triangulatory symbolism. The Sherrod incident in particular demonstrated that symbolism cuts both ways. Triangulatory symbolism may be practiced to assuage white fears of too much race consciousness in the post-racial black politician, but in the absence of robust policy content, it can also become a rather crude metric by which African Americans gauge the post-racial black politician's sensitivity to their concerns. Oddly then, the triangulator's efforts to deflect race may stimulate it in the minds of black voters in ways not necessarily favorable to the triangulator. Obama was pilloried for his handling of the Sherrod incident and for the transparency of his administration's motives in dispatching Sherrod without due process. One preeminent Democratic official reportedly complained that, "They're so panicky about looking anti-white that they overreact and do things so they can't be accused of being pro-black."[67] In academic circles, the assessment was just as blunt. Emory University professor Andra Gillespie summed it up: "They apologized, but the decision to fire her is the kind of knee-jerk reaction that people get concerned about with de-racialized candidates, such as Obama. The administration overacted in the Shirley Sherrod case to prove that they don't always side with the minorities, but they were wrong."[68] Race had been let loose for a wild-boar run by the post-racial black president's efforts to deflect it. Obama, himself a former professor, could only hope the views of the cognoscenti were not those of rank-and-file black voters, whose stalwart cohesion he would need more than ever for his reelection.

Triangulation had other unintended consequences for Obama. Clinton had successfully used his political triangulation to reposition himself to the political center for his reelection. But post-racial triangulation and political triangulation created a tense fusion for Obama where the former sometimes impeded the success of the latter. For instance, while Obama steadfastly defied the CBC's call for a jobs program directed at the hardest-hit communities, the outsized black and brown unemployment numbers were having a magnifying effect on overall unemployment. Few political analysts disputed that Obama's reelection prospects rested on the trend line for unemployment. To have targeted black (and Latino) unemployment would have been a way of favorably affecting the bottom line number. But Obama's determination not to be racialized suffocated his political thinking. Even as he tried to position himself in centrist terms by agreeing to slash entitlement and discretionary spending during the infamous debt-reduction negotiations in the summer of 2011, unemployment continued to eclipse all other issues in the electorate's mind. Obama's political triangulation was less effective because of the inhibitions he imposed on himself to achieve post-racial triangulation.

Obama's centrist debt-reduction capitulations were ineffective as political triangulation for another reason that also arose from his deployment of post-racial triangulation. These capitulations added to the impression of weak leadership—a continuation of his retreats during the racial implosions. In the wake of the debt-reduction negotiations in which the GOP won spending cuts but Obama achieved none of the new revenues he said were necessary for a "balanced approach," Democrats across the ideological spectrum began to call on Obama to "scrap his more cautious, conciliatory approach" and "be a lot less keep-it-cool Calvin Coolidge and a lot more give-'em-hell Harry Truman."[69] Drew Westen, an Emory psychology professor and a Democratic consultant, penned an essay in which he accused Obama of having a "deep-seated aversion to conflict" and failing to understand "bully dynamics—in which conciliation is always the wrong course of action, because bullies perceive it as weakness and just punch harder the next time."[70]

The difficulty with the Democrats' frustrations, though, was that they may have misconceived the core problem. To some observers, "Obama's preternaturally calm demeanor originated in his need to counter the stereotype of the angry black man."[71] Post-racial triangulation had no chance of success unless the triangulator was non-threatening. Social psychology reveals that latent stereotypes intrude upon whites' perception of black behavior, converting even ambiguously aggressive behavior into a definite threat. The threat perception by whites is greater when assertive conduct is engaged in by a black man.[72] Three-quarters of the way into his presidency, Obama's fear of being racialized seemed to have called into question his ability to lead by many of the very whites whom he had sought to appease by deracializing himself.

This paradox rested in large part on the uncertain terrain on which both Obama and white voters found themselves. For white voters, it was one thing to be comforted by a nonthreatening black man *in the positions to which they had become accustomed to seeing black people.* But transposing these expectations on the leader of the free world was like hamstringing a boxer but expecting him to go all nine rounds. White voters in a prematurely post-racial America had not yet sorted out how much assertiveness they could tolerate from a black president before they began to racialize him. And with their insistence that race be off the table of national conversation, there was simply no incentive or means for white voters to recognize their conflicting expectations of Obama. Obama, in turn, played into this confusion by attempting to accommodate these irreconcilable expectations by submerging race at almost every turn. Post-racial triangulation was suffocating Obama.

CONCLUSION

What is really new about the new politics of triangulation? Certainly not the fact that black voters are being triangulated. But black-on-black triangulation in a majority-white electorate breeds machinations and disabilities not seen heretofore and thus unexplored. These machinations multiply with the interlocking of political and post-racial triangulation. The tale of Obama's post-racial triangulation of African Americans is a cautionary one for black politicians. But it is most of all an admonition to black voters that despite the patina of equality, the election of blacks to the highest positions in the country layered new questions atop old about political accountability to and race solidarity within the black body politic. To these matters, we now turn.

CHAPTER 7

A Thousand Obamas? Black Electoral Ambition and Accountability to Black Voters

If he [Obama] comes and speaks out for black people in the middle of this, he will lose his reelection, and you know it. He has to temper this in such a manner so we can get him reelected, and once he's a lame-duck president, I think we'll see lots of changes and lots of movement toward the black community.

—Representative Frederica S. Wilson (D-Fla.)[1]

If we go after the president too hard, you're going after us. When you tell us it's all right and you unleash us and you're ready to have this conversation, we're ready to have the conversation. We're getting tired, y'all. We want to give him every opportunity. But our people are hurting. The unemployment is unconscionable.... When you let us know it is time to let go, we'll let go.

—Representative Maxine Waters (D-CA)[2]

He's a consummate politician, and he is not writing anything new here that hasn't already been done. So at least from my perspective, the goal is not to be triangulated. That's a goal knowing that the President of the United States is capable of triangulating.

—Representative Jesse Jackson, Jr. (D-IL)[3]

Frederica Wilson's, Maxine Waters's, and Jesse Jackson, Jr.'s statements portray the complexity of African Americans holding the first black president accountable to their policy agenda. Consider Congresswoman Wilson's extraordinary assessment that Obama would be a more effective president for African Americans as a lame duck. We ordinarily think of lame-duck elected officials in precisely the opposite way. Or take Representative Waters's statement that criticism of Obama, if not correctly calibrated, is a criticism of a broader swath of African Americans, and her request to her audience to allow her to offer criticism of Obama. Finally, consider Jesse Jackson, Jr.'s note of caution that blacks must ensure that they are not triangulated by the first black president even as he and the rest of black America staunchly support Obama.

There is a fair amount of consternation within black America and among black leaders regarding how and when to criticize the first black president in order to ensure some measure of political accountability to African Americans. Yet this dilemma is not limited to President Obama. It is a dilemma that black voters have faced and will continue to face as post-racial black politicians multiply. Black voters in Alabama, California, Florida, Massachusetts, Tennessee, Newark, Philadelphia, and Washington, D.C.—like black voters nationwide— have been presented with black candidates who eschew the orthodoxy of traditional black politics and who seek an electoral base beyond the African American vote. How can African Americans support the electoral ambitions of the post-racial black politician without being triangulated?

Obama personifies this question by virtue of occupying the highest office in the land. His election suggested that the black American agenda might be more hydraulic than at any time since the Great Society. That is, given Obama's moderately liberal politics while running for president and his identification with African Americans, there was some hope that African American concerns could once again be heard and addressed at the very highest level of government. But in the decades between Lyndon Baines Johnson's Great Society and Obama's election, black politics, like the American liberalism of which it is a variant, has been marginalized. The notion of political accountability to African Americans has been defined by this marginalization. The resultant siege mentality among black voters often pits accountability against solidarity. Quite ironically, the new black politics and the post-racial black politician do nothing to change this dynamic—the quandary simply percolates to the higher offices that these black politicians seek.

There are few norms of political accountability to blacks, who are electorally captured by the Democratic Party and for whom the Republican Party offers little aside from a rightward stake in the country's culture wars. In contrast, in the minute period since its formation, the Tea Party has developed a norm of electoral accountability within the Republican Party that (1) led to the defeat of incumbent Republican Senator Robert Bennett of Utah as well as the defeats of no fewer than four establishment Republicans in the Senate primaries in Colorado, Delaware, Florida, and Nevada during the 2010 election cycle and (2) fundamentally altered the Republican Congressional Caucus so as to make compromise with President Obama virtually unacceptable. The absence of a structure of accountability at all comparable to what the Tea Party has achieved in such a short period is a deficiency of traditional black politics that has helped to enable the new politics of triangulation. With siege defining its relationship to the broader electorate and with few settled metrics for holding its own accountable, traditional black politics finds itself laid bare by the criticisms of Obama, whose triangulation of black voters is premised on the porous nature of black political accountability that preceded him. To understand Obama's post-racial triangulation of black voters—and black voters' strategic willingness to tolerate it—we must place his actions in the broader context of political accountability to black voters.

Moments of Accountability, Right and Left

The problems of political accountability to African Americans are rooted in poverty, classic collective action problems, and electoral capture by the Democratic Party. All of these are significant factors in debating Obama's accountability, yet Obama lacks a clear historical parallel. Some recent moments of electoral accountability shed light on the complexity of electoral accountability to African Americans.

Former Congressional Black Caucus (CBC) member Harold Ford, Jr., believes that politicians and the public should stop being so critical of Wall Street, because "Wall Street and Main Street are the same."[4] This is an extraordinary statement coming from a former CBC member from Memphis, where the Great Recession brought on in substantial part by Wall Street's conduct has devastated the black middle class.[5] But this type of out-of-sync disposition was not unusual for Ford even when he represented the majority-black, Memphis-based Ninth Congressional District. As a congressman, Ford was a member of the conservative Blue Dog Coalition and the Democratic Leadership Council, which he would chair after his unsuccessful Senate bid.[6] He routinely endorsed conservative fiscal and foreign policies, including military action against Iraq, that had the backing of President George W. Bush.[7] His record in Congress earned him an unenviable sobriquet in the progressive black blogosphere: "the most anti-Black, pro-Republican member of the CBC."[8]

Ford's ability to be reelected in his liberal-leaning, majority-black district was in part attributable to his family name—his father represented the district before him. But the junior Ford's moment of accountability to black voters would not come during a reelection campaign for the House of Representatives. It instead came during a close United States Senate campaign. Continuing to burnish the conservative credentials that he had built during his tenure in the House, Ford ran a campaign of "situational deracialization."[9] Political scientist Sekou Franklin explains situational deracialization as a highly elastic strategy by African American candidates to normalize their images to white voters by campaigning on moderate to conservative positions on cultural and economic issues while making carefully contained race-conscious appeals to black voters.[10] Ford's campaign appeared to have mastered this split messaging, accusing his Republican opponent of raising taxes and proclaiming himself an evangelical Christian to appeal to white Tennesseans, while using surrogates and handbills in black communities to portray himself as a defender of the social welfare state.[11]

On election night, the race turned out to be surprisingly close. Ford garnered a highly respectable share of the white vote in racially conservative Tennessee, but he still ran behind the top of the Democratic ticket among white voters by 20 percent to 25 percent.[12] Ford, however, had anticipated a heavy black turnout to offset racially polarized voting in white precincts. Arguably, he lost his Senate bid by the margin of his neglect of the black community. While garnering near unanimous support among African American voters, black turnout was lower than had been predicted and than was needed for a Ford victory.[13] Although not framing the outcome in terms of accountability per se, Franklin notes that "Ford's split messaging approach, while earning him strong support in the African-American community, did not go far enough in convincing the requisite number of African Americans to go to the polls."[14] Ford had neglected his black base by failing to mobilize this group and by outsourcing mobilizing to surrogates.[15]

Former congressman Artur Davis of Alabama attempted a strategy similar to Ford's in his effort to ascend from representing one of the poorest districts in the country to becoming the first black governor of Alabama. If Ford continues his apostasy of black interests by equating Wall Street to Main Street, Davis's estrangement is perhaps more dramatic. Although he sought to become Alabama's first black governor, Davis contributed to the gubernatorial campaign of conservative white Republican Phil Bryant of Mississippi.[16] Bryant was running against Hattiesburg mayor Johnny Dupree, the first African American major party nominee for governor in Mississippi since Reconstruction.

Davis's positioning of himself to become Alabama's first black governor arguably went a bridge too far. He had been called "the Obama of Alabama."[17] This was a misnomer. Davis was perceptibly to Obama's right. When Davis was the lone member of the CBC to vote against President Obama's signature health-care legislation, the Reverend Jesse Jackson decried his decision, charging, "You can't vote against healthcare and call yourself a black man."[18] Jackson's reaction seemed to reflect the view of Alabama's black electorate, not just on health care, but on Davis's overall maneuver to the right.[19] Davis lost the heavily black Democratic gubernatorial primary by a stunning 26-point margin to the state's white agricultural commissioner.[20]

If black voters occasionally demand accountability from post-racial black politicians who veer too far to the right, they also exact electoral vengeance against stalwart black progressives, albeit not necessarily under circumstances that are affirming of their own political power. The affable and progressive Hank Johnson unseated Congresswoman Cynthia McKinney, an outspoken black progressive with a national following, running on a curious theme in a majority-black congressional district. Johnson candidly admits that part of his strategy in unseating McKinney was to exploit her perceived neglect of the northern side of Georgia's Fourth Congressional District where most of the district's white voters reside. "[Y]ou can never ignore a substantial part of your constituency," Johnson explained, referring to the district's white voters.[21]

To be sure, in losing to Johnson, the controversial McKinney ran a terrible campaign, as she did when she lost to Denise Majette four years earlier.[22] Given credible opponents like Johnson and Majette, and given her championing of nonmainstream causes such as Palestinian rights, McKinney's disorganized campaigns violated a cardinal rule for a political outsider. "It's not enough," Congresswoman Waters said in an election postmortem, "to take principled and courageous stands on the issues. Black and progressive elected officials have to know that when you speak truth to power...powerful interests will target you, will mobilize their resources...and come after you. We have to defend those correct and principled positions by hitting the street and organizing our own communities...."[23]

But the decisive role of white voters in a Democratic primary in a marginally black-majority district[24] raises intriguing—and perhaps troubling—questions about political accountability to African American voters. In 2002, Majette lost the black vote to McKinney handily, but still prevailed in the primary.[25] The data in the Johnson-McKinney matchup is less clear, but based on county commission district vote breakdowns provided by Johnson, McKinney prevailed in the predominantly black commission districts, while Johnson prevailed by even wider margins in the majority-white commission districts.[26]

Voting rights scholar Janai Nelson has analyzed the problems of the fragmentation of black voter preferences in majority-black districts that allows for the election of a white candidate, an outcome in Tennessee's Ninth Congressional District after Harold Ford, Jr.'s departure. Nelson observes that "the legal operation of majority-minority districts does not always comport with the normative behavior of minority groups within the district. Indeed, while the Voting Rights Act aims to protect minority communities against direct and inadvertent forms of discrimination in the electoral process, internecine conflicts, and outside interests can serve to frustrate these goals to the point of failure."[27] But the purposes of the Voting Rights Act are also arguably defeated where a black candidate is elected in a majority-black district—particularly one mandated as a remedy under the act—but is not the preferred candidate of a majority of black voters. Johnson's representational style appears to have acquitted him, as he received more than 75 percent of the vote in his 2010 reelection. Still, future concerns linger that as majority-black districts become more racially variegated, the candidate preferences of black voters, along with accountability to these voters, will suffer.

The moments of accountability to black voters sketched above portray the complexity of the issue even before Obama ascended to the presidency. With an African American in the White House, matters have become more layered.

Sharpton versus West: Elite Skepticism and the Hydraulics of Black Leadership and Race

I worry about you, brother, because you could be easily manipulated by those in the White House who do have the interests of Wall Street oligarchs, who have the interests of corporate plutocrats who you oppose. And you end up being the public face of Barack Obama, being another black mascot....

—Cornel West (to Al Sharpton)[28]

My response is that what I've said is not to give cover to President Obama, but don't give cover to anybody. I think you can't just hold President Obama accountable. You must hold all of us account-able, members of Congress, those of us that lead civil rights organi-zations, faith groups. I think that if we put everything on President Obama we do two things. One, we feed into the misperception that he was elected Messiah rather than president. And, second, that there is not responsibility for everyone. Some of our members of Congress have been there decades before President Obama, chaired committees, and didn't do as much as we wanted.

—Reverend Al Sharpton (elaborating on his earlier response to West)[29]

The fault lines in the debate over President Obama's accountability to black voters are clear. On the one hand, the president has incurred scathing critiques from Cornel West, Tavis Smiley, Congressman John Conyers, and Congresswoman Waters, among others. On the other hand is the pushback, most prominently from Al Sharpton, who with a nightly cable television show, now has a national platform. For the most part, neither the president's black critics nor his defenders want to see him defeated, for however averse to addressing issues of race Obama might be, any Republican alternative would be much more so. Sharpton's defense of the president portrays skepticism about the brand of black politics that predated Obama. He notes, for instance, that only one member of the CBC voted against the authorization to use military force in Afghanistan.[30] Sharpton's professed concern is that "we can't have different standards" for the president and other black politicians like CBC members.[31] But then again, Sharpton has made clear that his defense of the president against black critics is as protective and strategic as it is substantive: "I've seen this movie before," Sharpton continued. "We had the first black Mayor of New York, David Dinkins. And we got mad every time he went to a non-black event and we pouted until some of us didn't vote, he lost and we got eight years of Giuliani."[32]

The logic of a no-critics zone for President Obama in the black community is best captured in this statement by Atlanta mayor Kasim Reed, who himself was elected in a racially polarized contest in which his advice concerning Obama could have (indeed may have) applied equally to him: "If you weaken President Obama in the black community, you seriously hamper his chances of being re-elected. A small depression among the African American electorate could be devastating to this president. And I'd also like folks on the other side of the conversation to tell me who the alternative is that's going to do such a better job for black people. Will it be Michele Bachmann? I mean, will it be Mitt Romney? Rick Perry?"[33]

But if the need to protect black politicians who are in a state of siege from skeptical white voters extends all the way down to mayoralties, how much further down does it extend? Moreover, how and when do black Americans hold black politicians accountable? At what level of government is the issue of racial inequality as such addressed if black politicians, as they should, increasingly attempt to transcend the majority-black and plurality-black districts in which many begin their careers? And how precisely can any politician, black or white, be held accountable if the needs, desires, and political bare minimums of a voting bloc such as African Americans are not the subject of public discussion? These are among the hard questions presented by the tug of war between Obama's black critics and his high-profile black surrogates.

This debate was not supposed to happen—or at least it was theoretically avoidable. Sharpton implies that critics of Obama have placed too much responsibility on the president for black-centric concerns: "He shouldn't lead the civil rights marches against himself. Everybody's sitting around acting like we can't do anything; Obama's going to do it. That's hogwash."[34] Under this view, race needs to be hydraulic, distributed up and down the chains of black leadership, presumably in strategic proportion to each level's ability to weather its volatility. It's a fascinating theory that elides yet another fundamental question: what should happen when race percolates to the top and the president happens to be black?

Former mayor of Gary, Indiana, Richard Hatcher chaired Jesse Jackson's historic 1984 presidential campaign and is a stalwart of the civil rights movement as well as an admirer of Obama. Hatcher tells the story of the Black Caucus of the U.S. Conference of Mayors meeting with then-presidential candidate Jimmy Carter in North Carolina. The Caucus met with Carter to discuss preconditions of their support for his candidacy. One of their requests was that, if elected, Carter should appoint blacks to 10 percent of his cabinet positions, reflecting what was then the black percentage of the U.S. population. Hatcher, however, pointed out during the meeting that blacks were 25 percent of the Democratic Party and should therefore receive 25 percent of the cabinet appointments. Hatcher recalls: "I said 25 percent and almost—almost got beaten up and run out of the room by my colleagues telling me, you know, that's too much, that's too much."[35] As if his request for proportional representation were not hubris enough in the eyes of his colleagues, Hatcher requested that Carter put his commitments to the Black Caucus in writing. "I almost got run out of the room again," the former mayor recalls.[36]

Hatcher's vignette uncovers a point that has been largely obscured in the debate about Obama's accountability to black voters: blacks almost never allow race to percolate to the top. That is, more than 30 years ago, in the Carter era, black leaders relented in various ways on the insistence that the issues of black America be among the foremost in the Oval Office. Today, as then, politics is about "who gets what and how much."[37] But even after years of discrimination and neglect, and even with a black president in office, the abiding rule in today's politics, says Hatcher, is that blacks are not allowed any "catch-up."[38] With this rule in mind, referencing Obama specifically, Hatcher asks, "Why would he suddenly become really focused on the needs of black people and poor people in this country? Unless he is just a truly principled person, and he may be. But unless he is, there is nothing there that said, wow…these are the people who put me here, and this is what I need to do to make sure that their needs are met. It's almost illogical."[39]

These are the rules. This is the political reality—at least at the top. From Sharpton's perspective, "If you gave a pass in the past, why are you so vociferous now?"[40] Obama seemed to show his pique with black critics at a CBC gala when he told the audience, "I expect all of you to march with me and press on. Take off your bedroom slippers, put on your marching shoes. Shake it off. Stop complaining, stop grumbling, stop crying. We are going to press on. We've got work to do, CBC."[41] The president's remarks widened the rift between him and his critics and contributed to the perception that he was triangulating blacks. Congresswoman Waters responded,

> I found that language a bit curious because the president spoke to the Hispanic Caucus and certainly they are pushing him on immigration and despite the fact that he's appointed [Justice Sonia] Sotomayor to the Supreme Court, he has an office for excellence in Hispanic education right in the White House, they're still pushing him and he certainly didn't tell them to stop complaining. And he never would say that to the gay and lesbian community who really pushed him on Don't Ask, Don't Tell. Or even in a speech to AIPAC [American Israel Public Affairs Committee], he would never say to the Jewish community "stop complaining" about Israel.[42]

The president, in turn, insisted that there was "only a handful of African-Americans who have been critical. They were critical when I was running for president. There's always going to be somebody who is critical of the president of the United States."[43] Matters were not as simple as the president suggested. The state of siege had muted black criticism of Obama. Race was a rallying point among blacks even for a race-averse president. Members of the CBC carefully qualified any critique of Obama's responsiveness to black concerns by noting the role that race has played during his tenure or the dire alternatives to not supporting Obama. "[W]e might have gotten more [from a white progressive Democrat] because a white person would not be under attack as much as a black president would for targeting programs to the black community," opined Congresswoman Donna Christensen in a generally supportive but not glowing assessment of the president.[44] To Congresswoman Wilson, given the inclination of the Tea Party and its sympathizers to portray Obama in radical and racial terms, "[T]he president is doing the best he can with what he has."[45] Even Congressman Danny Davis of Obama's hometown of Chicago, an enthusiastic supporter of the president, couches his support in the language of relativity—that is, if not Obama, then who?—that is emblematic of the state of siege:

> [T]here's certain kinds of criticism [of Obama], but you look at the self-interest. I mean, it's in your best interests to do whatever you can do in your power to get Barack reelected. I say that to people who are disjointed and who are jaundiced. Don't think about Barack; think about you. Is it in your best interest to get Barack elected, or does it make sense for you to elect Michele Bachmann? Somebody [referring to Bachmann] will get elected who say[s] that...black children have a better chance of living in a two-parent family during slavery than they do now.[46]

In the state of siege that typifies black politics, a black politician's count of the number of blacks who publicly criticize him is not necessarily an indication that he is meeting the needs or expectations of African Americans. Instead, it is at least in part a reflection of the tacit understanding in black America of the constraints of race and the absence of viable political alternatives.

The real debate concerning Obama's accountability is between the many willing to quietly uphold this implicit compact until an ever-elusive safe harbor permits public debate about it, and those who wish to change it. For now, however, let us accept that there is a binding understanding on African Americans regarding legitimate expectations of Obama. We are then led back to a discomforting question. If one axiom of the hydraulics of race in politics is that blacks cannot push a president, no matter what his race, too hard on the issues most important to them, then where does race go? To the CBC? To black state legislators? To county commissioners? To local councilmen? Sharpton's arguments do not as easily slalom on these questions.

To the degree that Sharpton implies that the CBC has not done its job relative to the needs of African Americans, members of the CBC readily push back at charges of ineffectualness. Unsurprisingly, they qualify their assessment of their own performance in terms of the institutional obstacles they face as a minority caucus. In other words, no matter that they may hail from a safe black-majority or black-plurality district, the state of siege accompanies the black representative who seeks to legislate on behalf of blacks and the disadvantaged in a majority-white legislative body.

Two decades ago, Lani Guinier warned that the creation of majority-minority electoral districts would not ensure the substantive representation of black interests.[47] Guinier cautioned that the black electoral success theory of which the creation of majority-minority districts was a central part "fails to provide a realistic enforcement mechanism for establishing either leadership accountability within the black community or representational effectiveness within the legislative deliberation and coalition-building process. The theory marginalizes black leadership and leads to token representation. Black electoral success theory has failed to comprehend, or even to examine, the nature of representation within collective decision-making bodies controlled by prejudice and external inequalities."[48] Guinier rebuts the hydraulic premise of Sharpton pushing responsibility for race down to the CBC and below when she notes that the racial polarization that necessitates black districts does not cease once blacks are elected to the legislature. Black legislators face the same racial headwinds within a white legislative body that Obama faces as president within a white electorate—an obstacle that Guinier refers to as the legislative or deliberative gerrymander.[49]

The pushdown of race is also complicated because even when a majority-black district provides relative electoral safety to a black representative, institutional assimilation creates enticements for advancement within the body that may conflate individual success with group interests.[50] Moreover, the increased size and geographic diversity of the CBC in particular has affected its cohesion. Political scientist and legal theorist Kareem Crayton confirms this point empirically in his regression analysis of the CBC's voting patterns. Although the Caucus continues to be among the most cohesive in Congress, that cohesion varies with vote context.[51] Specifically, on economic issues, senior members have demonstrated a statistically significant greater likelihood to toe the CBC line than younger members.[52]

At least two factors explain these results and the larger challenge to CBC cohesion. The first is the simple ambition of members like Artur Davis and Harold Ford, ambitions over which black voters have a greater check where the representative hails from a majority-black district. Increasingly, however, black representatives are being elected from non-majority-black districts, a trend that the 2010 census suggests will only increase in the future as blacks leave the urban centers that formed the core of the first generation of CBC districts.[53] Guinier cautioned that even when a black elected from a majority-white jurisdiction receives decisive black support, they "do not necessarily feel obligated to black voters."[54] According to Guinier, black-voter electoral ratification of a black candidate in a majority-white setting "fails to furnish a consistent mechanism for establishing community-based credentials or leadership accountability"—the essence of the accountability debate surrounding Obama.[55]

The difficulties with the pushdown of race to the CBC only replicate themselves when race is pushed further down the electoral chain to states and localities. For instance, Prince Georges County, Maryland, is often viewed as a paradigm of black suburban political prowess. Yet political scientist Valerie Johnson details a history of the county's black lawmakers thwarting black unity and interests in order to advance their own ambitions.[56] Apart from political ambition, as demographic changes render majority and plurality-black congressional districts less black, state legislative and city and county council districts are likewise affected. Finally, not unlike the conditions under which the reins of the country were handed over to Obama, many blacks have ascended to power at the local and county level at a time when the economy, budget shortfalls, and the ongoing urban crisis have conspired to remove matters of racial inequality from the local agenda.

Race, in short, may have nowhere else to go but up in the current economic and political climate. Black officials at all levels of government bear increasing electoral liability in addressing issues of race. They also face governing constraints—albeit of a different scale than those of the president. And many of these individuals aspire to emulate the transracial success of Obama, disincentivizing them from emphasizing race. The trouble with addressing race in the American political process is not that race is not hydraulic enough to be addressed at all levels; rather, it is that it is too volatile and unwieldy an issue to be welcomed at any level.

A New Accountability?

The norm of accountability that appears to be emerging from the exchange between Obama's black critics and his African American defenders is a concerning one. Congressman John Conyers is one of the remaining black-centric purists in Congress. He has been an outspoken critic of Obama on Afghanistan and other policies, and Obama has taken umbrage at some of the criticism. Conyers recalls a telephone conversation with President Obama: "[Obama] called me and told me that he heard that I was demeaning him and I had to explain to him that it wasn't anything personal, it was an honest difference on the issues."[57] But the state of siege in black politics simply may no longer afford the luxury of criticism—even when the criticism is from the black Left and thus substantively might be shared by many or most blacks. Conyers is being challenged in a Democratic primary by a black candidate who has premised his campaign in part on Conyers's alleged disloyalty to the president.[58]

Jesse Jackson, Jr., another critic of the president on the black Left, has drawn a white primary opponent who is campaigning against him for criticizing the president too vigorously.[59] And CBC member Laura Richardson is being challenged by a black opponent for such acts of disloyalty as speaking what many understand to be the obvious: "I understand that you've got to be president for all people, but this administration has gone just too far; they really don't even say 'African-American' or talk about [our] specific issues....The president is smart enough to know he's the first African-American, and I think he's concerned—I would say afraid—that people are going to think he's favoring African-Americans."[60]

But it is not just CBC members who are critics of Obama that are drawing primary opponents whose campaigns are focused on support for Obama. The largely uncritical Bennie Thompson of Mississippi is being challenged for his seat by a black opponent who charges Thompson with not being vocally supportive enough of the president.[61]

The emerging accountability norm from the debate about Obama's accountability to black voters may simply be a doubling down in the state of siege in which critics on Obama's black Left are treated no differently than, say, Artur Davis, whose disagreements with Obama were not even arguably in the interests of his African American constituents. The consequences of such a norm would be bizarre. First, notwithstanding Sharpton's insinuation that Obama's black critics are subjecting the president to a double standard, the CBC has historically been more divided during Democratic administrations regarding support for the president because many members view a Democratic president, black or white, as the single best opportunity to encourage the party to respond to issues of concerns to the black community.[62] If there is a double standard at work, it is shared by Obama's black critics and defenders alike.

Second, Obama's performance has engendered criticism from white Democrats to the right and to the left of him. If it is fair to target Conyers and Jackson for left-leaning criticisms of Obama, what is black citizens' organized mechanism for punishing Senator Bernie Sanders of Vermont for his criticism of Obama? Sanders demurred when asked whether he was supporting Obama's reelection and said that Obama needs to remember who elected him: "It was not Wall Street, although they contributed. It was not the big money interests. It was working families, lower-income people and the middle class."[63]

Finally, some people understandably find criticism of Obama to be self-defeating. In the longer term, however, a prohibition on criticizing post-racial black politicians for fear of suppressing black support—if that, rather than a concern about perceptions among white voters, is the fear—will prove much more deleterious to the black body politic. Why? Because black voters, whose cohesion portrays a high degree of political sophistication, must learn and abide the ultimate mark of political sophistication: they must learn that disappointment with politics is cause to reengage the process, not abandon it. If politics is about who gets what and how much, it is also true that only the insistent get their due. This hard lesson, not the suppression of the expression of disappointment, is the foundation of a system of political accountability that will sustain itself beyond the next election.

CONCLUSION

What is striking about the accountability debate concerning President Obama is how it quickly and assuredly dissolved into African Americans pointing the finger at each other rather than addressing the core issue: whites require the triangulation of African Americans as the price of black electoral success in post-racial America, a precondition that is neither post-racial nor racially just. While the Black

Caucus of the U.S. Conference of Mayors may have been shy of the mark in requesting thirty-five years ago that just 10 percent of President Carter's appointments be black, the election of a black president governing under a state of siege by suspicious white voters makes that type of request for minimal fair representation unimaginable today. It would be racial treason to those blacks who seek a no-critics zone among blacks for the first black president. It would be fodder to further racialize the president for the Tea Party and Republican activists who have implicitly or explicitly made racialization of Obama a central tenet of their opposition. And, perhaps most importantly, the request would abridge the misguided norm of über-colorblindness on which white voters insist, notwithstanding its role in continuing racial inequality. (See chapter 6.) Clearly, then, there can be no norm of accountability to black voters until racial inequality is once again an acceptable part of the discourse in American politics. White resistance to this notion is the root of the current accountability debate.

Do African Americans Need a Black President? Of Movements, Not Men

President Barack Obama likely has no bigger defender in Congress than Representative Frederica Wilson of Florida. A veteran state legislator before being elected to Congress in 2010, Wilson's relationship to Obama is characteristic of the deep affinity that millions of African Americans have for the first black president. For Wilson, a former school principal, that attachment runs through Obama to the hundreds of African American males she has assisted in gaining entry into colleges through her mentoring program. By her own reckoning, Wilson was the first elected official in Florida to endorse Obama. Obama's election was a "prophecy fulfilled" that she had been inculcating in young black men for decades. "I tell my boys all the time, you can be anything you want to be. You can be President of the United States," Wilson said proudly on a humid September afternoon in her office on Capitol Hill.[1] Wilson was one of Florida's electors to the Electoral College; she took two hundred of her young mentees to the state capital to witness the signing ceremony for Florida's electors.[2] This is the kind of undeniable pride that Obama's election engendered among African Americans, especially those like Wilson, who had spent decades in the civil rights and political arenas and understood well the arc of history represented by Obama's victory.

Who would deny the importance of Obama's election? Yet, it is equally undeniable that there are important lessons beyond Obama himself to be gleaned from Obama's election and first term in office. They share two common threads. First, race mattered during Obama's term in office more than perhaps any president's term since

Lyndon B. Johnson's. But it did not matter in a transformative sense. Rather, a black president fearful of the reactions of white Americans was constantly crouched into a defensive position about race and his relationship to black voters. Meanwhile, many conservative white voters mobilized race (and racism) against the president and his policies. Most black voters probably understand both of these dynamics and their relationship to each other. To many blacks, Obama's triangulation of black voters is a forgivable sin precisely because Obama's presidency "smoked out" the country's continuing racism in a way no white president could have. But the revivification of race as an overt phenomenon in politics during Obama's term, and Obama's less than ideal way of defining his relationship to the black voters who are his core, hold a much more strategic lesson for black voters than the fact that racism endures. Black voters are in dire need of a coherent political movement more than a black president, for without such a movement, there is no organized structure through which to hold politics accountable to black interests—even when the leader of the free world happens to be black. Ironically then, Obama's presidency has taught African Americans that race matters, but not necessarily the race of the president.

THE RACIAL EDUCATION OF PRESIDENT BARACK OBAMA

President Obama's attempt at Clintonian triangulation was unsuccessful because political triangulation requires the cooperation of the Right to cut deals. Republican and Tea Party opposition to Obama was obdurate. After the humiliating debt-ceiling negotiations during the summer of 2011 in which Obama won no concessions from Republicans, who extorted concessions from Obama and the Democrats on the threat of causing the country to default on its debt, Obama realized that Republicans would oppose anything he supported.[3] Republicans were desperate to deny Obama any political victory and were willing to forestall the sputtering economic recovery in order to achieve this end. As Senate Minority Leader Mitch McConnell declared shortly before the Republicans' midterm sweep, "[T]he single most important thing we want to achieve is for President Obama to be a one-term president."[4] Faced with this reality and the demoralization of his progressive base, Obama pivoted left to restore his reelection prospects. He proposed a $447 billion jobs bill and reversed his earlier willingness to increase the Medicare eligibility age and to include Social Security as part of deficit reduction.[5]

Obama's lurch to his left, however, did not necessarily portend a public embrace of his black political base. Drawing the line in the sand on Medicare and protecting Social Security had been standard Democratic positions for decades, even under Bill Clinton. Moreover, Obama's new jobs bill contained none of the more race-ameliorative ideas the Congressional Black Caucus (CBC) had pressed him to adopt, such as targeting distressed communities or ensuring a set percentage of overall federal funding for communities with enduring rates of poverty.[6] To be sure, Obama worried about the erosion of his black base and rejiggered his campaign to begin greater outreach to black voters.[7] This tact, however, followed the routine of past Democratic candidates, albeit at perhaps a slightly earlier point in the election cycle. Obama's outreach also resembled his and the Democratic Party's largely belated attempt to motivate black voters during the 2010 midterm elections, an effort that fell short and cost Democrats several contests. The problem with focusing on black voters only when an election approaches, but focusing on independents and other voter groups continuously, is that it treats blacks as voters who need only to be mobilized rather than persuaded. Maintenance of this neglectful Democratic political tradition suggested that Obama continued to believe that whites would reward him for maintaining a healthy political distance from African Americans, even as his presidency was being racialized in spite of that distance.

If Obama's essay at Clintonian triangulation failed for lack of a willing partner on the Right, it begs the question, what was so different about President Obama as opposed to President Clinton? Did race either motivate the congressional Republicans' opposition to Obama or, at the very least, did it influence the form and intensity of their opposition? As discussed in chapter 5, several members of the CBC believed that race was at work. Even those who felt that a white Democrat would have endured similar opposition as President Obama believed that Obama's race provided a unique and visceral channel for Republicans to exploit.

Racial animus is difficult to ferret out in a society with an egalitarian veneer that encourages closeting one's biases. But as Charles Lawrence III persuasively argued in his seminal application of cognitive psychology to discrimination, unguarded "slips of the tongue" reveal much about the way in which racism operates unconsciously to influence its host's perceptions and behavior.[8] There were quite a few such slips during Obama's first term. To the extent these statements were not misstatements, intentional statements the racist implications of which the speaker fails to grasp likewise show the workings of unconscious bias.[9] Had the statements been limited to fringe members of the Tea Party, perhaps less weight might be accorded them. But U.S. senators, congressmen, and governors made it acceptable once again to deploy race overtly and aversively for political gain.

What was the difference between Obama and Clinton? Former Republican Senate Majority Leader Trent Lott explained it in terms of geography and culture, neither of which elides race: "You know with Clinton the chemistry was right. He was a good old boy from Arkansas, I was a good old boy from Mississippi, and Newt, he was from Georgia. So he knew what I was about, and I knew where he was coming from."[10] To Senator Tom Coburn of Oklahoma, understanding Obama's political ideology requires understanding that, "As an African American male, coming through the progress of everything he experienced, he got tremendous benefit through a lot of these programs. So he believes in them."[11] In former Republican House Speaker and presidential aspirant Newt Gingrich's view, Obama has engaged in "Kenyan, anti-colonial behavior" as president and is America's "greatest food stamp president."[12] To Republican Congressman Joe Walsh, the so-called benefits of being black helped Obama to gain the presidency and would help him to be reelected:

> Reagan was beautiful because Reagan simplified everything, so let's simplify it. This guy [Obama] pushed every one of the media's buttons. He was liberal, he was different, he was new, he was black. Oh my God, it was the potpourri of everything. They are so vested in our first black president not being a failure that it's going to be amazing to watch the lengths they go to protect him. They [the media], I believe, will spout this racist line if some of their colleagues up here aren't doing it aggressively enough. There is going to be a real desperation.[13]

There is a tendency to attempt to dismiss statements like these as mere anecdotes reflecting the views of individuals rather than segments of a party or population. This position, however, decontextualizes the statements from the overall racially regressive character of the modern Republican Party. (See chapter 3.) White conservative Republicans have been given leeway to make these kinds of statements with impunity because their sentiments reflect the racial predispositions of a good number of their party's base.

Some have attempted to equate Republicans' racialized—and in the cases of Gingrich and Walsh, racist—statements to comments by members of Obama's own party. For instance, Senate Majority Leader Harry Reid commented that Obama lacked a "Negro dialect," and when he was a contender for the Democratic nomination, Joe Biden paid an awkward compliment to Obama that Obama was "articulate and bright and clean." These statements almost certainly portray stereotypes about blacks, *but neither was deployed oppositionally to perpetuate or exploit those stereotypes.* Observing that Obama lacks a "Negro dialect" is certainly not comparable to referring to Obama as "Barack the Magic Negro" in a campaign ad, as a leading candidate for the chairmanship of the Republican National Committee did.[14] Moreover, even if we were naively to accept the false equivalency between statements that exploit racial stereotype for political gain versus statements that merely reflect such stereotypes, the very ubiquity of black stereotypes during the election and first term of the first black president underscores the degree to which his presidency was susceptible to becoming and did become racialized.

The sense that Obama's election had caused Republicans to be overcome by race rage was widespread and was even shared by a former U.S. president, Jimmy Carter:

> I think an overwhelming portion of the intensely demonstrated animosity toward President Barack Obama is based on the fact that he is a black man, that he's African American....I live in the south, and I've seen the south come a long way, and I've seen the rest of the country that shared the south's attitude toward minority groups at that time, particularly African Americans. And that racism inclination still exists. And I think it's bubbled up to the surface because of the belief among many white people, not just in the south but around the country, that African Americans are not qualified to lead this great country. It's an abominable circumstance, and it grieves me and concerns me very deeply.[15]

The racialization came not merely in the form of slips of the tongue like a Colorado Republican congressman's reference to Obama as a "Tar Baby," but also in acts of outright disrespect.[16] Yes, there was Congressman Joe Wilson's infamous and unprecedented outburst at the president during his State of the Union address—"You lie!" But a Tea-Party-backed Republican governor of Maine also told Obama to "go to hell."[17] House Republicans attacked the president with such personal vitriol during the debt-ceiling debate that the acting Republican Speaker of the House had to issue a warning that "disparaging remarks directed at the President of the United States are inappropriate."[18]

Some CBC members observed from the floor of the House that the Republicans' treatment of Obama had been unprecedented.

Sheila Jackson Lee of Texas invited her colleagues to "read between the lines": "I am particularly sensitive to the fact that only this president…has received the kind of attacks and disagreements and inability to work.…I do not understand what I think is the maligning and maliciousness of this president. Why is he different? In my community that is the question we raise. In the minority community that is a question being raised. Why is this president being treated so disrespectfully?"[19] Representative Jesse Jackson, Jr. also confronted the issue on the House floor, arguing that, "No other president has been stook up, shook down, or held hostage as president of the United States over this debt vote. This is fundamentally unfair, Mr. Speaker, to change the rules in the middle of the game."[20]

If Obama had intended that his lacunae around issues of race and his orchestrated distance from "black" issues would take race off the table during his term, his calculations had gone badly awry by the summer of 2011. The issue of race had gone mainstream. A *USA Today* columnist invoked the treatment of ex-slave turned abolitionist Frederick Douglass in explaining the congressional Republican leaders' treatment of Obama during the debt-ceiling negotiations. The columnist quoted Douglass's open letter to his former master: "I am your fellow man, but not your slave."[21]

Obama entered the White House believing that an overemphasis on race diluted the potential of enduring coalitions among whites and voters of color. In *The Audacity of Hope*, he wrote, "[P]roposals that solely benefit minorities and dissect Americans into 'us' and 'them' may generate a few short-term concessions when the costs to whites aren't too high, but they can't serve as the basis for the kinds of sustained, broad-based political coalitions needed to transform America.…[U]niversal appeals around strategies that help all Americans…can serve as the basis for such coalitions.…"[22] In cautioning against too much race, however, Obama was writing about a prospect of which the country had arguably never been in danger—not even during Reconstruction. As Darren Hutchinson has observed in his study of white responses to calls for racial equality, whites have historically claimed to be exhausted with issues of racial equality ab initio and indeed have deployed the rhetoric of race overkill to prevent the achievement of equality.[23] Obama's starting posture on race risked acting as an unwitting accomplice to a history of American racial neglect. Moreover, if an overemphasis of race destroyed potentially broad-based coalitions, surely too little emphasis would not facilitate these coalitions, unless blacks were to participate as supplicants rather than partners—that is, unless they were to be triangulated.

Setting to one side Obama's views at the beginning of his term, it was not clear what his own racialization as leader of the free world had taught him about race and the limits of his strategy of ensuring that race is not overwrought. Whatever lessons he had internalized were slow to be reflected in his relationship with black voters, who remained at an electorally safe distance and even were the object of a "Sister Souljah" moment by Obama when he called upon his black base to "stop complaining."[24] But what lesson should Obama have learned? That a country that would require him to triangulate blacks as the price of electoral success was one where race was still far too important for that triangulation to pay its expected dividends. Moreover, if emphasizing race was divisive, post-racial triangulation was no less so, for it gave legitimacy to white characterizations of black-identified issues as "special interests." In truth, human vulnerability is a universal condition, and the fact that some vulnerabilities arise from one's race should not make our political process any less inclined to address them on their own terms.[25]

That Obama may not have achieved the fairest calibration of the nation's racial cross-pressures in his first term is neither surprising nor indictable. But ignoring his arguable failure to accord blacks equal concern and respect risks making it an accepted norm of treatment for African American voters. Both Obama as the first black president and the nation faced a learning curve. Trial and error is intrinsic to that education process.

THE EDUCATION OF BLACK AMERICA

For African Americans, the learning curve took an ironic twist. Consider this exchange between CNN talk-show host Piers Morgan and the actor Morgan Freeman:

> *Piers Morgan:* Has Obama helped the process of eradicating racism or has it, in a strange way, made it worse?
>
> *Morgan Freeman:* Made it worse. Made it worse. The tea partiers who are controlling the Republican party…their stated policy, publicly stated, is to do whatever it takes to see to it that Obama only serves one term. What underlines that? Screw the country. We're going to do whatever we can to get this black man out of here.…It just shows the weak, dark, underside of America. We're supposed to be better than that. We really are.[26]

On the day of Barack Obama's inauguration as president in 2009, 70 percent of Americans believed that race relations between blacks and whites were getting better.[27] By Martin Luther King, Jr.'s birthday in 2011, that number had fallen to just 38 percent.[28] What happened in between is no mystery. The nation witnessed virulent opposition to its first black president even though Barack Obama had bested his Republican opponent by eight million votes and had won an Electoral College landslide. Certainly Obama had a greater mandate than Bill Clinton, who had been elected with a mere plurality, or George W. Bush, who lost the popular vote to his opponent but was installed to the presidency by the United States Supreme Court.

African Americans appeared to be particularly struck by the stridency of the opposition. A year into the Obama presidency, 59 percent of African Americans believed that black-white race relations would always be problematic for the nation—a 14-point increase from the early days of the Obama presidency.[29] Obama's election had marked a fleeting respite in a long-term pessimistic trend among blacks concerning race relations. In 1964, 70 percent of blacks believed that there would be an eventual solution to the black-white racial divide.[30] By 2007, the year before Obama's election, that number had declined to 41 percent, according to a Gallup Poll.[31] Even with the spike in black optimism over race relations brought about by Obama's election, white Americans were significantly more likely than black Americans to believe that the nation's race-relations issues would be worked out.[32] By early 2010, a majority of blacks believed that opposition to Obama's policies was significantly influenced by race.[33] Whatever beliefs about race neutrality Obama may have harbored before or during his presidency, black Americans saw events unfolding in distinctly racial ways.

Obama could not—or at least would not—campaign among African Americans for his reelection based on specific achievements for African Americans. Nor, ironically, could Obama rely much on his race-neutral achievements that disproportionately benefited African Americans. To be sure, they existed—health care chief among them. But with black unemployment and poverty spiraling out of control—even if not entirely Obama's fault—it would take something more to recreate the enthusiasm among African Americans that helped to propel Obama to the presidency. That something more was the racism that many white Americans had displayed in the aftermath of Obama's historic election. One legacy of Obama, a president who scrupulously avoided race, is the indelible confirmation of race's continuing significance in American life.

The actor Morgan Freeman witnesses Obama's treatment from the citadel of Hollywood and bristles just the same as the black janitor.

It must occur to everyday black Americans, "If white Americans can treat someone as accomplished as Obama as they have after electing him to the highest post in the free world, I can imagine how little they think of me." Just as Representative Wilson saw in Obama what she had seen in so many young black men who were her students, African Americans see themselves in Obama, even when Obama has kept them at arm's length. The tragic irony of Obama's post-racial triangulation is that it has not been post-racial at all. Many of the white voters whom it was primarily intended to placate have helped to revivify race for years to come. One is left to wonder whether a more honest reckoning with race by Obama would have better succeeded in reducing its importance during his first term. Understandably, electoral imperatives eclipsed such lofty goals. Now, with the erosion of white support, Obama must turn to a fundamental tenet of traditional politics, black voter cohesion, and nudge black voters to perform like never before.

Obama has taught black Americans seemingly contradictory lessons. First, they do not need a black president. They need a president who advances a black-friendly agenda, regardless of his or her race. Yet race was relevant to many of the white factions opposing Obama. And it was relevant to whites who were supporters but whose skittishness around issues of race might easily lead them to misinterpret the president's embrace of black-identified issues as racial partiality. It is undeniable that the perceptions of white voters—opponents and supporters alike—drove Obama's calculus concerning his public relationship to African American voters. Race was relevant after all, but infrequently in a manner that respected blacks. In an America that had pronounced itself prematurely post-racial, perhaps this was the best blacks could hope for. Or perhaps Obama's first term in office demonstrates the need for a more enduring, independent black political movement than traditional black politics—and certainly the new black politics—has been able to provide. In short, maybe black Americans need a "Tea Party" of their own, albeit of the progressive sort more akin to the liberationist tenor of the original Boston Tea Party. What would such a movement look like?

The Unrepresentative Senate

The United States Senate is a blight on American democracy. This is not because of the familiar criticism that according small states equal representation to larger ones inhibits the will of the nation's majority. Nor is it solely because the Senate has needlessly and illogically imposed on itself a supermajority requirement for doing business by making the filibuster applicable to far too many votes. The United States Senate is an embarrassment to democracy because in 2011, it had no black members, and of its two Latino members, one was a doctrinaire conservative who provided mere descriptive representation to many Latinos. Moreover, though the Senate had two Asian members, both hailed from the island state of Hawaii where people of Asian descent constitute nearly 40 percent of the population.

The absence of African Americans in the Senate has been the norm for the vast majority of this country's history. Prior to Barack Obama's election to the Senate, only four African Americans had served in that body.[34] Obama and his appointed replacement brought the total number to only six in the more than 220-year history of the Senate. The absence of African Americans in the Senate renders that body unrepresentative and artificially conservative. Alabama, Georgia, Louisiana, Mississippi, and South Carolina are all states with black populations of 25 percent or more, yet they are each represented in the Senate by two arch-conservative white Republicans who routinely disregard the interests of black voters. If one takes into account the possibility of coalitions between blacks and Latinos, Texas fits a similar bill, with blacks and Latinos constituting nearly 50 percent of the state's population but being represented by two white conservative Republicans. If each of these states had elected at least one moderate-to-liberal senator reflective of the politics of its minority citizens, imagine how different the trajectory of Obama's first term might have been. And if those senators were people of color, imagine how much more representative of the American population the Senate would be.

Americans of all races fail to comprehend the importance of the Senate. From the standpoint of African Americans and Latinos, one of its most significant functions is its advice-and-consent powers, which include confirming federal judges. An illustration best captures the importance of this function. Suppose President Obama adopted the CBC's approach to unemployment and focused on impoverished zip codes first and foremost. As I demonstrated in chapter 5, this would likely disproportionately benefit people of color. But disparate impact is insufficient to demonstrate an impermissible racial classification. Until it is. For we also learned early on in chapter 2 that the United States Supreme Court treats whites who complain of racial discrimination differently than people of color who do the same. The white plaintiffs in *Shaw v. Reno* had no injury to their right to vote, yet the Court upheld their claims. The plaintiffs in *Crawford v. Marion County Election Board* suffered an injury to their right to vote when

Indiana imposed a government-issued photo identification requirement on in-person voting that would render it more difficult for
minorities, the elderly and the poor—groups that disproportionately
lack such identification—to vote. Yet the Court afforded these voters no remedy. Does the Supreme Court really discriminate against
minority claimants? In the words of one constitutional scholar who is
hardly alone in his analysis,

> [B]y design or effect, the Court's equality doctrine reserves judicial
> solicitude primarily for historically privileged classes and commands
> traditionally disadvantaged groups to fend for themselves in the often-
> hostile majoritarian branches of government. In its equal protection
> decisions, the Court has effectively inverted the concepts of privilege
> and subordination; it treats advantaged classes as if they were vulner-
> able and in need of heightened judicial protection, and it views socially
> disadvantaged classes as privileged and unworthy of judicial solicitude.
> This paradoxical jurisprudence reinforces and sustains social subjuga-
> tion and privilege.[35]

For voters of color, the legislative process is only as good as the jurists
who adjudicate the meaning and constitutionality of the laws passed.
Conservative presidents, aided and abetted by an artificially conservative Senate, have stacked the courts with jurists whose oath of impar-
tiality is often belied by a record of hostility to minority interests.
Since the conservative judicial revolution sparked by President Ronald
Reagan thirty years ago, the Court has often (1) given a narrow construction to a constitutional provision so as to withdraw its protection
from minority litigants; (2) searched for a constitutional infirmity in
federal enactments important to minorities; or (3) given a narrow
construction to those enactments, often necessitating congressional
intervention to overturn its incorrect interpretation. The results of
this judicial activism have made affirmative action more difficult to
implement,[36] majority-minority districts more difficult to draw,[37]
voting rights more difficult to protect,[38] employment discrimination
suits more difficult to bring,[39] unions more difficult to organize,[40]
racial profiling more difficult to punish,[41] the racially disparate application of the death penalty more difficult to correct,[42] unwanted
pregnancies more difficult to end,[43] and free speech by government
employees more difficult to exercise.[44] Now the Court will likely
decide whether the federal government can offer the health-care coverage that President Obama touts as a signature achievement.[45] As
it turns out, the Senate is ground zero for voters of color protecting

their political and economic rights, for the Senate ultimately confirms the judiciary that the Constitution makes the final arbiter of its meaning and the validity of legislation.

So how do states like Alabama, Georgia, Louisiana, Mississippi, South Carolina, and Texas manage to elect such unrepresentatively conservative Senate delegations? Senators throughout our country are elected on a statewide, at-large basis instead of by district, as House members are. This allows a bloc-voting white majority to dilute the votes of citizens of color and allied whites in many states. But if these states were cut into two districts for purposes of electing their senators, and if minority voters were largely placed into the same district, both greater racial and ideological diversity would be present in their Senate delegations. There is nothing in the text of the Constitution to prevent doing this. The provision under which House members are elected from districts reads quite similarly to the Seventeenth Amendment, which concerns the election of senators.

Here is Article I, Section 2, Clause 1 of the Constitution:

The House of Representatives shall be composed of Members chosen every second Year by the People of the several States, and the Electors in each State shall have the Qualifications requisite for Electors of the most numerous Branch of the State Legislature.

And here is the text of the Seventeenth Amendment to the Constitution:

The Senate of the United States shall be composed of two Senators from each State, elected by the people thereof, for six years, and each Senator shall have one vote. The electors in each State shall have the qualifications requisite for electors of the most numerous branch of the State legislatures.

Neither provision authorizes the use of districts; both merely require election by inhabitants of the state. Thus, if districting is permissible to elect congressmen, it is also permissible to elect senators.[46]

There are now-familiar arguments that attempt to distinguish the purposes and functions of the Senate from those of the House. These arguments are, in turn, used to justify a different mode of electing senators, namely on a statewide basis. As a matter of original intent, however, the function of the Senate was always uncertain; the Constitution's framers simply knew they wanted a bicameral legislature.[47] The principal concern among the framers regarding the method of election was what role the people would play. Once it was decided that the House would be directly elected by the people, a mistrust of excessive democracy led the framers originally to assign to state legislatures the power to appoint senators.[48] This original method of selection has created a lingering misunderstanding about the representative capacity of the Senate. The Senate, it is often assumed, represents states in their sovereign capacity; the House represents the people. The House can be districted because people can be districted. A state's sovereignty, on the other hand, is indivisible. But this was not the understanding of the Federalists who prevailed during the campaign to ratify the U.S. Constitution. They argued that states did not possess sovereignty; only people did.[49] Once all sovereignty was reposed in the people, the question of how they would be represented in the Senate—whether at-large or by district—rested with the people of each state in the absence of explicit direction from the Constitution.[50] The original purpose of the Senate was simply to act as a check on the House, not to represent states.[51]

The Seventeenth Amendment gave citizens of states the right to directly elect their senators and thereby made the Senate even more analogous to the House. The story of the passage of that amendment is as complex as the story of the original intent behind the creation of the Senate. Like that story, the saga behind the passage of the Seventeenth Amendment cannot be fully imparted in these pages. But that story, too, belies common understandings. One irony of the current absence of blacks in the United States Senate is that the debates surrounding the Seventeenth Amendment were as much about black enfranchisement as they were about the merits of directly electing senators. This was because southerners had sought a partial repeal of the Fifteenth Amendment, which gave blacks the nominal right to vote, as the price of enacting the Seventeenth.[52] In sending the Seventeenth Amendment to the states for ratification free of the southerners' "race rider," the Sixty-Second United States Congress reaffirmed not only blacks' right to vote, but also the full remedial scope of the Fifteenth Amendment—including its application to Senate elections.

The Fifteenth Amendment is the enabling provision for the Voting Rights Act of 1965, a federal law that functionally has given blacks and other minorities a right to an effective vote. Thus, voting structures for legislative bodies that allow minorities to cast a vote only to have their votes consistently canceled out by a white bloc-voting majority are subject to challenge under the Voting Rights Act. Vote dilution is precisely what is happening in Senate elections in the South today. And this is precisely why traditional civil rights organizations, as well as black and progressive Latino and white state legislators, must spearhead a movement to change the method of electing senators in several southern jurisdictions.

Speak with members of the CBC, and they will lament that much of their agenda is continually stymied by an overly white, artificially conservative United States Senate. Having black representation in the House but not in the Senate is like having outfielders but no first, second, or third basemen. Black politics is simply inchoate and weak without representation in the "upper house" that many consider the most powerful legislative body in the world.

Black Money, Black Power

There is economic inequality between black and white Americans, yet there is considerable aggregate wealth within black America. How that wealth is deployed has helped to magnify political inequality between blacks and whites. In this regard, "economic conservatism"—the arguments of Booker T. Washington and latter-day black conservatives that traditional civil rights overemphasizes political equality—contrives a false distinction.[53] Campaign finance law and the interests that exploit its many loopholes to become wealthy or wealthier underscore the often symbiotic relationship between politics and economic empowerment. If economic empowerment were distinct from political rights, then corporations would not have sought the political right of free expression in *Citizens United*. And if leveraging the political process did not help to create or maintain wealth, there would be little reason for AT&T, Inc. to have contributed more than $47 million to federal candidates since 1989,[54] or for the National Beer Wholesalers Association to have contributed more than $24 million,[55] or for cigarette manufacturer Altria Group to have contributed in excess of $25 million as well.[56] "Substitution of the rule of cash for the rule of law," is how one former chief executive officer of a major financial services outfit described our current campaign finance system.[57] Money is political power because the Supreme Court treats money as speech. Political power, in turn, can and does translate into wealth.

African Americans have an annual disposable income of nearly a trillion dollars.[58] Disposable income, also known as buying power, is the amount of money that remains after taxes are paid.[59] The trillion-dollar figure means that if black Americans were a country unto themselves, they would have the sixteenth largest gross domestic product (GDP) in the world.[60] Like other Americans, many blacks—too many—emulate wealthier Americans in their consumptive spending. One theory of why this occurs is that some blacks use consumption as an expression of their alienation—that is, consumption is a means of purchasing the status that eludes them in their everyday lives.[61] Another critique views black conspicuous consumption as the expression of defiance. Under this view, black subcultures caricature mainstream white America by purchasing its goods and "altering the image or blackening the most mass of mass/masked produced goods so as to subvert domination and the generally received meaning of the thing."[62] Blacks bleaching their hair blond or gang members donning the gear of professional athletic teams are examples of this theory.[63]

Both these critiques of black consumptive behavior share one thing in common: each is a play on the consumptive habits of wealthier citizens. But why stop with the purchase of goods and services? If blacks desire to imitate the consumptive behavior of the rich, why not purchase political capital as the wealthy do? Why not divert a fraction of the trillion—let us say $50 million or well under one-half of one percent annually—to support candidates who embrace issues that enhance the lives of black Americans and to defeat those who do not? Fifty million dollars is about $1.28 for every African American. And what might these dollars buy? More wealth. A jobs program targeted at communities with historically high unemployment. More job opportunities through a fairer judicial interpretation of Title VII, the federal antidiscrimination in employment law, by electing senators who will refuse to confirm the conservative jurists who have scaled back Title VII. More educational opportunities through the revitalization of affirmative action—again, by electing senators who will not confirm the conservative jurists who have vanquished race-based affirmative action in the name of a notion of colorblindness that simply calcifies white privilege. A local police force less inclined to mistreat black inhabitants by electing a mayor who understands police misconduct and brutality. And so on. In the tradition of the wealthy, blacks must begin to vote with their dollars as well as their ballots.

Given that the vast majority of whites do not contribute to political campaigns, socializing blacks to spend money on political capital is admittedly challenging, though Barack Obama's 2008 campaign arguably marked the infancy of this socialization.[64] Ironically, blacks' current consumptive spending in many instances subsidizes their political opponents. The Republican Party receives only minimal black voter support, but it has received the lion's share of cigarette-maker Altria Group's political contributions to federal candidates since 1989.[65] According to the American Lung Association, in 2008, about 21 percent of African Americans smoked cigarettes.[66] The association points out that as the rate of cigarette smoking declines in the United States, cigarette makers have increasingly "bombarded" the African American community with advertising. Indeed, blacks were considerably more likely to have seen a cigarette ad than many other demographic groups.[67] Black smokers may vote Democratic but they indirectly subsidize Republicans with their purchases. The same can be said of black purchases of much gasoline and many fast food and pharmaceutical products—all industries that, according to the Center for Responsive Politics, have given disproportionately to Republican federal candidates since 1989.[68]

The rejoinder to all of this is familiar: facing discrimination, a declining economy, and myriad personal struggles, the average black American is in no position to consider how her purchases affect her political rights. Fair enough. But blacks do show discernment when they feel disrespected. A 2007 survey revealed that over half of the African Americans interviewed had boycotted sponsors of television programming they believed contained controversial racial stereotypes and language.[69] Another common reason why blacks boycott a product is that its manufacturer is the subject of a discrimination suit. Fifty-five percent of respondents indicated that they had stopped buying a product for this reason.[70] Black voters are being disrespected in the political process on a daily basis. Indeed, President Obama himself has been disrespected by the American political process, which demonstrates the need for a system of accountability to black voters that goes beyond merely electing black officials.

Corporations are not currently required to disclose all political contributions.[71] A starting point for a black accountability project revolving around campaign contributions would be insisting on passage of a law requiring disclosure. Failing that, black civil rights organizations such as the National Association for the Advancement of Colored People (NAACP) should insist on voluntary disclosure. There is simply no reason why corporate America should be allowed to traffic its goods in black communities throughout this country but not disclose to these communities that it is supporting candidates or causes that work against their political and economic interests.

Apart from disclosure, an infrastructure is needed to educate African Americans on the importance of political giving and to collect and distribute contributions. Churches are currently far too restricted in the political activities in which they can engage. Yet, among other quasi-political activities, churches can educate their congregations and the community about issues of consequence to them.[72]

Fifty-five percent of black congregations engaged in voter education and registration programs in 2010, according to a study by the Hartford Seminary.[73] The dissemination of information regarding a black accountability project intended to assist blacks in achieving political equality is of the same basic civic category as voter education and registration.

A church wishing to maintain its tax-exempt status could not be the actual instrumentality through which contributions were raised and distributed in support of candidates. For this, African Americans might create a multicandidate political action committee (PAC) that would function independently of candidates' campaigns and therefore be permitted to receive unlimited contributions from individuals and businesses after *Citizens United*. The seed money and personnel for the initial formation of such a PAC would come from white progressive groups like ACTBLUE.org and the Democratic Party. White progressives and the Democratic Party should not be able to rely on overwhelming black support without helping to enable black political empowerment.[74]

Regardless of the specific form the accountability project takes, three years after the election of the first black president, and more than 40 years after the passage of the Voting Rights Act of 1965, it is clear that blacks must put their dollars where their votes go in order to be politically effective.

A Black Party?

It is a perennial question in black politics: whither an independent black party? There is a rich history, if not tradition, of black political parties in the United States. Moreover, as detailed in chapter 2, the Supreme Court's ballot-box jurisprudence over the past two decades has invited a revival of the third-party practice by scrutinizing race in redistricting much more minutely than partisanship. The effect of this jurisprudence has been to saddle black voters with the burdens of race without conferring the full benefits of partisanship, even though blacks are the most loyal partisans. This is certainly a major incentive for blacks to exit the two-party process.

What is often unstated in discussions of black third-party alternatives is that a primary negative impetus for such a movement is the failure of white Democrats to uphold their end of the partisan coalitional bargain. From Harold Washington's tumultuous election as the first black mayor of Chicago with just a fraction of the white vote normally taken by a Democrat, to David Dinkins's defeat after one term as the first black mayor of New York City because of the defection of traditional white Democrats, many white Democrats are in the habit of being fair-weather partisans when the party's nominee is black. Indeed, there would be less need for majority-minority districts if white Democrats behaved as Democrats regardless of the race of the nominee. A history of white voter defections has left many black pols convinced of the continuing need for majority-minority districts. Representative Lacy Clay, Jr. has noted that the creation of a majority-minority district was the only way to secure black congressional representation from Missouri because, "You're not going to win a Senate seat."[75] Noting that white Democrats had a history of attempting to dismantle his majority-minority district, Clay stated that one rule of engagement in redistricting for African Americans is that "you take care of your own…so that Black people have a voice in this august body [the House]."[76] Congresswoman Eleanor Holmes Norton underscores the limited options for ensuring black representation in noting that, "Whites have not shown definitively that they will elect blacks except in the majority black districts."[77]

Mention of black third-party movements reflexively elicits responses that a third party is impractical and may ultimately harm black interests by helping to elect conservative Republicans. (The same arguments, ironically, are used against the creation of majority-minority districts within the two-party system.) Concerns such as these have led some to attempt to build a third-party movement not grounded in "identity politics." Lenora Fulani, who has run for multiple offices on third-party tickets, has more recently helped to lead the New York City Independence Party. True to its name, the party offers itself as a postpartisan alternative to the two major parties. Fulani insists that African Americans stand to benefit from a multiracial, independent third-party movement because, "It's not clear to me that we grow by virtue of isolating out our issues in the ways that we have in the past."[78] Fulani cites her coalition's successful efforts to woo black support for then–Republican mayor Michael Bloomberg—who Fulani viewed as responsive to the black community—as an example of the cross-racial coalitions an independent party movement is capable of.[79]

New York state law allows for fusion candidacies or cross-endorsing. Under fusion law, there is less downside to joining a third party in New York than in almost all other states because minor parties and major parties can nominate the same candidate, and the votes for that candidate on each party's line are consolidated for purposes of determining the election outcome. Thus, it is possible for an

African American to be a member of the Independence Party and to simultaneously vote for his party's candidate and the Democratic or Republican candidate. Absent fusion, third-party choices by blacks carry the risks traditionally associated with such a vote—wasted votes and/or the election of a conservative Republican. (Bloomberg, though a Republican, was not considered conservative.)

Fusion-party systems are quite beneficial to racial minorities and other outsiders seeking to exert pressure on the traditional two-party system to accommodate their interests.[80] But they are aberrational in modern American politics.[81] Discussions of black and other third-party movements have tended to be candidate-centric rather than focusing on the structural barriers to meaningful third-party participation. A third-party movement must begin, not with a candidate, but rather with a sustained effort to modify state laws to adopt fusion and other alterations—such as less onerous ballot-access requirements—that will create a more neutral terrain on which major and minor parties can coexist. Even then, however, strategic questions will persist regarding the wisdom of a third-party campaign in a given election.

Today, African Americans function as a satellite party to the Democrats. That is, they theoretically operate within the Democratic Party to bend its policies and practices in the direction of their goals.[82] But history and present circumstances demonstrate that electoral capture and stasis are just as likely under this arrangement as is transformation of the party. In the absence of a practical third-party option, blacks must function more effectively as a satellite party—as effectively as the Tea Party and other conservative elements within the Republican Party. The perpetual "hostage dilemma"—"if you don't support the Democrats, the Republicans (who are much worse) will win"—has not deterred the Tea Party from insisting that the Republicans accommodate their interests, moving that party ever further to the right. Having witnessed that a black president ensures them little more than the white Democratic status quo, if that, African Americans are now faced with a choice: they can remain second-class partisans or they can pursue their role as a satellite party as vigorously as the Tea Party has done.

Think for a moment what would happen to the nation's politics if blacks responded in kind to the fair-weather white Democrats who suddenly become swing voters when the party's nominee is black. Consider, for instance, Alan Hevesi, the former state comptroller of New York, who had an improbable political career, thanks largely to black voters. Hevesi, who is white, was elected New York City comptroller in 1993, the year New York City's first black mayor, David

Dinkins, was being swept from office. New York City is one of the most heavily Democratic jurisdictions in the country. Hevesi lost the white vote, but blacks and Latinos provided his margin of victory. White Democrats did not reciprocate on behalf of Dinkins. In 1997, when Reverend Al Sharpton sought the right to take on the racially divisive Rudy Giuliani as the Democratic mayoral candidate, Hevesi announced that he would not back Sharpton even if Sharpton won the Democratic primary.[83] So here was a white Democrat who owed his election to city-wide office to black voters declining to endorse a black Democrat for mayor. (There was a similar flight of Democratic Party support when black Democrat Kendrick Meek was the party's Florida Senate nominee in 2010.) The Tea Party-like response would be to punish Hevesi electorally.

Black voters must learn to hold white candidates and white Democratic voters responsible for their failure to uphold their end of the coalitional bargain. Sometimes insisting on accountability may well mean running an independent or a third-party candidate against a Democrat in response to their breach of the coalitional covenant. The strategically sound way to do this is to select an office that will not harm the most significant interests of African Americans. In Hevesi's case, the office of city comptroller is important, but it simply does not impact the daily quality of life for African Americans in New York City in the way the positions of mayor and governor do. It is therefore a perfectly reasonable office to target in response to white Democrats' failure to behave as Democrats during Dinkins's reelection contest and Sharpton's subsequent pursuit of the mayor's office.

By the same logic, it makes little strategic sense to sit out or exercise a third-party or an independent option in a presidential contest—unless all other means of exerting pressure have failed. But the likelihood of such a failure is far less if African Americans begin operating as a "strike group," selecting down-ballot offices as vehicles for the expression of their disapproval of Democrats' disrespect and, as discussed previously, exerting financial pressure on the party to accommodate their interests. Since such down-ballot offices are often the feeders of candidates for higher office, and because money is privileged in politics, the Democratic Party apparatus will be compelled to take notice and be responsive.

CONCLUSION

Politics are about movements, and movements must be larger than any one personality in order to be sustainable. This reality is easily obscured by Barack Obama's election. Until African American voters understand and comport their behavior to this basic premise, triangulation of one sort or another will define their relationship to the political process. The racialized obstructionism of the Republican Party and the Tea Party movement have given African Americans a compelling reason to ignore their own triangulation and to rally around President Obama. But the unfair and disrespectful treatment of the first black president is not only cause to fortify him; it is most of all a reminder to blacks that race matters a great deal in American life and that their racial cohesion in the face of continuing societal bias must be channeled into something greater and more sustainable than the next election or the next black candidate.

Conclusion

American politics requires of its African American denizens feats that no other demographic group must perform. Blacks must maintain political cohesion in the face of economic and social divergences among themselves and external solicitations by the likes of black conservatives to disaggregate their political power. Their cohesion, in turn, is the very lifeblood of the American two-party system. For their Herculean efforts on behalf of American democracy, they are not rewarded but instead are asked to engage in self-censorship so as not to risk alienating white voters. This is the current price of black electoral success in a white electorate. This is what post-racialism—prematurely declared—looks like for African American voters.

The post-racial black politician must be especially attentive to the need for self-censorship, for, as Sumi Cho observes, "[O]ne who points out racial inequities risks being characterized as an obsessed-with-race racist who is unfairly and divisively 'playing the race card'—one who occupies the same moral category as someone who consciously perpetrates racial inequities."[1] With this albatross—this inhibiting, suffocating, constraint of post-racialism—the post-racial black politician finds himself in a bind. He can pursue race-neutral equality, but the nation's fiscal crisis—and the victory of austerity over prime-the-pump, Keynesian economics—makes this proposition more rhetorical than real. The sensible and moral recourse when government cannot do a lot is to do what it should for those to whom it owes the greatest reparations—African Americans. But no post-racial black politician would ever make such an argument. So what they offer instead is as much of the already inadequate social safety net as the conservative assault has not dismantled, policy incrementalism (i.e., health-care reform with no public option), and plenty of unthreatening racial symbolism. These are the ingredients of post-racial triangulation that attempt to mask its actual lopsidedness in favor of maintenance of white privilege.

The responsibility for displacing post-racialism with a national progressive race consciousness lies with African Americans and whatever multiracial allies they can recruit. The responsibility of the post-racial black politician is, at a minimum, never to stand in the way or otherwise deprecate this endeavor. Post-racial triangulation by an African American president abrogates this fundamental responsibility to African American voters. In case there were ever any doubt, the Obama presidency serves notice to these voters that black electoral success is distinct from electoral accountability. To ensure accountability, African Americans must actively counteract the premise of post-racial triangulation: the racially prejudiced yet widely shared idea that an identification with African American issues (and voters) is verboten in our politics.

Notes

Introduction

1. This definition of black politics will be unsatisfying to those who are engaged in the philosophical project of explicating the contours of black politics. For instance, Harvard professor Tommie Shelby insists that "the only interests that blacks share on account of their being black and that can also serve as a stable and legitimate basis for political unity are race-related ones...." *See* Tommie Shelby, We Who Are Dark: The Philosophical Foundations of Black Solidarity 154 (2005). Of course, what is or is not race related is subject to both capacious and restrictive interpretations. There is, however, simply no need to engage this debate within this work. Normative arguments aside, my definition of black politics accurately reflects how it has historically functioned in the electoral realm with which I am primarily concerned.
2. Terry Smith, *Parties and Transformative Politics*, 100 Colum. L. Rev. 845, 847 (2000).
3. Barack Obama, The Audacity of Hope 34 (2006).
4. Robert S. Becker, *Triangulation or Strangulation? Obama + Clinton = Bush III?*, Open Salon (July 19, 2010), http://open.salon.com/blog /robert_s_becker/2010/07/19/triangulation_or_strangulation _obama_clinton_bush_iii.
5. Peter Wallsten, *It's Rahm Emanuel's Mayoral Race in Chicago, But Obama's Record Is the Ammunition*, Wash. Post (Jan. 15, 2011, 12:00 AM), http://www.washingtonpost.com/wp-dyn/content/article /2011/01/14/AR2011011406835.html; Chris Cillizza, *Obama vs the Congressional Black Caucus?*, Wash. Post (Aug. 2, 2010, 4:44 PM ET), http://voices.washingtonpost.com/thefix/white-house /president-obama-vs-the-congres.html.
6. Caroline May, *African-American Leaders and Intellectuals Express Dissatisfaction with President Obama*, Daily Caller (Aug. 24, 2010, 9:19 PM), http://dailycaller.com/2010/08/24/african-amer ican-leaders-and-intellectuals-express-dissatisfaction-with-president -obama/.
7. *Blacks Upbeat about Black Progress, Prospects: A Year after Obama's Election*, Pew Res. Center. (Jan. 12, 2010), http://pewresearch. org/pubs/1459/year-after-obama-election-black-public-opinion.

8. Ibid.

9. Krissah Thompson, *Obama Reaches Out to African Americans*, WASH. POST (Dec. 22, 2009, 12:51 PM ET), http://voices.washingtonpost.com/44/2009/12/obama-reaches-out-to-african-a.html.

10. Hazel Trice Edney, *Sharpton: Obama Gets Bad Rap on Black Jobs*, SEATTLE MEDIUM (Jan. 26, 2011), http://seattlemedium.com/News/search/ArchiveContent.asp?NewsID=107233&sID= (Citing Bureau of Labor Statistics records from 1993–2000 that show the unemployment rate for blacks was roughly double that of whites during the Clinton presidency).

11. Thompson, *supra* note 9.

12. Earl Ofari Hutchinson, *What Does Bill Clinton Have That Obama Doesn't?*, HUFFINGTONPOST.COM (Oct. 19, 2010, 12:21 PM), http://www.huffingtonpost.com/earl-ofari-hutchinson/what-does-bill-clinton-ha_b_768203.html.

13. Terry Smith, *Autonomy versus Equality: Voting Rights Rediscovered*, 57 ALA. L. REV. 261, 295 (2005). ("[C]ourts often cannot distinguish race from politics, and when they do, voters of color are usually assigned to whichever category is most disadvantageous in a given case.")

14. Tom Diemer, *Bill Clinton Visit to White House: Is Obama Borrowing His 'Triangulation' Strategy?*, POLITICS DAILY (Dec. 10, 2010), http://www.politicsdaily.com/2010/12/10/bill-clinton-visit-to-white-house-is-obama-borrowing-his-trian/.

15. KEITH REEVES, VOTING HOPES OR FEARS?: WHITE VOTERS, BLACK CANDIDATES & RACIAL POLITICS IN AMERICA 21 (1997) ("[T]hough political contests between two white candidates may traffic in blatant or subtle appeals to race, *where a black candidate competes against a white opponent in a jurisdiction whose population is comprised overwhelmingly of white voters, race becomes a key factor in the campaign.*") (Emphasis in the original).

16. Frank Rich, *2006: The Year of the 'Macaca,'* N.Y. TIMES (Nov. 12, 2006), http://select.nytimes.com/2006/11/12/opinion/12rich.html?ref=georgefallen; Margaret Ann Campbell, *State Exit Polls: Senate Hangs in the Balance*, FOXNEWS.COM (Nov. 8, 2006), http://www.foxnews.com/story/0,2933,227979,00.html (Quoting an exit poll that nearly 60 percent of whites supported Allen in the senatorial election).

1   BLACK POLITICS: WHICH WAY IS LEFT?

1. MICHAEL C. DAWSON, BLACK VISIONS: THE ROOTS OF CONTEMPORARY AFRICAN-AMERICAN POLITICAL IDEOLOGIES 83 (2001). (Using public opinion survey data to divide black ideology into five categories, and finding that black conservatism garners the least support among African Americans.)

2. Claire Jean Kim, *The Racial Triangulation of Asian Americans*, 27 POL. & SOC'Y 105, 107 (1999).

3. The concept of vulnerability has undergone a redefinition in legal discourse, one that attempts to remove its stigma of victimhood and recognize the universality of vulnerability in the human condition. *See* Martha Albertson Fineman, *The Vulnerable Subject: Anchoring Equality in the Human Condition*, 20 YALE J.L. & FEMINISM 1, 9–10 (2008). Like humans, vulnerability inheres in social institutions—most relevantly for purposes of this book, in political parties. *See* Ibid. at 12. It is not necessary for me to subscribe entirely to the reconceptualization of vulnerability to advance my thesis. It is sufficient to note the duality of the implications of the use of the term.

4. *Concede Nothing to Bush: Black Consensus Remains Intact*, BLACK COMMENTATOR, http://www.blackcommentator.com/112/112_cover _election.html (last visited Jan. 31, 2011).

5. Terry Smith, *A Black Party? Timmons, Black Backlash and the Endangered Two-Party Paradigm*, 48 DUKE L.J. 1 (1998).

6. For a discussion of the legal significance of black voter cohesion, *see infra* Ch. 3.

7. ROBERT C. SMITH & RICHARD SELTZER, RACE, CLASS, AND CULTURE: A STUDY IN AFRO-AMERICAN MASS OPINION 10 (1992) [hereinafter SMITH & SELTZER, RACE, CLASS, AND CULTURE]; ROBERT C. SMITH & RICHARD SELTZER, CONTEMPORARY CONTROVERSIES AND THE AMERICAN RACIAL DIVIDE 10 (2000) [hereinafter SMITH & SELTZER, AMERICAN RACIAL DIVIDE]. (Black "opinions are deeply rooted in both the individual psyche and the collective memory of blacks, as well as in their dissatisfaction with their separate and unequal status in contemporary American society.")

8. SMITH & SELTZER, RACE, CLASS, AND CULTURE, *supra* note 7, at 38.

9. Ibid.

10. Ibid. at 41.

11. SMITH & SELTZER, AMERICAN RACIAL DIVIDE, *supra* note 7, at 26.

12. SMITH & SELTZER, RACE, CLASS, AND CULTURE, *supra* note 7, at 41.

13. Ibid. at 147–48.

14. KATHERINE TATE, BLACK FACES IN THE MIRROR: AFRICAN AMERICANS AND THEIR REPRESENTATIVES IN THE U.S. CONGRESS 91 (2003).

15. Robert C. Smith & Richard Seltzer, *The Deck and the Sea: The African American Vote in the Presidential Elections of 2000 and 2004, in* THE EXPANDING BOUNDARIES OF BLACK POLITICS 253, 261 (Georgia A. Persons ed., 2007).

16. Ibid.

17. *Blacks Upbeat about Black Progress, Prospects a Year after Obama's Election*, PEW RES. CENTER (Jan. 12, 2010), http://pewresearch. org/pubs/1459/year-after-obama-election-black-public-opinion.

18. Fineman, *supra* note 3, at 12–13.

19. Ibid at 12.

20. *See* TATE, *supra* note 14, at 93–94.

21. Crisitunity, *PVI/Vote Index for 2008*, SWING STATE PROJECT (May 4, 2009, 2:32 PM), http://swingstateproject.com/diary/4578/pvivote-index-for-2008. The specific methodology employed by the *Swing State Project* was to "rank every district from 1 to 435 in terms of how Democratic its presidential voting record is, rank every representative from 1 to 435 in terms of how liberal his or her voting record is, and find the difference, with a larger difference in one direction or the other meaning that representative is overperforming or underperforming the district's lean." Ibid. The first calculation is called a partisan vote index score, which measures the partisan tilt of a district by looking at its vote in presidential elections and determining how much more or less Democratic or Republican that district is in comparison to the national ticket's performance. *Introducing the Cook Political Report Partisan Voting Index (PVI) for the 111th Congress*, COOK POL. REP. (Apr. 9, 2009), http://cookpolitical.com/node/4201.

22. Crisitunity, *The PVI-Voting Pattern Index*, SWING STATE PROJECT (Mar. 28, 2008, 3:34 PM), http://www.swingstateproject.com/showDiary.do?diaryId=1637.

23. Terry Smith, *White Dollars, Black Candidates: Inequality and Agency in Campaign Finance Law*, 57 S.C. L. REV. 735, 740–41 (2006).

24. Ibid.

25. Stephanie Condon, *Jesse Jackson Slams Black Votes against Healthcare*, CBS NEWS (Nov. 19, 2009, 2:59 PM), http://www.cbsnews.com/blogs/2009/11/19/politics/politicalhotsheet/entry5712116.shtml?utm_source=feedburner&utm_medium=feed&utm_campaign=Feed%3A+CBSNewsPCAnswer+%28PC+Answer%3A+CBSNews.com%29.

26. ADOLPH REED, JR., STIRRINGS IN THE JUG: BLACK POLITICS IN THE POST-SEGREGATION ERA 205 (1999).

27. Ibid.

28. Cornel West, *Unmasking the Black Conservatives*, CHRISTIAN CENTURY, July 16–23, 1986 at 644.

29. ROBERT KUTTNER, THE SQUANDERING OF AMERICA: HOW THE FAILURE OF OUR POLITICS UNDERMINES OUR PROSPERITY 44–45 (2007).

30. LOUIS UCHITELLE, THE DISPOSABLE AMERICAN: LAYOFFS AND THEIR CONSEQUENCES 67 (2006).

31. David Cay Johnston, *Joe the Plumber's Taxes*, 121 TAX NOTES 471, 473 (2008).

32. UCHITELLE, *supra* note 30, at 67.

33. Peter Whoriskey, *With Executive Pay, Rich Pull Away from Rest of America*, WASH. POST (June 18, 2011), http://www.washingtonpost

.com/business/economy/with-executive-pay-rich-pull-away-from
-rest-of-america/2011/06/13/AGKG9jaH_print.html. Of the
top 0.1 percent of income earners in 2008, 41 percent were chief
executive officers, managers, or supervisors at nonfinancial companies. Ibid. The AFL-CIO reported in 2011 that CEO pay was
343 times workers' median compensation. In 1980, it was only 42
times higher. *See* Danielle Douglas, *Stock Awards and Bonuses Push
Up Compensation Totals*, WASH. POST (June 19, 2011), http://www
.washingtonpost.com/business/capitalbusiness/stock-awards-and
-bonuses-push-up-compensation-totals/2011/06/14/AGb74ibH
_story.html?hpid=z1.

34. Cedric Herring, *Who Represents the People? African Americans,
Public Policy, and Political Alienation during the Reagan-Bush
Years, in* AFRICAN AMERICANS AND THE NEW POLICY CONSENSUS:
RETREAT OF THE LIBERAL STATE 94 (Marilyn E. Lashley & Melanie
Njeri Jackson, eds., 1994) [hereinafter RETREAT OF THE LIBERAL
STATE]; Marilyn E. Lashley, *Reclaiming the State: Representative
Government and Public Policy Access, in* RETREAT OF THE LIBERAL
STATE 55.

35. Floyd W. Hayes III, *Government Retreat, the Dispossessed, and the
Politics of African American Self-Reliant Development in the Age of
Reaganism, in* RETREAT OF THE LIBERAL STATE, *supra* note 34, at
99–102.

36. KUTTNER, *supra* note 29, at 44–45.

37. *See* Hayes, *supra* note 35, at 110. ("What is important to note is
that traditional liberal African American leadership and conservative
African American policy spokespersons are both wedded to ideas,
programs, and strategies that look backward to the declining capital-
ist social order.")

38. *See* Terry Smith, *Reinventing Black Politics: Senate Districts, Minority
Vote Dilution and the Preservation of the Second Reconstruction*, 25
HASTINGS CONST. L.Q. 277, 281 (1998). ("The paucity of color
in the Senate is remarkable when contrasted with the House of
Representatives, where members are elected from districts rather
than entire states.")

39. Lani Guinier, *No Two Seats: The Elusive Quest for Political Equality*,
77 VA. L. REV. 1413, 1444–47 (1991).

40. Ibid. at 1494.

41. ROBERT SINGH, THE CONGRESSIONAL BLACK CAUCUS: RACIAL POLITICS
IN THE U.S. CONGRESS 203 (1998).

42. Ibid. at 205.

43. Bruce A. Dixon, *Black Politics Is Over: Black Politicians No Longer
Believe Social Justice Is Possible*, BLACK AGENDA REP. (Jan. 6, 2010,
15:22), http://blackagendareport.com/print/content/black-politics
-over-black-politicians-no-longer-believe-social-justice-possible.

44. GWEN IFILL, THE BREAKTHROUGH: POLITICS AND RACE IN THE AGE OF OBAMA 64 (2009) (Quoting Corey Ealons, the Obama campaign's director of outreach to African American media).

45. Interview with Congresswoman Donna Christensen, in Wash., D.C. (Sept. 15, 2011).

46. *See* SMITH & SELTZER, AMERICAN RACIAL DIVIDE, *supra* note 7, at 15 (Reviewing data through 1999).

47. U.S. Dep't of Labor, Bureau of Labor Statistics, *Employment Status of the Civilian Noninstitutional Population 25 Years and over by Educational Attainment, Sex, Race, and Hispanic or Latino Ethnicity*, http://www.bls.gov/cps/cpsaat7.pdf (Presenting data for 2009 and 2010).

48. IFILL, *supra* note 44, at 56.

2 RACE AND MONEY IN POLITICS

1. *See* Matthew Patane, *Lawmakers Override Nixon's Veto of Congressional Redistricting Map*, MISSOURIAN (May 4, 2011, 7:07 PM CDT), http://www.columbiamissourian.com/stories/2011/05/04/lawmakers-override-governors-veto-congressional-redistricting-map-date-may-4–2011/; Rebecca Berg, *Legislature Overrides Nixon Veto of Redistricting Map*, STLTODAY.COM (May 5, 2011, 12:45 AM), http://www.stltoday.com/news/local/metro/article_6995ad6c-813a-5d55-b094-eed9ef306c8e.html.

2. Philip Rucker, *Mitt Romney Says 'Corporations Are People' at Iowa State Fair*, WASH. POST (Aug. 11, 2011), http://www.washingtonpost.com/politics/mitt-romney-says-corporations-are-people/2011/08/11/gIQABwZ38I_story.html?wpisrc=emailtoafriend.

3. *See* Terry Smith, *Autonomy Versus Equality: Voting Rights Rediscovered*, 57 ALA. L. REV. 261, 265–74 (Identifying traditions of subgroup autonomy in the American political structure and arguing that the quest for black voting rights must be understood in light of this tradition).

4. Frank Newport, Jeffrey M. Jones, & Lydia Saad *Republicans Nationwide Are Similar in Composition to 2008*, GALLUP (Oct. 28, 2011), http://www.gallup.com/poll/150386/Republicans-Nationwide-Similar-Composition-2008.aspx.

5. Ibid.

6. Ibid.

7. ROBERT C. SMITH, CONSERVATISM AND RACISM, AND WHY IN AMERICA THEY ARE THE SAME 116 (2010).

8. *Civil War at 150: Still Relevant, Still Divisive*, PEW RES. CENTER (Apr. 8, 2011), http://people-press.org/2011/04/08/civil-war-at-150-still-relevant-still-divisive/1/ (Fifty-six percent of respondents found the Civil War to be of continuing relevance). Although another question in the poll attempts to elicit from respondents whether they

thought the war was about "states' rights" or slavery, the question itself is ill-informed to the extent that it suggests that "states' rights" was a concept independent of slavery during the Civil War. *See, e.g.*, Wilson R. Huhn, *Constantly Approximating Popular Sovereignty: Seven Fundamental Principles of Constitutional Law*, 19 Wm. & Mary Bill Rts. J. 291, 328 (2010). ("During the antebellum period 'states rights' became the battle cry of nullifiers and secessionists in support of slavery. After the Civil War, state sovereignty remained the principal argument in opposition to the protection of newly-freed slaves, and 'states rights' was the constant refrain of segregationists up to and throughout the Civil Rights Movement of the 1950s and 1960s.")

9. In 2009, whites composed about 64 percent of voters who identified themselves as Democrat. *See* Frank Newport, *Republican Base Heavily White, Conservative, Religious*, Gallup (June 1, 2009), http://www .gallup.com/poll/118937/republican-base-heavily-white-conse rvative-religious.aspx. The minority composition of the Democratic Party was 36 percent compared to the Republican Party's 11 percent. *See* Ibid. The nation's combined Asian, black, and Latino population in 2010 was 33.9 percent. *See* State & County QuickFacts, U.S. Census Bureau, http://quickfacts.census.gov/qfd/states/00000 .html (last visited Nov. 11, 2011). According to Gallup, "The results show clearly that the Republican Party today is first and foremost a political entity dominated by white Americans. Eighty-nine percent of rank-and-file Republicans are non-Hispanic whites, leaving just 5% who are Hispanic (of any race), 2% who are black, and 4% of other races." *See* Newport, *supra*.

10. Jill Lawrence, *Study: Sharp Drop in Black GOP Delegates*, USA Today (Sept. 2, 2008, 4:04 AM), http://www.usatoday.com/news/politics /election2008/2008–09–01-diversity_N.htm.

11. Ibid.

12. *See* David A. Bositis, Joint Ctr. for Political and Econ. Studies, Blacks and the 2004 Democratic National Convention 9 tbl.1 (2004) (providing black and white vote percentages in presidential elections from 1936 to 2000), *available at* http:// www.jointcenter.org/sites/default/files/upload/research/files /2004%20Democratic%20Convention%20Guide.pdf. The peak for Republicans between 1964 and 2000 is 15 percent. Ibid. In 2004, Republicans took 11 percent of the black vote. *See Election Results*, Cnn.com, http://www.cnn.com/ELECTION/2004/pages/results /states/US/P/00/epolls.0.html (last visited Nov. 12, 2011) [hereinafter *2004 Election Results*]. In 2008, their share slipped to 5 percent. *See Election Results 2008*, N.Y. Times (Nov. 5, 2008), http://elections .nytimes.com/2008/results/president/exit-polls.html [hereinafter 2008 *Election Results*].

13. *See* Bositis, *supra* note 12, at 9 tbl.1; *2004 Election Results*, *supra* note 12; *2008 Election Results*, *supra* note 12.

14. Shaw v. Hunt, 517 U.S. 899, 907 (1996).
15. "No State shall make or enforce any law which shall abridge the privileges or immunities of citizens of the United States; nor shall any State deprive any person of life, liberty, or property, without due process of law; nor deny to any person within its jurisdiction the equal protection of the laws." U.S. CONST. amend. XIV, § 1.
16. Terry Smith, *A Black Party: Timmons, Black Backlash and the Endangered Two-Party Paradigm*, 48 Duke L.J. 1, 23–24 (1998).
17. 478 U.S. 109, 144–45 (1986) (O'Connor, J., concurring).
18. Vieth v. Jubelirer, 541 U.S. 267 (2004), revisited *Davis*. In *Vieth*, four justices would have overturned *Davis* on "non-justiciability" grounds—that is, they would have found that federal courts are not competent to adjudicate gerrymandering claims because there are not judicially manageable standards by which to do so. Ibid. at 305–06. The majority in *Vieth*, however, declined to overrule *Davis*, though they could not agree on the standards for adjudicating a partisan gerrymander unconstitutional. Thus, *Davis* stood as good, albeit unhelpful, law. Two years after *Vieth*, in League of United Latin American Citizens v. Perry, 548 U.S. 399 (2006), the Court considered whether Texas's extraordinary mid-decade redistricting that had been undertaken for the evident purpose of yielding Republicans more congressional seats, violated *Davis*'s undefined prohibition on some forms of partisan gerrymandering. While reaffirming a putative constitutional claim, the Court once again found that no appropriate standard existed and thus declined to invalidate the Texas remapping on this ground. Ibid. at 416–21. *But see* Cox v. Larios, 542 U.S. 947 (2004) (*sum. affirm*) (Summarily affirming a district court decision that partisan gerrymandering was not a constitutional justification for departures from one-person, one-vote).
19. *Davis*, 478 U.S. at 131.
20. *See* Abrams v. Johnson, 521 U.S. 74 (1997); Shaw v. Hunt, 517 U.S. 899 (1996); Bush v. Vera, 517 U.S. 952 (1996). Lower court decisions following *Shaw* and striking down majority-minority congressional districts include Hays v. State of La. 936 F.Supp. 360 (W.D. La. 1996) (Striking down a majority-black district in Louisiana); Diaz v. Silver, 978 F.Supp. 96 (E.D.N.Y. 1997), *aff'd*, 118 S.Ct. 36 (1997) (Invalidating New York's congressional remapping as an unconstitutional gerrymander under *Shaw*); Moon v. Meadows, 952 F.Supp. 1141 (E.D.Va. 1997), *aff'd*, 521 U.S. 1113 (1997) (Striking down a majority-black congressional district in Virginia that sent the first black to Congress from the state since Reconstruction).
21. Shaw v. Reno, 509 U.S. 630, 647 (1993). The Court subjected the two districts to its most suspicious level of constitutional scrutiny, strict scrutiny, because it found that race had "predominated" in the creation of the districts. Yet North Carolina's congressional remapping left whites with a disproportionate share of congressional seats in

which they were a majority of the voters. So who precisely was denied "equal protection of the laws"? The plaintiffs in *Shaw* were white voters who resided in the two new majority-black congressional districts. Ibid. at 638. They could not demonstrate that their votes had been diluted by North Carolina's plan because white voters throughout the state continued to control more than their proportionate share of congressional districts. Rather, they claimed that "the deliberate segregation of voters into separate districts on the basis of race violated their constitutional right to participate in a 'color-blind' electoral process." Ibid. at 641–42.

Although the Court purported to understand the folly of insisting on "color-blindness" in elections, its own analysis did not veer far from the white plaintiffs' claim. Finding that the odd shapes of the two black congressional districts were proof of an intent to segregate voters on the basis of race, the Court identified a constitutional harm that the dissent believed to be "imagin[ed]" and "entirely new." Ibid. at 659 (White, J., dissenting). White voters whose votes were undiluted by a remapping could nevertheless state a constitutional claim because:

> A reapportionment plan that includes in one district individuals who belong to the same race, but who are otherwise widely separated by geographical and political boundaries, and who may have little in common with one another but the color of their skin, bears an uncomfortable resemblance to political apartheid. It reinforces the perception that members of the same racial group—regardless of their age, education, economic status, or the community in which they live—think alike, share the same political interests, and will prefer the same candidates at the polls. We have rejected such perceptions elsewhere as impermissible racial stereotypes.

Ibid. at 647.

The Court also expressed concern that the redistricting threatened "to stigmatize individuals by reason of their membership in a racial group and to incite racial hostility." Ibid. at 643. It feared that the districts would exacerbate racially polarized voting and signal to the black congressmen elected from the districts "that their primary obligation is to represent only [blacks], rather than their constituency as a whole." Ibid. at 648. These special "representational" harms were present, where, as in North Carolina, race predominated in the drawing of a district.

The injury to white voters that the five-justice majority described was indeed imagined. Prior to *Shaw*, a plaintiff complaining of an injury in the electoral process had to show an injury to his right to vote—dilution, for instance. *See* Smith, *A Black Party, supra* note 16, at 49. The Court's invocation of apartheid was factually inapposite since the black voting-age population of the new districts was only 53.40 percent and 53.34 percent, respectively. *See* State Appellees'

Brief, Shaw v. Reno, 509 U.S. 630, 647 (1993) (No. 92–357), 1993 WL 476425, at *5 n.6. This begged the question whether the Court would view the districts as segregated if whites held a slight voting-age majority. The notion that majority-black districts created racial hostility was subject to a similar turnabout: Do white districts do the same thing? Moreover, to the extent that the hostility with which the Court was concerned was that of whites angry at being in the minority, the Court failed to explain why this type of hostility was entitled to constitutional protection. *See* Smith, *A Black Party*, *supra* note 16, at 45. Nor did it explain who was stereotyped by such districts. We ordinarily think of stereotype as an unfair generalization that risks ignoring the individual character or potential of its object. Yet, both black and white voters in the new majority-black districts could defy whatever stereotype was imposed on them by simply voting as they wished. In any case, to the extent that the Court was concerned specifically with black stereotype and stigma, not allowing blacks a controlling hand in government was surely a greater harm to them than creating majority-black districts.

The Court's concern with an uptick in racially polarized bloc voting made no doctrinal sense in the context of the new claim it was recognizing. Racially polarized bloc voting is the concern of *vote dilution*, the very claim that the white plaintiffs could not make out. Ibid. Apart from this, however, there was evidence that majority-minority districts actually decrease racially polarized voting. Voters in majority-minority districts had been shown to be more willing to support a white candidate than were voters in a majority-white district to support a black candidate. *See* Ibid. at 46. Kareem Crayton has tested *Shaw*'s hypothesis that majority-minority districts increase racially polarized voting and found no support for the Court's speculation. *See* Kareem U. Crayton, *Beat'em or Join'em? White Voters and Black Candidates in Majority-Black Districts*, 58 Syracuse L. Rev. 547, 571–72 (2008). Finally, the Court in *Shaw* engaged in stereotyping of its own by suggesting that a black representative would have fealty only to his black constituents. In *Davis*, the Court assumed the opposite—"[a]n individual or a group of individuals who votes for a losing candidate is usually deemed to be adequately represented by the winning candidate and to have as much opportunity to influence that candidate as other voters in the district." 478 U.S. at 132.

22. Section 5 of the Voting Rights Act of 1965 requires covered jurisdictions to receive administrative approval from the U.S. Department of Justice (DOJ) or a declaratory judgment from the United States District Court for the District of Columbia before making a change to "any voting qualification or prerequisite to voting, or standard, practice, or procedure with respect to voting." 42 U.S.C. § 1973c(a) (2006).

23. Thornburg v. Gingles, 478 U.S. 30, 50–51 (1986).

24. 129 S.Ct. 1231, 1243–45 (2009).
25. Terry Smith, *Disappearing Districts: Minority Vote Dilution Doctrine as Politics*, 93 MINN. L. REV. 1680, 1690 (2009). ("If a state may inflict [Shaw's harm of stereotyping voters] by adjoining what the Supreme Court concluded were unrelated communities of color for purposes of maximizing the number of black congressional districts, it is difficult to see why a racial group is not similarly harmed when it is overaggregated into a single district.")
26. MICHAEL TESLER & DAVID O. SEARS, OBAMA'S RACE: THE 2008 ELECTION AND THE DREAM OF A POST-RACIAL AMERICA 5 (2010).
27. Smith, *Autonomy Versus Equality, supra* note 3, at 275–79.
28. Ibid.
29. Election Center, *Exit Polls*, CNN.COM, http://www.cnn.com /ELECTION/2010/results/polls/#DES01p1 (last visited Nov. 14, 2011).
30. Election Center, *Exit Polls*, CNN.COM, http://www.cnn.com /ELECTION/2010/results/polls/#val=NVS01p1 (last visited Nov. 14, 2011).
31. Election Center, *Exit Polls*, CNN.COM, http://www.cnn.com /ELECTION/2010/results/polls/#val=ILG00p1 (last visited Nov. 14, 2011).
32. *See* Bush v. Gore, 531 U.S. 98 (2000).
33. *See* BOSITIS, *supra* note 12, at 10 tbl.2.
34. To put a finer point on it, consider the 2004 presidential election. If that election had been held only among whites, George W. Bush would have carried most "blue" or Democratic states won by John Kerry. In the 40 jurisdictions for which data is available, only in the District of Columbia and Washington State did the Democrat win the white vote. *See* Smith, *Autonomy v. Equality, supra* note 3, at 279.
35. *See* Judith Browne Dianis, *Five Myths About Voter Fraud*, WASH. POST (Oct. 7, 2011), http://www.washingtonpost.com/opinions/five -myths-about-voter-fraud/2011/10/04/gIQAkjoYTL_story.html ?wpisrc=emailtoafriend; Spencer Overton, *Voter Identification*, 105 MICH. L. REV. 631, 659 (2007).
36. Crawford v. Marion County Election Bd., 553 U.S. 181, 191 (2008) (Requiring only "relevant and legitimate state interests" to justify a state voter photo ID law, rather than the "compelling interest" required by strict scrutiny). Gilda Daniels, the former chief of the U.S. Department of Justice's Voting section, has referred to voter ID and other superfluous election administration laws as "conniving methods" intended to rid the electoral process of the "unwanted voter." *See* Gilda R. Daniels, *A Vote Delayed Is a Vote Denied: A Preemptive Approach to Eliminating Election Administration Legislation that Disenfranchises Unwanted Voters*, 47 U. LOUISVILLE L. REV. 57, 58–59 (2008). The majority in *Crawford* demonstrates no such skepticism of this type of legislation.

37. 532 U.S. 234 (2001).

38. Ibid. at 245.

39. Smith, *Autonomy Versus Equality, supra* note 3, at 280–81.

40. Terry Smith, Commentary, *For Black Caucus, Race Can't be the Only Factor,* PHILA. INQUIRER, Nov. 17, 2010, at A19. (Describing blacks as "a political group that faces discrimination based on race.")

41. Smith, *Equality versus Autonomy, supra* note 3, at 282. ("[O]ne is hard-pressed to think of a single example where black voters have preferred the black candidate in a bi-racial contest in which that candidate has been politically conservative.")

42. Rogers v. Lodge, 458 U.S. 613, 651–52 (1982) (Steven, J., dissenting) (citation omitted).

43. *See* Robert E. Hogan and Joel A. Thompson, *Minorities and Campaign Contributions, in* CAMPAIGN FINANCE IN STATE LEGISLATIVE ELECTIONS 139, 148 & 154 (Joel A. Thompson & Gary Moncrief, eds., 1998) (Examining the state legislative campaigns of 755 non-Hispanic white candidates and 81 minority candidates and concluding that "the general pattern is that minority candidates, for the most part, raise and spend less than non-Hispanic white candidates," a disparity that is exacerbated in biracial contests in non-Hispanic white districts); JOHN THEILMANN & AL WILHITE, DISCRIMINATION AND CONGRESSIONAL CAMPAIGN CONTRIBUTIONS 77–78 (1991) (Examining congressional races during the 1980s and concluding that incumbent black representatives received significantly lower large contributions from individual donors than did white incumbents in three of five election cycles); Samantha Sanchez, *Money and Diversity in State Legislatures, 2003*, at 5 (2005), http://www.follow themoney.org/press/Reports/200505111.pdf (Noting that in 42 out of 50 states minority legislators raised less on average than their white counterparts). *See also* LINDA CASEY, NAT'L INST. ON MONEY IN STATE POLITICS, DIVERSITY IN STATE JUDICIAL CAMPAIGNS, 2007–2008 (Jan. 13, 2010), *available at* http://www.followthe money.org/press/PrintReportView.phtml?r=412 (Examining contested partisan judicial elections for state high courts in 2007–2008 and finding that "the average $414,677 raised by members of an ethnic or racial minority was less than the average $771,509 raised by all other candidates in partisan high court races. . . ."). In nonpartisan high court contests, minority candidates were, on average, outraised $193,531 to $256,366. Ibid. In contested partisan races for state appellate courts, racial minorities were outraised on average by $94,348 to $137,409. *See* Ibid. In nonpartisan appellate contests, minority candidates were outraised on average by $71,445 to $75,047. Ibid.

   During the 2005–2006 election cycle for contested state high court races, African American candidates were outraised on average by $323,329 to $631,909. *See* RACHEL WEISS, NAT'L INST. ON MONEY

IN STATE POLITICS, DIVERSITY IN HIGH COURT CAMPAIGNS, 2005–2006, at 8 (June 2007), *available at* http://www.followthemoney.org/press/Reports/200706191.pdf.

44. *Contributions to Candidates for the 109th Congress*, TECHPOLITICS (June 30, 2004), http://www.techpolitics.org/congress/fec630042.php?sort_field=cbc%20desc,%20netreceipts&sort_order=desc.

45. *See, e.g.*, Sekou Franklin & Pearl K. Ford, *Barack Obama and the Presidential Election in Georgia: Symbolic Racism, Electoral Mobilization, and Campaign Contributions, in* AFRICAN AMERICANS IN GEORGIA: A REFLECTION OF POLITICS AND POLICY IN THE NEW SOUTH 67, 86 (Pearl K. Ford, ed., 2010) (Examining the 2008 presidential contest in Georgia and concluding that donors in black communities were more likely to contribute to Obama's campaign than donors residing in white communities, a finding that mimicked racially polarized candidate preferences in the state). Obama, however, out-fundraised his Republican opponent both in Georgia and nationally. No scholar has suggested that Obama's fundraising prowess is generalizable to most candidates, let alone black candidates.

46. Interview with Congressman William Lacy Clay, Jr., in Wash., D.C. (July 26, 2011).

47. Ibid. Clay disputes the notion that the relative safety of many black districts justifies the degree of discrimination against minority candidates in the distribution of funds by progressive causes. He notes that, safe district or not, all members have obligations, such as member dues, that require campaign dollars to fulfill. Ibid.

48. Interview with Congresswoman Yvette Clarke, in Wash., D.C. Sept. 15, 2011).

49. Ibid.

50. Ctr. for Responsive Politics, Communications, *Money Wins Presidency and 9 of 10 Congressional Races in Priciest U.S. Election Ever*, OPENSECRETSBLOG (Nov. 5, 2008, 3:19 PM), http://www.opensecrets.org/news/2008/11/money-wins-white-house-and.html.

51. President Barack Obama, Remarks by the President in State of the Union Address (Jan. 27, 2010), *available at* http://www.whitehouse.gov/the-press-office/remarks-president-state-union-address.

52. Citizens United v. FEC, 130 S.Ct. 876 (2010).

53. These contribution limitations, however, favor the well-to-do. Despite the much-heralded small contributor to campaigns, individuals may currently contribute up to $2,500 per federal candidate per election and a combined total of $117,000 to candidates and various party committees and PACs. *See Contribution Limits 2011–12*, FED. ELECTION COMM'N, http://www.fec.gov/pages/brochures/contrib.shtml#Contribution_Limits (last visited Nov. 14, 2011). These are thresholds that are simply beyond the capacity of the ordinary American. During the current 2011–12 reporting cycle, as of early November 2011, only .11 percent of the American population

contributed $200 or more to a federal candidate, party committee, or PAC. *See* Ctr. for Responsive Politics, *Donor Demographics*, OPENSECRETS.ORG, http://www.opensecrets.org/overview/DonorDemographics.php (last visited Nov. 14, 2011). (In order for a contribution to be itemized on a Federal Election Commission report, it must be $200 or greater.) Yet that .11 percent of Americans contributed 66.1 percent of all direct contributions to individual candidates, party committees, and PACs.

54. Buckley v. Valeo, 424 U.S. 1, 25–28 (1976).

55. Ibid. at 48–49 (Internal quotations deleted).

56. *Citizens United*, 130 S.Ct. at 903 (Quoting Austin v. Mich. Chamber of Commerce, 494 U.S. 652, 660 (1990)).

57. Ibid. at 905.

58. Richard H. Pildes, *Is the Supreme Court a 'Majoritarian' Institution?*, 2010 SUP. CT. REV. 103, 112 n.37 (2010).

59. Dan Eggen, *The 2012 Election Brings a New Kind of Fundraiser: The Super Bundler*, WASH. POST (Aug. 16, 2011), http://www.washingtonpost.com/politics/the-2012-election-brings-a-new-kind-of-fundraiser-the-super-bundler/2011/08/05/gIQALQZCJJ_story.html?wpisrc=emailtoafriend.

60. *See* Nicholas Confessore, *Lines Blur Between Candidates and PACs With Unlimited Cash*, N.Y. TIMES (Aug. 27, 2011) http://www.nytimes.com/2011/08/28/us/politics/28donate.html?pagewanted=2&_r=1&emc=eta1#.

61. Terry Smith, *Race and Money in Politics*, 79 N.C. L. REV. 1469, 1486–87 (2001).

62. Camille Gear Rich, *Marginal Whiteness*, 98 CAL. L. REV. 1497, 1587 (2010).

63. ROBERT SPERO, THE DUPING OF THE AMERICAN VOTER: DISHONESTY AND DECEPTION IN PRESIDENTIAL TELEVISION ADVERTISING 96–98 (1980).

64. KATHLEEN HALL JAMIESON, DIRTY POLITICS: DECEPTION, DISTRACTION, AND DEMOCRACY 109 (1992).

65. Mary Jacoby, *'98 is not Sen. Moseley-Braun's Year*, ST. PETERSBURG TIMES, Oct. 31, 1998, at 1A, LEXIS, St. Petersburg Times File.

66. *See* Amanda Terkel, *West Virginia Conservative Foundation's New Ad Warns Of Rep. Nick Rahall's Outreach to Arab-Americans*, HUFFINGTONPOST.COM (Oct. 4, 2012, 11:19 AM), http://www.huffingtonpost.com/2010/10/04/west-virginia-conservative-foundation-nick-rahall-ad_n_748213.html.

67. *See* Greg Sargent, *Sharron Angle Ad Shows Mexican Border—After She Insisted Her Ads Weren't About Latinos*, WASH. POST (Oct. 25, 2010, 4:59 PM ET), http://voices.washingtonpost.com/plum-line/2010/10/sharron_angle_ad_shows_mexican.html.

68. KEITH REEVES, VOTING HOPES OR FEARS? WHITE VOTERS, BLACK CANDIDATES & RACIAL POLITICS IN AMERICA 59 (1997).

(Demonstrating through a content analysis of news publications concerning biracial elections that "the press has the uncanny ability to shape race as a variable and thereby undercut one's appeal as a candidate.")

69. *See* William P. Marshall, *The Last Best Chance for Campaign Reform*, 94 Nw. L. Rev. 335, 366 n.176 (2000) (Surveying the divergent findings of empirical research regarding the effectiveness of political ads).

70. Tali Mendelberg, The Race Card: Campaign Strategy, Implicit Messages, and the Norm of Equality 4 (2001).

71. Ibid.

72. Ibid. at 20–21.

73. Charlton D. McIlwain & Stephen M. Caliendo, Race Appeal: How Candidates Invoke Race in U.S. Campaigns 30 (2011). ("By far, the strongest factor associated with ads' racist potential is the percentage of Whites in the electorate.")

74. *See* Guy-Uriel E. Charles, *Racial Identity, Electoral Structures, and the First Amendment Right of Association*, 91 Cal. L. Rev. 1209, 1248–49 (2003). (Surveying the Supreme Court's First Amendment freedom of association cases and concluding that "[t]he main principle of the political association cases is that of effective aggregation: an individual must have a reasonable opportunity to join with like-minded others for the purpose of acquiring political power. Stated differently, association enables individuals to amplify their voices to further common political beliefs.")

75. *Buckley*, 424 U.S. at 19.

76. A word about the concept of "state action" is in order. Some might attempt to distinguish the Court's treatment of money from its treatment of race based on differences in the public nature of the conduct engaged in by the racial interests versus monied interests. The argument is that an individual's or a group's expenditure of money is a private act, while the speech medium of black voters seeking the creation of a majority-minority district requires government action. Yet government action is as much a part of the expenditure of campaign dollars as private action is a part of the black voters' lobbying efforts. The congressional districts for which the money is used do not exist in the state of nature. Their creation requires state action. Legislatures can and do draw districts where certain kinds of candidates will have to spend more money to get elected and other candidates will have to spend less. In a marginal district, for instance, small shifts in voter preference can change outcomes because neither party is particularly dominant. *See* Michael J. Klarman, *Majoritarian Judicial Review: The Entrenchment Problem*, 85 Geo. L.J. 491, 541 (1997). Competition and the need for the expenditure of large sums of money to retain control of the district are thus greater in such a district.

Our system of campaign finance is public-oriented in another respect. To the degree that donors give in order to receive, they must petition the government for the salutary outcomes they seek. Why is it acceptable for Carl Linder to use his money to encourage favorable treatment of Chiquita bananas, *see* RANDALL ROBINSON, THE DEBT: WHAT AMERICA OWES TO BLACKS 103 (2000) (Arguing that the Clinton administration sought to accommodate Carl Linder, who gave a large amount in campaign contributions, by seeking favorable European treatment of Linder's Chiquita Brands bananas), but constitutionally objectionable for black voters to use their voice to encourage the Georgia legislature to create a majority-black district? The fact that black voters speak through the prism of race can only delegitimize their conduct if the Court limits its view of race to race as biology rather than race as a reality that these voters have been forced to live.

Finally, even if one is inclined to believe that donating or expending money in connection with a campaign is a private act, *Shaw v. Reno* and its progeny reveal that the Court is quite willing to regulate private expression that influences the public sphere. For instance, in *Shaw*, one alleged harm to the white plaintiffs in a newly created majority-minority district was that the creation of such a district "reinforces the perception that members of the same racial group...will prefer the same candidates at the polls." 509 U.S. at 647. If such a preference existed, it would admittedly be private—as private as the act of registering that preference in the voting booth, and moreover, as private as giving a campaign contribution to a candidate for whom one had a racial preference. The Court is undeterred in regulating this private preference because "the Court is rejecting as harmful an official acceptance that racial identity reliably translates into political perspective." Nan D. Hunter, *Expressive Identity: Recuperating Dissent for Equality*, 35 HARV. C.R.-C.L. L. REV. 1, 15 (2000). But if *Buckley* is correct that "[i]n the free society ordained by our Constitution it is...the people—individually as citizens and candidates and collectively as associations and political committees—who must retain control over the quantity and range of debate on public issues in a political campaign," 424 U.S. at 57, then the Court must respect concerted black action to create majority-minority districts and, moreover, must respect the judgment of these voters concerning who should represent their district. Yet *Shaw* illustrates that for all the debate about whether or not campaign finance involves state action sufficient to invoke the Fourteenth Amendment, the Court is quite at ease with regulating private speech and association when it views such regulation as necessary to achieve its vision of the polity.

77. *See* Smith, *A Black Party*, *supra* note 16, at 34–39. *See also* Ricci v. DeStefano, 129 S.Ct. 2658, 2684–85 (2009) (Alito, J., concurring).

(Using the advocacy of black leaders in New Haven to demonstrate that the city's discarding of firefighter test results that had a disproportionately high black applicant failure rate was done to discriminate against white firefighters.)

78. Money's potential for racial distraction is not limited to racial cuing. A highly successful busing program credited with integrating the school system in Wake County, North Carolina, was rolled back when four Republican candidates financially backed by organizations receiving funding from the billionaire Koch brothers and wealthy donor James Pope, secured seats on the local school board. *See* Andy Kroll, *How the Koch Brothers Backed Public-School Segregation*, MOTHER JONES (Aug. 15, 2011, 2:00 AM PDT), http://motherjones .com/mojo/2011/08/koch-brothers-school-segregation-ame ricans-prosperity and Sue Sturgis, *NC Voters Reject Pope-Backed Candidates in Local School Board Battle over Resegregation*, FACING SOUTH (Oct. 12, 2011), http://www.southernstudies.org/2011/10/ nc-voters-reject-pope-backed-candidates-in-local-school-board-battle -over-resegregation.html. Antiaffirmative action champion Ward Connerly's ballot initiatives banning affirmative action and attempting to ban the collection of data regarding race have been heavily funded by white conservatives whose wealth was (ironically) generated from corporations that make significant profits from African American consumers—i.e., Coors Beer. *See* David A. Love, JD, *Color of Law*, BLACK COMMENTATOR, http://www.blackcommentator.com/262/262_color_of_law_ward_connerly.html (last visited Nov. 14, 2011) and Christian Berthelsen, *Sacramento / Prop. 54's Big-Money Backers Revealed / Measure Sought to Prevent Gathering of Racial, Ethnic Data*, SFGATE.COM (May 19, 2005), http://articles .sfgate.com/2005-05-19/bay-area/17374703_1_campaign-finance-initiative-joseph-coors.

79. *See* Smith, *Autonomy versus Equality, supra* note 3, at 270–72.

80. *See* Robert Moore, Ctr. for Pub. Integrity, *Black Candidates See Little of the Millions Their Parties Raise*, iWatch NEWS (Sept. 15, 2000, 7:23 PM), http://www.iwatchnews.org/2000/09/15/3269 /black-candidates-see-little-millions-their-parties-raise.

81. Ibid.

82. Terry Smith, *White Dollars, Black Candidates, Inequality and Agency in Campaign Finance Law*, 57 S.C. L. REV. 735, 737–38 (2006).

83. Ibid. at 738 n.22 (citing PUBLIC CAMPAIGN ET AL., COLOR OF MONEY: THE 2004 PRESIDENTIAL RACE 3 (2004), *available at* http://www .colorofmoney.org/report/2004_cofm_pres_ complete.pdf).

84. Ibid. at 738.

85. INST. FOR POLITICS, DEMOCRACY & THE INTERNET, SMALL DONORS AND ONLINE GIVING 1 (2006), *available at* www.cfinst.org/pdf /federal/president/IPDI_SmallDonors.pdf.

86. Ibid. at 11–16.

87. Ibid. at 15–16. This conclusion is consistent with available data from the 2000 presidential primaries that demonstrated people of color were "grossly underrepresented" in the $100-or-less contribution category. *See* Spencer Overton, *The Donor Class: Campaign Finance, Democracy, and Participation*, 153 U. PA. L. REV. 73, 118 n.162 (2004).

88. Theodore S. Arrington & Gerald L. Ingalls, *Race and Campaign Finance in Charlotte, N.C.*, 37 W. POL. Q. 578, 579–80 (1984).

89. Ibid. at 580.

90. Bradley A. Smith, *Regulation and the Decline of Grassroots Politics*, 50 CATH. U. L. REV. 1, 9 (2000). Smith cites two studies from the 1980s in support of this assertion. *See* ibid. at 9 n.25.

91. 540 U.S. 93, 125, 146–52 (2003), overruled by Citizens United v. Federal Election Com'n, 558 U.S. 310 (U.S. Jan 21, 2010).

92. Ibid.

93. Ibid.

94. Cf. Lani Guinier, *The Triumph of Tokenism: The Voting Rights Act and the Theory of Black Electoral Success*, 89 MICH. L. REV. 1077, 1108–09 (1991). ("Electoral success by culturally and ethnically black candidates in majority-white jurisdictions does not necessarily mean that black concerns will be addressed. For example, where 'authentic blacks' are elected by whites with significant black support, electoral ratification by a majority of those blacks voting may not in fact send a recognizable message regarding substantive policies. Especially in winner-take-all electoral systems, 'the aggregation device of the election garbles these messages, producing winners while obscuring the reasons for their victories.' Thus, even where black support provides a critical margin, successful black candidates in majority-white electorates do not necessarily feel obligated to black voters.") (Quoting Kathryn Abrams, *"Raising Politics Up": Minority Political Participation and Section 2 of the Voting Rights Act*, 63 N.Y.U. L. REV. 449, 487 (1988)).

95. Even election law textbooks purporting to survey the area of campaign finance have in the past accorded little or no treatment of the subject. *See* SAMUEL ISSACHAROFF, PAMELA S. KARLAN & RICHARD H. PILDES, THE LAW OF DEMOCRACY: LEGAL STRUCTURES OF THE POLITICAL PROCESS 450–543 (rev. 2d ed. 2002); DANIEL HAYS LOWENSTEIN & RICHARD L. HASEN, ELECTION LAW: CASES AND MATERIALS 717–1024 (3d ed. 2004).

96. Pub. L. No. 109–8, 119 Stat. 23.

97. Abid Aslam, *New Bankruptcy Law Could Sink Katrina Survivors—Lawmakers, Rights Groups*, ONEWORLD.NET (Sept. 15, 2005), *available at* http://www.commondreams.org/headlines05/0915–02.htm.

98. Ibid.

99. *Black Caucus Conservatives Attempt to Clone Themselves*, BLACK COMMENTATOR (May 12, 2005), http://www.blackcommentator .com/138/138_cover_cbc_clones.html [hereinafter *Black Caucus Conservatives*].

100. Ibid.

101. Ibid.

102. Ctr. for Responsive Politics, *David Scott: Campaign Finance/Money*, OPENSECRETS.ORG, http://www.opensecrets.org/politicians/summary.asp? CID=N00024871&cycle=2006 (last visited Nov. 15, 2011).

103. *See Black Caucus Conservatives, supra* note 99.

104. Ibid.

105. *How to Fix the Fractured Black Caucus*, BLACK COMMENTATOR (Apr. 28, 2005), http://www.blackcommentator.com/136/136_cover_black_caucus.html.

106. *See Black Caucus Conservatives, supra* note 99; Ctr. for Responsive Politics, *Total Raised and Spent, 2006 Race: Georgia District 2: Sanford Bishop*, OPENSECRETS.ORG, http://www.opensecrets.org/races/summary.asp?ID=GA02&Cycle=2006 (last visited Nov. 16, 2011); Ctr. for Responsive Politics, *Total Raised and Spent, 2006 Race: Alabama District 7: Artur Davis*, OPENSECRETS.ORG, http://www.opensecrets.org/races/summary.php?cycle=2006&id=AL07 (last visited Nov. 16, 2011); Ctr. for Responsive Politics, *Total Raised and Spent, 2006 Race: Louisiana District 2: William Jefferson*, OPENSECRETS.ORG, http://www.opensecrets.org/races/summary.php?cycle=2006&id=LA02 (last Nov. 16, 2011); Ctr. for Responsive Politics, *Total Raised and Spent, 2006 Race: Georgia District 13: David Scott*, OPENSECRETS.ORG, http://www.opensecrets.org/races/summary.asp? ID=GA13&Cycle=2006 (last visited Nov. 16, 2011); Ctr. for Responsive Politics, *Total Raised and Spent, 2006 Race: Maryland District 4: Albert Wynn*, OPENSECRETS.ORG, http://www.opensecrets.org/races/summary.php?cycle=2006&id=MD04 (last visited Nov. 16, 2011).

107. *See* McConnell v. FEC, 540 U.S. at 136 (Describing the interests that justify contribution limitations as preventing both "'actual corruption'" and "'the eroding of public confidence in the electoral process through the appearance of corruption'" (Quoting FEC v. Nat'l Right to Work, 459 U.S. 197, 208 (1982))).

108. Ibid.

109. Terry Smith, *White Dollars, Black Candidates, supra* note 82, at 741.

110. Eric Lipton & Eric Lichtblau, *In Black Caucus, a Fund-Raising Powerhouse*, N.Y. TIMES (Feb. 13, 2010), http://www.nytimes.com/2010/02/14/us/politics/14cbc.html?emc=eta1&pagewanted=print.

111. Ibid.

112. Ibid.

113. Ibid.

114. Ibid.

115. *See* Smith, *Autonomy and Equality, supra* note 3, at 276–77 (Noting that in her 2002 primary against Denise Majette, McKinney took

83 percent of the black vote in a district that was 53 percent black, but still lost).

116. Ctr. for Responsive Politics, *Politicians & Elections: Earl F. Hilliard,* OPENSECRETS.ORG, http://www.opensecrets.org/politicians/summary .php?cid=N00003008&cycle=2002 (Nov. 16, 2011).

117. Ctr. for Responsive Politics, *Politicians & Elections: Artur Davis,* OPENSECRETS.ORG, http://www.opensecrets.org/races/summary .php?cycle=2002&id=AL07 (last visited Nov. 16, 2011).

118. Compare Ctr. for Responsive Politics, *Politicians & Elections: Cynthia A. McKinney,* OPENSECRETS.ORG, http://www.opensecrets.org/ politicians/summary.php?cid=N00002511&cycle=2002 (last visited Nov. 16, 2011) and Ctr. for Responsive Politics, *Politicians & Elections: Denise L. Majette,* OPENSECRETS.ORG, http://www.opensecrets.org /races/summary.php?id=GA04&cycle=2002 (last visited Nov. 16, 2011).

119. 42 U.S.C. § 1973(b) (2006).

120. Johnson v. DeGrandy, 512 U.S. 997, 1020 (1994).

3 BLACK TEA: BLACK CONSERVATIVES AND THE RHETORIC OF SOCIAL CONSERVATISM

1. Rashaverak, *Fried Chicken, Potato Salad, and a History Lesson,* DAILY KOS (July 14, 2009, 11:36 AM PDT), http://www.dailykos .com/story/2009/07/14/753389/-Fried-Chicken-Potato-Salad -and-a-History-Lesson.

2. Jennifer Steinhauer, *Black Hopefuls Pick This Year in GOP Races,* N.Y. TIMES, May 4, 2010, at A14.

3. Abdon M. Pallasch, *Steele Urges GOP to Heed the Tea Party; Republican Chief Tells DePaul Students Both Parties Need to Pay Better Attention,* CHI. SUN-TIMES, Apr. 21, 2010, at 8.

4. *See* PAUL FRYMER, UNEASY ALLIANCES: RACE AND PARTY COMPETITION IN AMERICA 7-10 & 87 (1999); Betrall L. Ross II & Terry Smith, *Minimum Responsiveness and the Political Exclusion of the Poor,* 72 LAW & CONTEMP. PROBS. 197, 201 (2009).

5. EARL OFARI HUTCHINSON, THE EMERGING BLACK GOP MAJORITY 13 (Middle Passage Press 2006).

6. *Jesse Helms "Hands" ad,* YOUTUBE (Oct. 16, 2006), http://www .youtube.com/watch?v=KIyewCdXMzk.

7. Holder v. Hall, 512 U.S. 874, 903 (1994).

8. HUTCHINSON, *supra* note 5, at 143.

9. *House Exit Polls,* N.Y. TIMES, http://elections.nytimes.com/2010 /results/house/exit-polls (last visited Jan. 31, 2011).

10. MICHAEL K. FAUNTROY, REPUBLICANS AND THE BLACK VOTE 79–87 (2007).

11. Jonathan Tilove, *Obama Made Inroads with White Voters except in Deep South,* NOLA.COM (Nov. 8, 2008), http://www.nola.com/news /index.ssf/2008/11/obama_made_inroads_with_white.html.

12. Frank Rich, *The Great Tea Party Rip-Off*, N.Y. TIMES (Jan. 16, 2010), http://www.nytimes.com/2010/01/17/opinion/17rich.html.

13. Andrew DeMillo, *Republican Leader Says Party Must Court Blacks*, DIVERSE ISSUES IN HIGHER EDUCATION (Sept. 23, 2009), *available at* http://diverseeducation.com/cache/print.php?articleId=13074.

14. Pallasch, *supra* note 3.

15. Christopher S. Parker, Univ. of Wash. Inst. for the Study of Ethnicity, Race & Sexuality, *Multi-State Survey on Race & Politics*, http://depts.washington.edu/uwiser/racepolitics.html (last visited Jan. 31, 2011).

16. Kate Zernike & Megan Thee-Brenan, *Poll Finds Tea Party Backers Wealthier and More Educated*, N.Y. TIMES, Apr. 14, 2010 at A1; *New York Times/CBS News Poll: National Survey of Tea Party Supporters*, http://documents.nytimes.com/new-york-timescbs-news-poll-national-survey-of-tea-party-supporters?ref=politics (last visited Jan. 31, 2011).

17. *Tea Party Federation Expels Tea Party Express*, MSNBC.COM, http://www.msnbc.msn.com/id/38299783/ns/politics/ (last visited Jan. 31, 2011).

18. Anderson Cooper 360 (CNN television broadcast Jan. 25, 2011).

19. Stephanie McCrummen, *At Rick Perry's Texas Hunting Spot, Camp's Old Racially Charged Name Lingered*, WASH. POST (Oct. 1, 2011), http://www.washingtonpost.com/national/rick-perry-familys-hunting-camp-still-known-to-many-by-old-racially-charged-name/2011/10/01/gIQAOhY5DL_story.html. White conservatives accused of racial insensitivity or racism often defend the charge by highlighting the number of blacks they have appointed to various positions. Governor Perry's proponents did the same. *See* Amy Gardner, *Perry Built Complicated Record on Matters of Race*, WASH. POST (Oct. 3, 2011), http://www.washingtonpost.com/politics/perry-built-complicated-record-on-matters-of-race/2011/10/02/gIQAaJ5DJL_story.html?wpisrc=emailtoafriend. Inasmuch as these black appointees are typically unrepresentative of the views of most African Americans, counting black faces is a quota defense by opponents of affirmative action. Notwithstanding such appointments, the median viewpoint of blacks—that is, the substance of blackness—is rejected, while the far less important aesthetic of race is used to distract from the myriad ways in which conservatism marginalizes blacks as group.

20. *Glenn Beck: Obama Is a Racist*, CBS NEWS (July 29, 2009, 12:07 PM), http://www.cbsnews.com/stories/2009/07/29/politics/main5195604.shtml.

21. Burgess Everett, *Williams: "My Analogy Was Extreme,"* POLITICO.COM (OCT. 4, 2011, 1:25 PM), http://www.politico.com/blogs/onmedia/1011/Williams_My_analogy_was_extreme.html.

22. Huma Khan, *NAACP vs. Tea Party: Racism Debate Heats Up as Sarah Palin Joins the Fray*, ABC NEWS (July 13, 2010), http://abcnews

.go.com/Politics/naacp-tea-party-race-debate-heats-sarah-palin /story?id=11153935. The organization's president, Ben Jealous, decried the racialism of the Tea Party in graphic terms:

> For more than a year we've watched as Tea Party members have called congressmen the N-word, have called congressmen the F-word. We see them carry racist signs and whenever it happens, the membership tries to shirk responsibility.

23. News Release, Pew Res. Center, Trends in Political Values and Core Attitudes: 1987–2009 (May 21, 2009), *available at* http://people -press.org/reports/pdf/517.pdf.

24. *Race and Ethnicity*, http://www.pollingreport.com/race.htm (last visited Jan. 31, 2011).

25. KEVIN PHILLIPS, AMERICAN THEOCRACY: THE PERIL AND POLITICS OF RADICAL RELIGION, OIL, AND BORROWED MONEY IN THE 21st CENTURY 180 (2006).

26. Edward G. Carmines & Robert Huckfeldt, *Party Politics in the Wake of the Voting Rights Act, in* CONTROVERSIES IN MINORITY VOTING: THE VOTING RIGHTS ACT IN PERSPECTIVE 117, 130 (Bernard Grofman & Chandler Davidson eds., 1992). ("What are the political consequences of the Democratic party's reliance on black voters? White voters are frequently unwilling to support a party that depends heavily upon black support, and the decline in white support for Democratic presidential candidates has been most pronounced among working-class whites.")

27. STEVEN F. HAYWARD, THE AGE OF REAGAN: THE FALL OF THE OLD LIBERAL ORDER: 1964–1980, at 58 (2009).

28. JACOB S. HACKER & PAUL PIERSON, WINNER-TAKE-ALL POLITICS: HOW WASHINGTON MADE THE RICH RICHER—AND TURNED ITS BACK ON THE MIDDLE CLASS 97 (2010).

29. Ibid.

30. Mark Knoller, *Bush Administration Adds $4 Trillion to National Debt*, CBS NEWS (Sept. 29, 2008, 12:20 PM), http://www.cbsnews .com/8301-500803_162-4486228-500803.html.

31. Interview with Representative Frederica Wilson, in Wash., D.C. (Sept. 15, 2011).

32. TAYLOR BRANCH, AT CANAAN'S EDGE: AMERICA IN THE KING YEARS, 1965–68, at 400 (Simon & Schuster 2006).

33. Eric Zorn, *Why Stop Short? The Clintons Are Lying about Obama's Remarks on Reagan*, CHI. TRIB. (Jan. 22, 2008), http://blogs .chicagotribune.com/news_columnists_ezorn/2008/01/obamarea-gan.html.

34. Terry Smith, *Speaking against Norms: Public Discourse and the Economy of Racialization in the Workplace*, 57 AM. U. L. REV. 523, 543 (2008).

35. HUTCHINSON, *supra* note 5, at 104–05.

36. *Concede Nothing to Bush: Black Consensus Remains Intact*, BLACK COMMENTATOR, http://www.blackcommentator.com/112/112 _cover_election.html (last visited Jan. 31, 2011).

37. BRIAN MORIN, A MATTER OF FAITH 226–27 (Aardvark Press 2005).

38. Angela Onwuachi-Willig, *Just Another Brother on the SCT?: What Justice Clarence Thomas Teaches Us About the Influence of Racial Identity*, 90 IOWA L. REV. 931 (2005). For a comprehensive history of black conservatism in the U.S., *see* CHRISTOPHER A. BRACEY, SAVIORS OR SELLOUTS: THE PROMISE AND PERIL OF BLACK CONSERVATISM, FROM BOOKER T. WASHINGTON TO CONDOLEEZA RICE (2008). Neither nonvictimology nor self-reliance are the exclusive domains of black conservatism. Rather, these values, like religiosity, remain conservative remnants within black liberalism, the dominant philosophy among blacks. *See* ROBERT C. SMITH, CONSERVATISM AND RACISM, AND WHY IN AMERICA THEY ARE THE SAME 73 (2010). Importantly, modern black conservatives cite traditional precepts like self-reliance to justify denigration of government programs that benefit blacks. But traditions often require translation to a modern context in order to make sense. *See* Lawrence Lessig, *Fidelity in Translation*, 71 TEXAS L. REV. 1165, 1263 (1993). As argued in chapter 2, rich Americans and corporations contribute to political campaigns and expend billions each year lobbying the government in order to extract benefits from the government—benefits that often undermine the interests of African Americans. The idea that African Americans should not seek a return on the taxes they pay to local, state, and federal government makes no sense given the modern centrality of government to both the rich and the poor as well as to the public sphere and the free market.

39. Donald H. Smith, *Coretta Scott King Goes Home*, BLACK COMMENTATOR, http://www.blackcommentator.com/171/171_guest _smith_coretta.html?sms_ss=email (last visited Oct. 11, 2011).

40. BRANCH, *supra* note 32, at 168–81.

41. Rod McCullom, *Black Connecticut Church Focus of Gay Teen "Exorcism" Video*, DAILY VOICE (June 25, 2009, 2:26 PM), http:// thedailyvoice.com/voice/2009/06/black-connecticut-church-focus -002039.php.

42. Bill Berkowitz, *Black Conservatives in the Age of Obama*, ALTERNET (Aug. 21, 2009), http://www.alternet.org/news/141966/Black _conservatives_in_the_age_of_obama/.

43. Interview with Charles Butler, Host of "The Other Side," in Chicago, Ill. (Mar. 10, 2010).

44. *Steele: Gay Marriage Costs Small Business*, WASH. TIMES (May 17, 2009), http://www.washingtontimes.com/news/2009/may/17/gay -marriage-called-burden-on-business/.

45. THOMAS FRANK, WHAT'S THE MATTER WITH KANSAS: HOW CONSERVATIVES WON THE HEART OF America (2004).

46. Telephone Interview with Reverend C. T. Vivian (Apr. 15, 2009).

47. Interview with David J. Malebranche, Emory University School of Medicine, in Atlanta, Ga. (July 2009). Summarizing some of this research, Malebranche's specific observation was: "This whole sexuality conversation and comfort with it is couched in a foundation of racism and racial oppression. So if you feel at the beginning of the day that white men have the privilege in the society, and if you already see that, if that's your personal experience, many of the guys told us, like, well, I don't feel comfortable because I already have a disadvantage against me. So why am I going to scream at the top of my lungs that I'm homosexual and subject myself to other forms of discrimination if I'm already getting this? White guys can do it because they don't have to worry about that part of it, and it's a valid point to consider when you talk about all of this." Ibid.

48. Lani Guinier, *No Two Seats: The Elusive Quest for Political Equality*, 77 VA. L. REV. 1413, 1503 (1991).

49. *Public Backs Affirmative Action, But Not Minority Preferences*, PEW RES. CENTER (June 2, 2009), http://pewresearch.org/pubs/1240 /sotomayor-supreme-court-affirmative-action-minority-preferences.

50. *U.S. Voters Disagree 3–1 with Sotomayor on Key Case, Quinnipiac University National Poll Finds; Most Say Abolish Affirmative Action*, QUINNIPIAC UNIV., http://www.quinnipiac.edu/x1295.xml?Release ID=1307 (last visited Jan. 31, 2011).

51. *See The O'Reilly Factor: Are African-Americans Unhappy with Obama?* (Fox News television broadcast Aug. 17, 2011), *available at* http://nation.foxnews.com/allen-west/2011/08/18/rep-allen-west -im-modern-day-harriet-tubman-freeing-voters-democratic-partys -plantation [hereinafter *O'Reilly Factor*].

52. Juana Summers, *Jesse Jackson: "Plantation" Comments Insult Black Voters*, POLITICO.COM (Sept. 30, 2011, 4:20 PM EDT), http://www. politico.com/news/stories/0911/64841.html.

53. SMITH, CONSERVATISM AND RACISM, *supra* note 38, at 104. ("[T]here is nothing intellectually new or interesting about black neo-conservative thought....Rather, it is simply traditional conservative or neoconservative ideas applied to the problem of race in America.")

54. Clarence Thomas, *The Loneliness of the Black Conservative, in* BLACK AND RIGHT: THE BOLD NEW VOICE OF BLACK CONSERVATIVES IN AMERICA 6 (Stan Faryna, Brad Stetson & Joseph G. Conti eds., 1997).

55. Ibid.

56. *See* Hi-Voltage Wire Works, Inc. v. City of San Jose, 24 Cal. 4th 537 (2000).

57. Maura Dolan, *Bar Faults High Court Nominee in Key Areas*, L.A. TIMES (Apr. 26, 1996), http://articles.latimes.com/1996–04–26 /news/mn-63076_1_high-court.

58. Ibid.

59. Suzanne Espinosa Solis, *Affirmative Action Critic Used His Minority Status / UC Regent Got No-Bid State Contracts*, S.F. CHRONICLE (May 8, 1995), http://articles.sfgate.com/1995–05–08/news/17804951_1_affirmative-action-race-based-program-connerly-associates.

60. Charlie Savage, *Affirmative-Action Foe Is Facing Allegations of Financial Misdeeds*, N.Y. Times (Jan. 17, 2012), http://www.nytimes.com/2012/01/18/us/ward-connerly-faces-allegations-of-fiscal-misdoing.html?_r=3&hp.

61. Solis, *supra* note 59.

62. *See* Savage, *supra* note 60. ("One reason Mr. Connerly has been a particularly effective advocate is that he is black.")

63. Deborah Solomon, *Life of the Party: Florida's Freshman Congressman on the Changing Face of Republican Politics*, N.Y. TIMES MAG., Jan. 2, 2011, at 11.

64. *Herman Cain: "Racism in This Country Today" Doesn't Hold "Anybody Back in a Big Way,"* HUFFINGTONPOST.COM (Oct. 9, 2011, 6:30 PM ET), http://www.huffingtonpost.com/2011/10/09/herman-cain-racism_n_1002375.html. Cain has willingly offered himself up as a human shield to thwart charges of racism against the Tea Party movement and Republican Party. *See* Edward-Isaac Dovere, *GOP Dilemma: How to Handle Herman Cain*, POLITICO.COM (Oct. 19, 2011 5:26 PM EDT), http://www.politico.com/news/stories/1011/66411.html. ("Cain himself has talked often about how his candidacy rebuts charges of racism among Republicans and in the tea party base, and few in the party are eager to prove him wrong.")

65. Frank Rich, *Fourth of July 1776, 1964, 2010*, N.Y. TIMES (July 3, 2010), http://www.nytimes.com/2010/07/04/opinion/04rich.html (Citing two minority Republicans elected in South Carolina as examples). Although Republicans like Allen West are philosophically estranged from the Black political mainstream, this does not stop them from trading on their racial background to make political points on behalf of the Republican Party. After the Congressional Black Caucus embarked on a national jobs-fair tour to underscore the urgency of the unemployment rate among blacks and President Obama's neglect of the issue, West likened black Democrats to plantation overseers and himself to Harriet Tubman:

> So you have this 21st century plantation that has been out there where the Democratic party has forever taken the black vote for granted and you have established certain black leaders who are nothing more than the overseers of that plantation and now the people on that plantation are upset because they've been disregarded, disrespected and their concerns are not cared about. So I'm here as the modern day Harriet Tubman to kind of lead people on the underground railroad away from that plantation and to a sense of sensibility.

See O'Reilly Factor, supra note 51.

Left unstated by Representative West is the fact that he had advised his own unemployed brother to attend the CBC job fair, which his brother did. *See* icebergslim, *Rep. Alan West (R-FL) Told Unemployed Brother to Go to Rep. Maxine Waters (D-CA) for a JOB*, DAILY KOS (Aug. 18, 2011, 1:45 PM PDT), http://www.dailykos.com /story/2011/08/18/1008352/-Rep-Alan-West-% 28R-FL%29-told -unemployed-brother-to-go-to-Rep-Maxine-Waters-%28D-CA%29 -for-a-JOB?via=siderecent.

This was not the first time West had deployed his race even though he is unrepresentative of the politics of his race. West responded indignantly and unprofessionally in an email to floor remarks by Congresswoman Debbie Wasserman-Schultz, a fellow Floridian who like West represents numerous senior citizens. Wasserman-Schultz had criticized West for supporting cuts in Medicare. West later invoked racial symbolism to explain Wasserman-Schultz's criticism of him:

> I grew up in the inner city, strong values, came from a strong military family and background.... What we do is we totally invalidate the liberal social welfare policies and programs. And you know, I'm the threat because I'm the guy that got off their 21st-century plantation, and they cannot afford to have a strong voice such as mine out there, reverberating and resonating across this country.

See Adam Serwer, *Allen West and the "Plantation" Card*, WASH. POST (July 21, 2011, 11:08 AM ET), http://www.washington-post.com/blogs/plum-line/post/allen-west-and-the-plantation-card/2011/03/04/gIQAYajqRI_blog.html.

66. Ibid.
67. Terry Smith, A Black Party: Timmons, *Black Backlash and the Endangered Two-Party Paradigm*, 48 DUKE L.J. 1, 40–41 n.180 (1998). ("Even scholars who contend that race in its explicit form has disappeared as a partisan issue concede that it continues to be intertwined with a more general ideological divide between Republicans and Democrats and that the voting patterns created by explicitly racial issues beginning in 1964 have not disappeared.")
68. *News: Obama Fights Back against Black Critics*, BLACKNEWS2 (Dec. 22, 2009), http://Blacknews2.wordpress.com/2009/12/22/obama-fights-back-against-Black-critics/ (last visited Jan. 31, 2011).
69. HUTCHINSON, *supra* note 5, at 143.

4   CONTRADICTIONS IN A LATINO MOMENT:
LATINOS AS LESS BLACK?

1. Sumi Cho, *Post-Racialism*, 94 IOWA L. REV. 1589, 1593, n.7 (2009).
2. *Blacks Upbeat about Black Progress, Prospects a Year after Obama's Election*, PEW RES. CENTER (Jan. 12, 2010), http://pewresearch .org/pubs/1459/year-after-obama-election-black-public-opinion.

3. Rich Morin, *Black-White Conflict Isn't Society's Largest*, PEW RES. CENTER (Sept. 24, 2009), http://pewsocialtrends.org/2009/09/24 /black-white-conflict-isnt-societys-largest/.

4. Frank Newport, *Republicans Remain Disproportionately White and Religious*, GALLUP (Sept. 1, 2010), http://www.gallup.com/poll /142826/republicans-remain-disproportionately-white-religious .aspx.

5. Devon W. Carbado, *Race to the Bottom*, 49 UCLA L. REV. 1283, 1305 (2002).

6. *CNN Inside Politics: Lott on Defensive after Comments on Thurmond's 1948 Presidential Bid; Is Landrieu's Victory a Roadmap for Democratic Success?* (CNN television broadcast Dec. 10, 2002), *available at* http://transcripts.cnn.com/TRANSCRIPTS/0212/10/ip.00.html.

7. *See* John B. Judis, *You've Got Them All Wrong, Mr. President: Obama's Misguided View of the Independent Voter*, NEW REPUBLIC (Nov. 18, 2010, 12:00 AM), http://www.tnr.com/article/politics/79246 /independent-voters-barack-obama-midterms. (Citing a Pew Research Center survey of independents that distinguished four groups of Republican and Democratic leaners: "Shadow Republicans," "Disaffected Republicans," "Doubting Democrats," and "Shadow Democrats")

8. Sylvia R. Lazos Vargas, *The Latina/O And Apia Vote Post-2000: What Does It Mean to Move Beyond "Black And White" Politics?*, 81 OR. L. REV. 783, 788 (2002).

9. Ibid. at 806.

10. Ibid. at 802–03.

11. Ibid. at 807.

12. Ibid. at 806.

13. White v. Regester, 412 U.S. 755, 768 (1973).

14. Ibid. at 767.

15. Hernandez v. N.Y., 500 U.S. 352 (1991).

16. Bush v. Vera, 517 U.S. 952 (1996).

17. Terry Smith, *Autonomy versus Equality: Voting Rights Rediscovered*, 57 Ala. L. REV. 261, 287 (2005).

18. Darren Lenard Hutchinson, *"Unexplainable on Grounds Other Than Race": The Inversion of Privilege and Subordination in Equal Protection Jurisprudence*, 2003 U. Ill. L. REV. 615 (2003).

19. Smith, *Autonomy versus Equality, supra* note 17, at 288 n.205.

20. Juan F. Perea, *An Essay on the Iconic Status of the Civil Rights Movement and Its Unintended Consequences*, 18 VA. J. SOC. POL'Y & L. 44, 51–52 (2010).

21. Roy L. Brooks & Kirsten Widner, *In Defense of the Black/White Binary: Reclaiming a Tradition of Civil Rights Scholarship*, 12 Berkeley J. Afr.-Am. L. & Pol'y 107, 117–18 (2010).

22. Ibid. at 141.

23. Ibid. at 128.

24. Ibid. at 125 (internal quotations omitted).

25. Eduardo Bonilla-Silva, Racism without Racists: Color-Blind Racism and the Persistence of Racial Inequality in the United States 179 (3d ed. 2010).

26. Cristina Beltrán, The Trouble with Unity: Latino Politics and the Creation of Identity 101 (2010).

27. Ibid. at 103.

28. Ibid. at 116.

29. Ibid.

30. Ibid. at 124.

31. Ibid. at 125.

32. Philip D. Dalton, Swing Voting: Understanding Late-Deciders in Late-Modernity 9 (2006).

33. William G. Mayer, *What Exactly Is a Swing Voter? Definition and Measurement, in* The Swing Voter in American Politics, at 27 (William G. Mayer, ed., 2008).

34. Ibid.

35. Dalton, *supra* note 32, at 13. ("Targeting communication efforts at this key group has the potential to pay dividends, whereas advertising to voters faithful to the opponent's party would waste valuable campaign resources….")

36. Paul Frymer, Uneasy Alliances: Race and Party Competition in America 8–10 (1999).

37. Terry Smith, *Race and Money in Politics*, 79 N.C. L. Rev. 1469, 1517 (2001).

38. Dalton, *supra* note 32, at 25 & 139 (Noting that media stories often portray swing voters as consisting of women, Latinos, and suburbanites).

39. Mayer, *supra* note 33, at 8–12; Dalton, *supra* note 32, at 12.

40. Mayer, *supra* note 33, at 9 (Noting that several political dictionaries define swing voters as political independents).

41. *See* Frymer, *supra* note 36, at 185 (Discussing Mexican-Americans specifically).

42. Ibid. at 185.

43. Smith, *Race and Money in Politics, supra* note 37, at 1516 n.230.

44. Lazos Vargas, *supra* note 8, at 802.

45. Tanya Katerí Hernández, *Latino Inter-Ethnic Employment Discrimination and the 'Diversity' Defense*, 42 Harv. C.R.-C.L. L. Rev. 259, 271 (2007).

46. Ibid. at 272–74.

47. Jennifer Gordon & R.A. Lenhardt, *Rethinking Work and Citizenship*, 55 UCLA L. Rev. 1161, 1179–82 (2008).

48. Katherine Tate, Black Faces in the Mirror: African Americans and their Representatives in the U.S. Congress 90 (Discussing H.R. 2002, which would have barred the children of illegal immigrants from the public school system).

49. Raphael J. Sonenshein & Susan H. Pinkus, *Latino Incorporation Reaches the Urban Summit: How Antonio Villaraigosa Won the 2005 Los Angeles Mayoral Race*, 38 POL. SCIENCE & POL., 713, 718 tbl.4 (2005).

50. In the Democratic mayoral primary, Fernando Ferrer collected 52 percent of the black vote, while Mark Green collected only 34 percent. In the run-off, Ferrer secured 71 percent of the black vote, while Green secured just 29 percent. *See* Report of Allan J. Lichtman, The Voting Rights Implications of Nonpartisan Citywide, Borough President, and City Council Elections and Nonpartisan Succession Elections for Mayor in the City of New York (Aug. 2003), app. at 25, tbl.2, *available at* www.nyc.gov/html/charter/downloads/ . . . /report_affnychart2003.pdf. *See also* Adam Nagourney, *Squirming in Sharpton's Embrace; Fidgeting Without It*, N.Y. TIMES (Oct. 5, 2001), http://www.nytimes.com/2001/10/05/nyregion/squirming -in-sharpton-s-embrace-fidgeting-without-it.html.

51. Mirta Ojito, *The 2001 Elections: The Voters; City's Hispanics Shift, Moving toward G.O.P.*, N.Y. TIMES (Nov. 8, 2001), http://www .nytimes.com/2001/11/08/nyregion/the-2001-elections-the -voters-city-s-hispanics-shift-moving-toward-gop.html.

52. SAMUEL KIMBALL GOVE & JAMES DUNLAP NOWLAN, ILLINOIS POLITICS & GOVERNMENT: THE EXPANDING METROPOLITAN FRONTIER 32 (1996).

53. I do not mean to paint too sanguine a picture. In THE PRESUMED ALLIANCE: THE UNSPOKEN CONFLICT BETWEEN LATINOS AND BLACKS (2004), Nicolas C. Vaca examines a number of conflicts, such as the overrepresentation of blacks in the Los Angeles County government and the corresponding underrepresentation of Latinos. *See* ibid. at 52–56. But Vaca's arguments become strained and somewhat insupportable when he concludes that, "[I]n case after case it was clear that African Americans, in pursuing their own goals, are more likely to form coalitions, alliances, and support groups with whites than they are with Latinos." Ibid. at 188. On the contrary, African Americans have not wasted time flirting with the racially monochromatic Republican Party, as Latinos have done only to be betrayed time and again. And if, as Vaca appears to posit, black self-interest trumps their coalitional sensibilities, these practical concerns are no more causative of the black-Latino conflict than is Latinos' identification with whiteness and its tendencies to marginalize blacks, including black-skinned Latinos.

54. Randal C. Archibold, *Arizona Enacts Stringent Law on Immigration*, N.Y. TIMES (Apr. 23, 2010), http://www.nytimes.com/2010 /04/24/us/politics/24immig.html; Louis Provenzano, *Arizona's Immigration Law: Racial Profiling at Its Worst as 10 States Explore Copycat Legislation*, HUFFINGTONPOST.COM (May 7, 2010, 10:01 AM), http://www.huffingtonpost.com/louis-provenzano/arizonas -immigration-law_b_567590.html.

55. B. Drummond Ayres, Jr., *The 1994 Campaign: California; California Governor Suggests Requiring Citizenship Cards*, N.Y. TIMES, Oct. 27, 1994, at A1.

56. Julia Preston, *State Lawmakers Outline Plans to End Birthright Citizenship, Drawing Outcry*, N.Y. TIMES (Jan. 5, 2011), http://www.nytimes.com/2011/01/06/us/06immig.html.

57. David Jackson, *Obama Rejects Congressional Black Caucus Criticism*, USA TODAY (Dec. 3, 2009), http://content.usatoday.com/communities/theoval/post/2009/12/obama-rejects-congressional-black-caucus-criticism-/1.

58. The purpose of The Lilly Ledbetter Fair Pay Act is "to reverse the Supreme Court's ruling in Ledbetter v. Goodyear." H. REP. NO. 110–237, at 3 (2007). The act amends Title VII of the Civil Rights Act of 1964 and the Age Discrimination in Employment Act of 1967, and modifies the Americans with Disabilities Act of 1990 and the Rehabilitation Act of 1973 in terms of discriminatory compensation. Lilly Ledbetter Fair Pay Act of 2009, Pub. L. No. 111–2, 123 Stat. 5 (2009).

59. *Civil Rights*, WHITEHOUSE.GOV, http://www.whitehouse.gov/issues/civil-rights (last visited Oct. 7, 2011).

60. Martha A. Fineman, *The Vulnerable Subject: Anchoring Equality in the Human Condition*, 20 YALE J.L. & FEMINISM 1, 10 (2008).

61. A. Leon Higginbotham, Jr., *An Open Letter to Justice Clarence Thomas from a Federal Judicial Colleague*, 140 U. PA. L. REV. 1005 (1991). Higginbotham, a renowned federal judge, wrote in a public letter to Thomas, "I have read almost every article you have published, every speech you have given, and virtually every public comment you have made during the past decade. Until your confirmation hearing I could not find one shred of evidence suggesting an insightful understanding on your part on how the evolutionary movement of the Constitution and the work of civil rights organizations have benefitted you." Ibid. at 1011.

62. Russell Berman & Bob Cusack, *Dem to Obama: Push Immigration or Lose Latino Voters at Polls*, HILL (Apr. 20, 2010), http://thehill.com/homenews/house/93183-dem-to-obama-push-immigration-or-ill-tell-latino-voters-to-stay-home.

63. Ibid. Indeed, Obama has arguably been more aggressive on the question of immigration rights than he has been on the question of black voting rights. For instance, South Carolina's population is 28 percent black, and rough proportionality would presume that two of that state's seven congressional districts should be majority-black. Yet the Obama Justice Department did not object to a state redistricting plan that contained only one black district. *See* WACH Fox News Center, *SC's Congressional Map Approved, Lawsuit Expected*, MIDLANDSCONNECT.COM (Oct. 31, 2011, 2:20 PM), http://www.midlandsconnect.com/news/story.aspx?id=680838. In contrast,

when South Carolina passed Arizona-style immigration legislation empowering local police with unprecedented enforcement authority over immigration matters, the Obama administration quickly filed suit against the state. *See* Josh Gerstein, *South Carolina Immigration Law Sparks Suit from Justice Department*, POLITICO.COM (Oct. 31, 2011), http://www.politico.com/news/stories/1011/67274.html.

Obama's discriminating public solicitude can be observed with other "minority" groups. When a gay U.S. solder was booed by the audience at a Republican presidential debate for asking a question about "don't ask, don't tell," Obama lacerated the Republican candidates for not condemning the audience's behavior: "You want to be commander in chief? You can start by standing up for the men and women who wear the uniform of the United States, even when it's not politically convenient. We believe in a big America—a tolerant America, a just America, an equal America—that values the service of every patriot." *See* Amanda Terkel, *Obama HRC Speech 2011: President Talks Gay Rights at Human Rights Campaign Dinner*, HUFFINGTONPOST.COM (Oct. 1, 2011), http://www.huffingtonpost.com/2011/10/01/obama-hrc-speech-gay-rights_n_990574.html. Yet one is hard-pressed to think of an occasion on which Obama has so openly and strongly rebuked the Republicans for their racial politics, a corrosive politics often aimed at Obama himself.

64. Joseph Williams, *Barack Obama Speech Reopens Rift with Black Critics*, POLITICO.COM (Sept. 29, 2011, 5:03 AM EDT), http://www.politico.com/news/stories/0911/64680.html. ("In January 2008, speaking from the pulpit where King had family ties at Ebenezer Baptist Church in Atlanta, Obama told a large congregation that King's vision of a colorblind America is unrealized. But he raised some eyebrows when he said blacks bear some responsibility; clashes with Jews, suspicion of immigrants, and widespread homophobia in the African American community, he said, show 'none of our hands are entirely clean.'")

65. John C. Duncan, Jr., *Two "Wrongs" Do/Can Make a Right: Remembering Mathematics, Physics, & Various Legal Analogies (Two Negatives Make a Positive; Are Remedies Wrong?) the Law Has Made Him Equal, But Man Has Not*, 43 BRANDEIS L.J. 511, 517 n.18 (2005). ("There was never a true immigration by the Black Slaves, they were forcibly brought to the Americas. The very notion of immigration implies that it is a migration of one's own choosing.")

66. Jeff Diamond, *African-American Attitudes towards United States Immigration Policy*, 32 INT'L MIGRATION REV. 451, 451 (1998).

67. Ibid.

68. Ibid. at 451–52.

69. Ibid. at 452–53.

70. Ibid. at 454.

71. Ibid.

72. Ibid.

73. Ibid. at 457.

74. *See* Gordon & Lenhardt, *supra* note 47, at 1179–81.

75. Carol M. Swain, *The Congressional Black Caucus and the Impact of Immigration on African American Unemployment, in* DEBATING IMMIGRATION 182 (Carol M. Swain ed., 2007).

76. Ibid. at 181–82.

77. *See* Gordon & Lenhardt, *supra* note 47, at 1179–81.

78. Barack Obama and Hillary Rodham Clinton Hollywood Debate at Kodak Theater (Jan. 31, 2008), *available at* http://blogs.sun-times.com/sweet/2008/02/sweet_clinton_obama_hollywood.html [hereinafter Clinton, Obama Hollywood Debate].

79. SUSAN MINUSKIN AND MARK HUGO LOPEZ, THE HISPANIC VOTE IN THE 2008 DEMOCRATIC PRESIDENTIAL PRIMARIES, at 2 (Pew Hispanic Center, June 2008), *available at* http://pewhispanic.org /files/reports/86.pdf.

80. Clinton, Obama Hollywood Debate, *supra* note 78.

81. In the construction industry, even during the housing market slump, Latinos landed two out of every three new construction jobs in 2006. *See Construction Jobs Expand for Latinos Despite Slump in Housing Market,* PEW HISPANIC CENTER (Mar. 7, 2007), http:// pewhispanic.org/factsheets/factsheet.php?FactsheetID=28. Indeed, employers' current hiring practices may be having a deterrent effect on potential black applicants. Political commentator Earl Ofari Hutchinson observes, "[W]hen employers give the quick brush-off to young blacks and other young American workers who are willing to take lower-end jobs, they send the not-so-subtle message that they are not wanted or welcome. This is a powerful disincentive for them to pursue work in these areas of the job market. The end result is that an entire category of jobs on the ground rung of American industry is clearly marked as 'Latino only.'" *See* EARL OFARI HUTCHINSON, THE LATINO CHALLENGE TO BLACK AMERICA: TOWARDS A CONVERSATION BETWEEN AFRICAN AMERICANS AND HISPANICS 124 (2007).

82. Mackenzie Weinger, *President Obama to Halt Some Deportations,* POLITICO.COM (Aug. 18, 2011), http://www.politico.com/news /stories/0811/61655.html. Tellingly, in response to Latino protests that the record number of deportations was a breach of Obama's campaign promises, his administration announced a change of policy to focus primarily on illegal immigrants with criminal records or those with security risks. Ibid. Again, Latinos are permitted to voice clearly ethnic concerns in transparently ethnic terms. Only blacks are required to be opaque.

5   TRIANGULATION 101: THE OLD CONCEIVES THE NEW

1. John F. Harris & Ben Smith, *The Dirtiest Word in Politics: Has Barack Obama Been Caught Triangulating?*, POLITICO.COM (Dec. 10, 2010, 4:39 AM), http://www.politico.com/news/stories/1210/46218.html.

2. DICK MORRIS, BEHIND THE OVAL OFFICE: GETTING REELECTED AGAINST ALL ODDS (1999).

3. DICK MORRIS, BEHIND THE OVAL OFFICE: WINNING THE PRESIDENCY IN THE NINETIES 118 (1997).

4. Ibid. at 339.

5. David A. Super, *The New Moralizers: Transforming the Conservative Legal Agenda*, 104 COLUM. L. REV. 2032, 2095 n. 179 (2004).

6. Dan Froomkin, *Welfare's Changing Face*, WASH. POST (July 23, 1998), http://www.washingtonpost.com/wp-srv/politics/special/welfare/welfare.htm#pol.

7. CHRISTOPHER HITCHENS, NO ONE LEFT TO LIE TO: THE TRIANGULATIONS OF WILLIAM JEFFERSON CLINTON 80 (1999).

8. Harris & Smith, *supra* note 1 (Quoting White House Communications Director Dan Pfeiffer).

9. BARACK OBAMA, THE AUDACITY OF HOPE: THOUGHTS ON RECLAIMING THE AMERICAN DREAM 34 (2006).

10. Ibid. at 247.

11. Josh Gerstein, *New Obama Aide Crafted "Race-Neutral" Opportunity Agenda*, POLITICO.COM (Jan. 17, 2011), http://www.politico.com/blogs/joshgerstein/0111/New_ObamaBiden_aide_crafted_raceneutral_opportunity_agenda.html.

12. Ibid.

13. Memorandum from Bruce Reed and Elena Kagan to President Clinton (Nov. 11, 1997), *available at* http://www.clintonlibrary.gov/Documents/Kagan%20-%20Bruce%20Reed/Kagan%20-%20Bruce%20Reed%20%20Subject%20File%20Series/Box%20124%20Race%20Initiative%20Doc%209.pdf.

14. OBAMA, *supra* note 9, at 244.

15. Ibid. at 245. Obama would take this approach once in office. Responding to a question at a press conference from a Black Entertainment Network reporter, President Obama stated:

> So my general approach is that if the economy is strong, that will lift all boats as long as it is also supported by, for example, strategies around college affordability and job training, tax cuts for working families as opposed to the wealthiest that level the playing field and ensure bottom-up economic growth.
>
> And I'm confident that that will help the African-American community live out the American dream at the same time that it's helping communities all across the country.

See The President's News Conference, 1 PUB. PAPERS 584, 593 (Apr. 29, 2009), *available at* http://www.gpo.gov/fdsys/pkg/PPP-2009 -book1/xml/PPP-2009-book1-Doc-pg584.xml.

16. CHRISTOPHER EDLEY, JR., NOT ALL BLACK AND WHITE: AFFIRMATIVE ACTION AND AMERICAN VALUES 155 (1998).

17. The Patient Protection and Affordable Care Act contains a mandate requiring individuals not covered by a government health plan to acquire health insurance in the private market. The federal government will provide an income-based subsidy to those unable to afford insurance on their own. Progressives believe the act is flawed for its failure to include a public option that would have competed against private insurers and, in the view of many, helped to improve the delivery of health care and lower costs. *See* Helen A. Halpin & Peter Harbage, *The Origins and Demise of the Public Option*, HEALTH AFFAIRS, June 2010, at 1117, 1119. The impact of the new legislation on the health care of African Americans remains in question. Regardless of whether they have health insurance, African Americans receive inferior quality care and experience worse health outcomes. *See* Wilhelmina A. Leigh & Anna L. Wheatley, *U.S. Healthcare Reform, 2009–2010: Implications for African Americans*, 37 REV. BLACK POLIT. ECON., 191, 193 (2010). While coverage will be increased, cost-containment provisions for Medicare and Medicaid may have a disproportionate impact on African American recipients. Ibid. at 198–99.

18. Michael Gerson, *A Stalled Economy and A Presidency Adrift*, WASH. POST (June 27, 2011), http://www.washingtonpost.com/opinions /a-stalled-economy-and-a-presidency-adrift/2011/06/27 /AG52GDoH_story.html?wpisrc=emailtoafriend.

19. PAUL PIERSON & JACOB S. HATCHER, WINNER-TAKE-ALL POLITICS: HOW WASHINGTON MADE THE RICH RICHER AND TURNED ITS BACK ON THE MIDDLE CLASS 212 (2010).

20. Ibid. at 232.

21. Ibid. at 233.

22. Sheila C. Bair, *Short-Termism and the Risk of Another Financial Crisis*, WASH. POST (July 8, 2011), http://www.washingtonpost .com/opinions/our-focus-on-the-short-term-is-holding -the-economy-back/2011/07/06/gIQAw3cI4H_story.html ?wpisrc=emailtoafriend.

23. *See* Shan Carter & Amanda Cox, *Obama's 2012 Budget Proposal: How $3.7 Trillion Is Spent*, N.Y. TIMES (Feb. 14, 2011), http://www .nytimes.com/packages/html/newsgraphics/2011/0119-budget /index.html; Lori Montgomery, *Obama's Proposed Budget for Fiscal 2012 Focuses on Education, Energy, Research*, WASH. POST (Feb. 15, 2011), http://www.washingtonpost.com/wp-dyn/content/article/2011 /02/14/AR2011021406234.html; *Obama Budget Proposal: Cuts to Target Working Poor, Middle Class & Students*, HUFFINGTONPOST

.COM (Feb. 13, 2011, 11:55 PM), http://www.huffingtonpost.com/2011/02/13/obama-budget-proposal-cut_n_822689.html.

24. Ethan Pollack, Economic Policy Institute, Major Budget Proposals Pit Public Investment against Vital Services 1 (July 13, 2011), *available at* http://www.epi.org/page/-/EPI_PolicyMemorandum_187.pdf?nocdn=1.

25. *See* Ibid. at 2, tbl.1 (Listing spending categories covered by non-security discretionary spending).

26. Montgomery, *supra* note 23.

27. Nick Anderson, *Obama's Education Budget Would Spare Pell Grants, Increase Spending 11% Overall*, WASH. POST (Feb. 14, 2011, 1:05 PM), http://www.washingtonpost.com/wp-dyn/content/article/2011/02/14/AR2011021403265.html.

28. ROD PAIGE & ELAINE WITTY, THE BLACK-WHITE ACHIEVEMENT GAP: WHY CLOSING IT IS THE GREATEST CIVIL RIGHTS ISSUE OF OUR TIME 2 (2010).

29. Michael A. Rebell, *Poverty, "Meaningful" Educational Opportunity and the Necessary Role of the Courts*, 85 N.C. L. REV. 1467, 1518 (2007).

30. Robert Pear, *Administration Offers Healthcare Cuts as Part of Budget Negotiations*, N.Y. TIMES (July 4, 2011), http://www.nytimes.com/2011/07/05/us/05deficit.html?pagewanted=1&_r=1&hp.

31. Ibid.

32. Zachary A. Goldfarb, *On Debt, Credit Rating Firms Flex Muscle with Downgrade Warnings Despite U.S. Pleas*, WASH. POST (July 15, 2011), http://www.washingtonpost.com/business/economy/on-debt-credit-rating-firms-flex-muscle-with-downgrade-warnings-despite-us-pleas/2011/07/15/gIQApK33GI_story.html?wpisrc=emailtoafriend.

33. Ibid. Ironically, although the financial sector had played a major role in inducing the Great Recession, it was the first to recover, while household income and unemployment continued to ail. *See* Sudeep Reddy, *IMF Sees Global Impact from U.S. Debt Woes*, WALL ST. J., July 26, 2011, at A6 (Graphic entitled "Ranking Recoveries").

34. Paul Kane, *Debt Talks Bring Tensions between Democrats, Obama to Surface*, WASH. POST (July 21, 2011), http://www.washingtonpost.com/politics/debt-talks-bring-tensions-between-democrats-obama-to-surface/2011/07/21/gIQAXeVnSI_story.html?wpisrc=emailtoafriend.

35. Ibid.

36. Jackie Calmes, *Rightward Tilt Leaves Obama with Party Rift*, N.Y. TIMES (July 30, 2011), http://www.nytimes.com/2011/07/31/us/politics/31dems.html?emc=eta1.

37. Ibid.

38. Ibid.

39. Paul Krugman, *What Obama Wants*, N.Y. TIMES (July 7, 2011), http://www.nytimes.com/2011/07/08/opinion/08krugman.html?_r=2&hp.

40. Jonathan Chait, *Did Obama Get Rolled?*, NEW REPUBLIC (Aug. 1, 2011), http://www.tnr.com/blog/jonathan-chait/92991/did-obama-get -rolled.

41. Carl Hulse, *Long Battle on Debt Ending as Senate Set for Final Vote*, N.Y. TIMES (Aug. 1, 2011), http://www.nytimes.com/2011/08 /02/us/politics/02fiscal.html?emc=eta1; Ford Fessenden, Haeyoun Park & Archie Tse, *Comparing Deficit-Reduction Plans*, N.Y. TIMES, http://www.nytimes.com/interactive/2011/07/22/us/politics /20110722-comparing-deficit-reduction-plans.html?ref=politics#panel /11th-hour-deal (last updated Aug. 1, 2011).

42. Ezra Klein, *Wonkbook: A Deal That Found the Lowest Common Denominator*, WASH. POST (July 31, 2011, 11:52 PM), http://www .washingtonpost.com/blogs/ezra-klein/post/a-deal-that-found-the -lowest-common-denominator/2011/07/11/gIQAde9TmI_blog .html.

43. Peter Wallsten & David Nakamura, *Did Obama Capitulate—Or Is This a Cagey Move?*, WASH. POST (July 31, 2011), http://www. washingtonpost.com/politics/did-obama-capitulate-or-is-this -a-cagey-move/2011/07/31/gIQAhJXGmI_story.html?wpisrc =emailtoafriend.

44. Address Before a Joint Session of the Congress on the State of the Union, 1 PUB. PAPERS 79, 79 (Jan. 23, 1996).

45. Margaret Talev & Kevin G. Hall, *Back to the Future: Obama Turns to Clinton Economic Team*, MCCLATCHY (Jan. 6, 2011), http:// www.mcclatchydc.com/2011/01/06/106309/stimulus-act-obama- brings-back.html.

46. Jackie Calmes, *Behind Battle over Debt, a War over Government*, N.Y. TIMES (July 14, 2011), http://www.nytimes.com/2011/07/15/us /politics/15deficit.html?emc=eta1.

47. Ibid.

48. OBAMA, *supra* note 9, at 246.

49. Melissa Harris-Lacewell & Bethany Albertson, *Good Times? Under- standing African American Misperceptions of Racial Economic For- tunes*, 35 J. OF BLACK STUD. 650, 661 (2005).

50. Ibid. at 661–62.

51. Ibid. at 663.

52. Ibid. at 662.

53. Ibid. at 659.

54. Ibid. at 670.

55. KIRWAN INST., RACE RECOVERY INDEX: IS STIMULUS HELPING COMMUNITIES IN CRISIS? 5 (2010), *available at* http://fairrecovery .org/docs/Race-Recovery_FEB2010.pdf.

56. Ibid.

57. Harris-Lacewill & Albertson, *supra* note 49, at 661.

58. News Release, Kirwan Inst. for the Study of Race and Ethnicity, Five Month Trend: Blacks and Latinos Face Consistently Higher

Unemployment Rates (Nov. 18, 2010), *available at* http://490 9e99d35cada63e7f757471b7243be73e53e14.gripelements.com /NewsRelease/2010_1118_news_release_rr_index_nov.pdf.

59. Jesse Washington, *Black Economic Gains Reversed in Great Recession*, Associated Press (July 9, 2011), *available at* http://www.msnbc.msn. com/id/43645168/ns/business-eye_on_the_economy/t/blacks -economic-gains-wiped-out-downturn/.

60. Ibid. *See also* Miriam Jordan, *White-Minority Wealth Gulf Widens*, WALL ST. J., July 26, 2011, at A6, (Reporting on census data tabulated by the Pew Research Center that placed the 2009 median net worth of white households at $113,149 compared to a black median household net worth of $5,677, representing a "sudden and steep increase in wealth disparities" between 2005 and 2009, according to the Center).

61. Algernon Austin, *Joblessness, Discrimination, and Black Poverty*, HUFFINGTONPOST.COM (Sept. 28, 2010), http://www.huffington-post.com/algernon-austin/joblessness-discriminatio_b_741502. html.

62. Catherine Rampell, *Somehow, the Unemployed Became Invisible*, N.Y. TIMES (July 9, 2011), http://www.nytimes.com/2011/07/10 /business/the-unemployed-somehow-became-invisible .html?pagewanted=1&_r=1.

63. Janell Ross, *Blacks and Poor Americans List Unemployment as Larger Problem Than General Economy: Gallup*, HuffingtonPost.Com (June 12, 2011), http://www.huffingtonpost.com/2011/06/10/economy -or-jobs-which-pro_n_874975.html.

64. Carol E. Lee, *POTUS's Outlook on Black America*, POLITICO.COM (Dec. 21, 2009), http://www.politico.com/politico44/perm/1209 /obama_concedes_grumbling_d3f4e3ea-9672–407a-8c9c -2898cc184375.html.

65. Obama's appointment of Kagan can be viewed as part of his strategy to triangulate African Americans as well as the political Left. Prior to his nomination of Kagan, Obama suggested that the liberal judicial victories obtained during the 1960s and 1970s were the product of liberal judicial activism and that the conservative Roberts Court was now behaving similarly. *See* Charlie Savage & Sheryl Gay Stolberg, *Obama Says Liberal Courts May Have Overreached*, N.Y. TIMES (Apr. 29, 2010), http://www.nytimes.com/2010/04/30/us /politics/30court.html. Civil rights activists expressed concern over Obama's attempt to draw a moral equivalence between the eras of the Warren and Burger Courts and the rulings by the now dominant conservative judiciary. Ibid.

66. During the first two years of Obama's presidency, Democrats controlled both the Senate and the House. Despite the Congressional Black Caucus's introduction of some 40 pieces of jobs-creation legislation, none was adopted. CBC Chairman Emanuel Cleaver blamed

the Senate for the fate of the CBC's legislation: "The Senate does, you know, what the Senate does—which is nothing." *See* Cynthia Gordy, *Frustrated by Inaction from Capitol Hill, the CBC Is Trying a New Line of Attack on Unemployment: A Traveling Job Fair with a Twist*, THE ROOT (June 23, 2011), http://www.theroot.com/views /black-caucus-wants-get-you-job?page=0,0.

67. Ylan Q. Mui, *Lack of Jobs for Blacks Creates Tension between Black Lawmakers and Obama*, WASH. POST (Aug. 7, 2011), http://www. washingtonpost.com/business/economy/lack-of-jobs-for-blacks-creates-tension-between-black-lawmakers-and-obama/2011/08/05 /gIQAJL520I_story.html?wpisrc=emailtoafriend. The caucus had met with President Obama at least three times during 2011 to press their jobs proposals, which the president refused to back. Ibid. The caucus had grown frustrated with Obama's belief that the best way to fix black joblessness was to fix the overall economy. Members of the caucus thus embarked on a national, multicity jobs fair during the summer of 2011 to highlight the problem of black unemployment. Ibid.

68. ROBERT C. SMITH, CONSERVATISM AND RACISM, AND WHY IN AMERICA THEY ARE THE SAME 100 (2010). (Describing the War on Poverty's aims as "addressing the disproportionate incidence of poverty in the rural South and the urban ghettos.")

69. Adarand Contractors, Inc. v. Pena, 515 U.S. 200, 224 (1995). ("[A]ny person, of whatever race, has the right to demand that any governmental actor subject to the Constitution justify any racial classification subjecting that person to unequal treatment under the strictest judicial scrutiny.")

70. Ibid. at 206.

71. *See, e.g.*, Baranowski v. Hart, 486 F.3d 112, 125 (5th Cir. 2007) (Finding that maintaining order and controlling costs constitute compelling governmental interests justifying the prison's policy of refusing to comply with prisoners' kosher dietary requirements); Charles v. Verhagen, 220 F. Supp. 2d 937, 947 (W.D. Wis. 2002) (Finding that security and resource concerns constitute a compelling interest justifying the prison's religious feast regulation); Putzer v. Donnelly, No. 3:07-cv-00620-LRH-VPC, 2010 U.S. Dist. LEXIS 63708, at *20 (D. Nev. May 11, 2010) (Finding that limited staff concerns constitute a compelling governmental interest justifying the prison's practice regarding a candle lighting ceremony).

72. This, of course, is precisely what conservatives did in their efforts to thwart Johnson's War on Poverty, though the venue was the political arena rather than the courts. See SMITH, CONSERVATISM AND RACISM, *supra* note 68, at 100.

73. President Barack Obama, Press Conference by the President (July 11, 2011), *Available at* http://www.whitehouse.gov/the-press-office /2011/07/11/press-conference-president. ("We've got the potential

to create an infrastructure bank that could put construction workers to work right now, rebuilding our roads and our bridges and our vital infrastructure all across the country. So those are still areas where I think we can make enormous progress;" however, "[w]e are now in a situation where because the economy has moved slower than we wanted, because of the deficits and debt that result from the recession and the crisis…taking a [sic] approach that costs trillions of dollars is not an option. We don't have that kind of money right now. What we can do is to solve this underlying debt and deficit problem for a long period of time so that then we can get back to having a conversation about…some strategies that we could pursue that would really focus on some targeted job growth—infrastructure being a primary example.")

74. *See, e.g.,* Kenneth R. Davis, *Wheel of Fortune: A Critique of the Manifest 'Imbalance Requirement' for Race-Conscious Affirmative Action under Title VII,* 43 GA. L. REV. 993, 1022 (2009) (Arguing the national unemployment statistics reflect the effects of past and present discrimination: the black unemployment rate in 1962 was 124 percent higher than the white unemployment rate, and in 2007 it was still 104 percent higher); Julius Chambers, *Beyond Affirmative Action,* 27 CAP. U. L. REV. 1, 7 (1998) (Describing discrimination as a "pervasive" factor in black unemployment); MARGERY A. TURNER ET AL., OPPORTUNITIES DENIED, OPPORTUNITIES DIMINISHED: RACIAL DISCRIMINATION IN HIRING (1991) (Revealing white testers were 16 percent more likely to receive job offers than black testers).

75. United States Department of Labor, Bureau of Labor Statistics, *Employment Status of the Civilian Noninstitutional Population 25 Years and Over by Educational Attainment, Sex, Race, and Hispanic or Latino Ethnicity,* http://www.bls.gov/cps/cpsaat7.pdf (Presenting data for 2009 and 2010).

76. Laura Giuliano, David I. Levine & Jonathan Leonard, *Manager Race and the Race of New Hires,* 27 J. LAB. ECON. 589, 590 (2009).

77. Ibid. at 609.

78. Ibid. at 620.

79. U.S. Equal Emp't Opportunity Comm'n, Charge Statistics: FY 1997 Through FY 2010, http://www.eeoc.gov/eeoc/statistics/enforcement/charges.cfm (last visited Aug. 5, 2011); William R. Tamayo, *Symposium: The Evolving Definition of the Immigrant Worker: The Intersection between Employment, Labor, and Human Rights Law: Speeches: The EEOC and Immigrant Workers,* 44 U.S.F. L. REV. 253, 260 (2009).

80. David Jackson, *Obama Rejects Congressional Black Caucus Criticism,* USA TODAY (Dec. 3, 2009), http://content.usatoday.com/communities/theoval/post/2009/12/obama-rejects-congressional-black-caucus-criticism-/1.

81. Laura Meckler & Carol E. Lee, *Obama Aims to Keep White Voters on Board*, WALL ST. J. (Aug. 17, 2011), http://online.wsj.com/article_email/SB10001424053111904253204576512713681895884-lMyQjAxMTAxMDEwODExNDgyWj.html?mod=wsj_share_email.

82. *See* Economic News Release from the Bureau of Labor Statistics, tbl.A-3, http://www.bls.gov/news.release/empsit.t03.htm (last modified Aug. 5, 2011); Economic News Release from the Bureau of Labor Statistics, tbl.A-2, http://data.bls.gov/cgi-bin/print.pl/news.release/empsit.t02.htm (last modified Aug. 5, 2011).

83. Michael Muskal, *Rep. Maxine Waters Says It's Time for Obama to Fight*, L.A. TIMES (Aug. 18, 2011, 10:05 AM), http://www.latimes.com/news/politics/la-pn-maxine-waters-obama-20110818,0,6519191.story. Even a conservative black Republican, Congressman Allen West, joined in the criticism of the president for failing to visit black communities on his tour. Ibid.

84. For a more detailed discussion of this phenomenon of unintended consequences, *see* chapter 6.

85. Terry Smith, *Speaking against Norms: Public Discourse and the Economy of Racialization in the Workplace*, 57 AM. U. L. REV. 523, 526 (2008).

86. U.S. Dept. of Health and Human Servs., African American Profile, http://minorityhealth.hhs.gov/templates/browse.aspx?lvl=3&lvlid=23 (last visited Aug. 5, 2011).

87. Health Care Reform, N.Y. TIMES (Aug. 2, 2011), http://topics.nytimes.com/top/news/health/diseasesconditionsandhealthtopics/health_insurance_and_managed_care/health_care_reform/index.html.

88. MICHAEL TESLER & DAVID O. SEARS, OBAMA'S RACE: THE 2008 ELECTION AND THE DREAM OF A POST-RACIAL AMERICA 155 (2010).

89. Michael Tesler, President Obama and the Growing Polarization of American Politics by Racial Attitudes and Race (2011) (Ph.D. dissertation, UCLA), *available at* http://mst.michaeltesler.com/uploads/Sample_1.pdf.

90. TESLER & SEARS, *supra* note 88, at 62.

91. Ibid. at 6.

92. Ibid. at 77.

93. Greg Sargent, *What Coburn Really Said about Obama, Race, and Dependency*, WASH. POST (Aug. 18, 2011, 1:55 PM), http://www.washingtonpost.com/blogs/plum-line/post/what-coburn-really-said-about-obama-race-and-dependency/2011/03/03/gIQAdBywNJ_blog.html.

94. Interview with Representative Eleanor Holmes Norton, in Wash., D.C. (July 26, 2011).

95. Interview with Representative Jesse Jackson, Jr., in Wash., D.C. (July 27, 2011).

96. Interview with Representative William Lacy Clay, Jr., in Wash., D.C. (July 26, 2011).

6   THE NEW POLITICS OF TRIANGULATION: OBAMA AND
POST-RACIALISM

1. Regents of the University of California v. Bakke, 438 U.S. 265, 407 (1978) (Blackmun, J., concurring in judgment in part and dissenting).
2. GWEN IFILL, THE BREAKTHROUGH: POLITICS AND RACE IN THE AGE OF OBAMA 54 (2009).
3. ROBERT C. SMITH, CONSERVATISM AND RACISM, AND WHY IN AMERICA THEY ARE THE SAME 118–19 (2010) (Emphasis in the original).
4. KEITH REEVES: VOTING HOPES OR FEARS?: WHITE VOTERS, BLACK CANDIDATES & RACIAL POLITICS IN AMERICA 87 (1997) (Emphasis in the original).
5. Ibid. at 90.
6. Terry Smith, *Speaking against Norms: Public Discourse and the Economy of Racialization in the Workplace*, 57 AM. U. L. REV. 523, 535–36 (2008). I have argued that precepts of cognitive psychology that inform the concept of unconscious discrimination or aversive racism also inform sociopolitical discourse:

> Professor Linda Krieger has observed in her highly regarded application of cognitive psychology to status-based discrimination, individuals seldom process information sui generis; rather, they simplify it into broader categories to expedite an understanding, albeit an imperfect one, of persons and events. These cognitive processes can result in stereotyping and other forms of biased intergroup judgment previously attributed to motivational processes. Once in place, stereotypes operate as a latent schema for perceiving other people and information about other people. No intent is necessary to summon the stereotypes into operation. Indeed, a decision-maker is often unaware that he harbors them.
>
> The processing of language is not significantly different from the cognitive processing of people and information about people, for as sociolinguists observe, people may be just as biased in the interpretation of conversation or media messages. Discourse plays an integral role in the reproduction of societal prejudice and discrimination. The process is symbiotic. On the one hand, the manner in which whites discuss minorities, both in everyday conversation and in the media and other elite conduits, reinforces in-group racial hegemony and out-group racial stereotypes. On the other hand, the same social cognition that affects whites' discourse about minorities also affects their perception and interpretation of minority speech.

Ibid. at 534–35 (Citations omitted) (Internal quotations omitted).
7. CHARLTON D. MCILWAIN & STEPHEN M. CALIENDO, RACE APPEAL: HOW CANDIDATES INVOKE RACE IN U.S. CAMPAIGNS 10–15 (2011).

8. Ibid. at 43.
9. Ibid. at 54.
10. Ibid. at 54, 64.
11. Ibid. at 56.
12. Ibid. at 59, 64.
13. Ibid. at 92. The authors find the same disdain for racial appeals among black voters when a black candidate attempts to appeal to racial "authenticity" in a black-on-black contest. Ibid. at 82–84. This context is not relevant to our discussion.
14. Ibid. at 92.
15. *See* Ibid. at 166–68.
16. Smith, *supra* note 6, at 563.
17. Ibid. at 562 n.178.
18. Ibid. at 560; Darren Lenard Hutchinson, *Racial Exhaustion*, 86 WASH. L. REV. 917, 919 (2009) ("[A]n abundance of statistical data consistently demonstrates that persons of color tend to believe that racism remains a substantial barrier to their social and economic advancement, while whites tend to dismiss racial status as a contemporary marker of disadvantage and privilege. These data suggest that whites have, in fact, grown frustrated with ongoing claims of racial injustice.") (Footnotes omitted). Hutchinson further explains:

    Historically, opponents to racial egalitarian measures have portrayed such policies as redundant given prior legislation and societal commitments to antiracism, too extreme and overwhelming in terms of substance and duration; harmful to whites because they discriminate in reverse, invade whites' individual rights, and make persons of color special favorites of the law; futile because they attempt to legislate matters beyond the law's competence; and unnecessary because persons of color have ample opportunity to advance without additional legal protection and any barriers they face come from nonracial sources, such as poverty or lack of merit. These same rhetorical strategies have framed contemporary opposition to race-based remedies among lawmakers, the Supreme Court, countermovements to antiracism, and individual whites.

    Ibid. at 953.
19. Brian Knowlton & Jodi Kantor, *Obama Camp Caught Up in Minister's Controversial Remarks*, N.Y. TIMES (Mar. 17, 2008), http://www.nytimes.com/2008/03/17/world/americas/17iht-campaign.5.11196520.html.
20. For a full transcript of Wright's post-9/11 sermon, *see* http://www.theatlantic.com/daily-dish/archive/2008/03/the-wright-post-9–11-sermon/218678/.
21. Smith, *supra* note 6, at 557 n.157.

22. In 1991, a majority of whites believed that blacks were less patriotic. *See Poll Finds Whites Use Stereotypes*, N.Y. TIMES (Jan. 10, 1991), http://www.nytimes.com/1991/01/10/us/poll-finds-whites-use-stereotypes.html. The efforts to disapprove Barack Obama's citizenship and to attribute to him Islamic as opposed to Christian faith, underscore the ongoing susceptibility of African Americans to the insinuation of lack of patriotism. *See* Jim Rutenberg, *The Man behind the Whispers about Obama*, N.Y. TIMES (Oct. 12, 2008), http://www.nytimes.com/2008/10/13/us/politics/13martin.html?_r=1&hp; Nicholas Kristof, *Was Obama a Kenyan Citizen?*, N.Y. TIMES (Aug. 29, 2008, 6:37 PM), http://kristof.blogs.nytimes.com/2008/08/29/was-obama-a-kenyan-citizen/; Jon Cohen & Michael D. Shear, *Poll Shows More Americans Think Obama Is a Muslim*, WASH. POST (Aug. 19, 2010), http://www.washingtonpost.com/wp-dyn/content/article/2010/08/18/AR2010081806913.html; Stephanie Condon, *Poll: One in Four Americans Thinks Obama Was Not Born in U.S.*, CBS NEWS (Apr. 21, 2011 10:24 AM), http://www.cbsnews.com/8301–503544_162–20056061–503544.html.

23. *Anderson Cooper 360 Degrees: Interview with Illinois Senator Barack Obama; Severe Storms Strike Atlanta* (CNN television broadcast Mar. 14, 2008), *available at* http://transcripts.cnn.com/TRANSCRIPTS/0803/14/acd.01.html.

24. *Bill Moyers Journal* (PBS television broadcast Apr. 25, 2008), *available at* http://www.pbs.org/moyers/journal/04252008/transcript1.html.

25. Ibid.

26. *Barack Obama's "A More Perfect Union" Speech*, NAT'L PUB. RADIO (Mar. 18, 2008), http://www.npr.org/templates/story/story.php?storyId=88478467.

27. http://www.pollingreport.com/race.htm (CBS News/New York Times Poll, July 7–14, 2008).

28. http://www.pollingreport.com/race.htm (CNN/Essence Magazine/Opinion Research Corporation Polls, March 26–April 2, 2008).

29. http://www.pollingreport.com/race.htm (Gallup Poll, June 8–25, 2006).

30. http://www.pollingreport.com/race.htm (ABC/Washington Post Poll, January 12–15, 2010).

31. *Barack Obama's "A More Perfect Union" Speech, supra* note 26.

32. http://www.pollingreport.com/race.htm (CBS/New York Times Poll, July 7–14, 2008) (Sixty-eight percent of black respondents could recall a specific instance in which they were discriminated against because of their race, while only 26 percent of whites could.).

33. *See* Richard Delgado, *Rodrigo's Reconsideration: Intersectionality and the Future of Critical Race Theory*, 96 IOWA L. REV. 1247, 1286

(2011). (Describing white privilege as "the opposite side of the coin of discrimination and exploitation.")

34. Julie Bosman, *Obama Sharply Assails Absent Black Fathers*, N.Y. TIMES (June 16, 2008), http://www.nytimes.com/2008/06/16/us /politics/15cnd-obama.html.

35. Ibid.

36. Jeff Zeleny, *Jesse Jackson Apologizes for Remarks on Obama*, N.Y. TIMES (July 10, 2008), http://www.nytimes.com/2008/07/10/us /politics/10jackson.html.

37. Frank Rudy Cooper, *Our First Unisex President?: Black Masculinity and Obama's Feminine Side*, 86 DENVER U. L. REV. 633, 652 (2009).

38. Larry Elder, *A Christmas Story—in the Mall Parking Lot*, REALCLEARPOLITICS.COM (Jan. 4, 2007), http://www.realclear politics.com/articles/2007/01/a_christmas_story_in_the_mall. html. *See also* Dave Urbanski, *"You've Damaged Your Own Race": Philly Mayor Blasts Teens, Flash Mobs*, THE BLAZE (Aug. 9, 2011, 11:02 AM), http://www.theblaze.com/stories/youve-damaged-your-own-race-philly-mayor-blasts-teens-flash-mobs/. (Comments of Philadelphia Mayor Michael Nutter denouncing a black teenage flash mob by saying "you've damaged your own race.")

39. *See* Terry Smith, *Parties and Transformative Politics*, 100 COLUM. L. REV. 846, 846 n.4 (2000).

40. Ibid. at 846.

41. Joseph Margulies, *Deviance, Risk, and the Law: Reflections on the Demand for the Preventive Detention of Suspected Terrorists*, 101 J. CRIM. L. & CRIMINOLOGY 729, 734 (2011).

42. Ibid.

43. For a panoply of health disparity and unemployment statistics, *see* U.S. Dept. of Health and Human Servs., Office of Minority Health, African American Profile, http://minorityhealth.hhs.gov/templates /browse.aspx?lvl=2&lvlID=51 (last visited Aug. 25, 2011). The expected black male life span is on average six years less than that of white men. *See* Vernellia R. Randall, *Inequality in Health Is Killing African Americans*, 36 HUM. RTS. 20 (2009).

44. Michael Barbaro & Fernanda Santos, *Bloomberg to Use Own Funds in Plan to Aid Minority Youth*, N.Y. TIMES (Aug. 3, 2011), http://www .nytimes.com/2011/08/04/nyregion/new-york-plan-will-aim-to -lift-minority-youth.html?_r=1&emc=eta1.

45. Ibid.

46. The Obama administration's specific programs to address black male parental responsibility were anemic and did not focus on job creation for this subgroup. *See* Cynthia Gordy, *The Root: Obama Helps Dads Do It Better*, NATIONAL PUBLIC RADIO (June 16, 2011), http://www .npr.org/2011/06/16/137217614/the-root-obama-helps-dads-do -it-better

47. Zeleny, *supra* note 36.

NOTES ❖ 203

48. Katie Zezima & Abby Goodnough, *Harvard Scholar Won't Be Charged*, N.Y. TIMES (July 21, 2009), http://www.nytimes.com/2009/07/22/us/22gates.html.

49. Ben Smith, *Obama: Cambridge Police Acted "Stupidly*," POLITICO.COM (July 22, 2009, 9:05 PM), http://www.politico.com/blogs/bensmith/0709/Obama_Cambridge_police_acted_stupidly.html.

50. Ibid.

51. http://www.pollingreport.com/race.htm (CNN/Opinion Research Corporation Poll, July 29-August 3, 2009). Blacks were not entirely sympathetic to Gates, however. Forty-four percent found that he, too, acted stupidly; fifty-eight percent of whites were in accord. Ibid.

52. Ibid.

53. Jonathan Weisman & Simmi Aujla, *Obama Scrambles to Defuse Race Flap*, WALL ST. J. (July 25, 2009), http://online.wsj.com/article/SB124844815302279253.html.

54. http://www.pollingreport.com/race.htm (CNN/Opinion Research Corporation Poll, July 29-August 3, 2009).

55. Weisman & Aujla, *supra* note 53.

56. Ibid.

57. Smith, *Obama: Cambridge Police Acted "Stupidly," supra* note 49.

58. *Were Obama's Race Remarks Too Risky?* N.Y. TIMES (July 23, 2009, 7:39 PM), http://roomfordebate.blogs.nytimes.com/2009/07/23/were-obamas-race-remarks-too-risky/.

59. Krissah Thompson, *A Year Later, Sherrod Won't Go Away*, WASH. POST (June 15, 2011), http://www.washingtonpost.com/politics/a-year-later-sherrod-wont-go-away/2011/06/07/AGjHEVWH_story.html?wpisrc=emailtoafriend.

60. Karen Tumulty & Ed O'Keefe, *Fired USDA Official Receives Apologies from White House, Vilsack*, WASH. POST (July 22, 2010), http://www.washingtonpost.com/wp-dyn/content/article/2010/07/21/AR2010072103871.html.

61. Thompson, *supra* note 59.

62. Tumulty & O'Keefe, *supra* note 60.

63. Teun A. van Dijk, *Denying Racism: Elite Discourse and Racism*, *in* RACISM AND MIGRATION IN WESTERN EUROPE 179, 184 (J. Solomos & J. Wrench eds., 1993), *available at* http://www.discourses.org/OldArticles/Denying%20racism%20-%. 20Elite%20discourse%CC20and%20racism.pdf [hereinafter Elite Discourse].

64. *See* Ibid.

65. Smith, *supra* note 6, at 560.

66. Ibid. at 561.

67. Thomas M. Defrank, *Obama's Bungling of Shirley Sherrod Issue Overshadows Administration's Legislative Accomplishments*, N.Y. DAILY NEWS (July 25, 2010), http://articles.nydailynews.com/2010-07-25/news/27070755_1_president-obama-robert-gibbs-quinnipiac-poll.

68. Thompson, *supra* note 59.

69. Karen Tumulty & Peter Wallsten, *Nervous Democrats Say President Obama Must Be Bolder on Economy*, WASH. POST (Aug. 10, 2011), http://www.washingtonpost.com/politics/nervous-democrats -say-president-obama-must-be-bolder-on-economy/2011/08/10 /gIQA8SZS7I_story.html?hpid=z1.

70. Drew Westen, *What Happened to Obama?*, N.Y. TIMES (Aug. 6, 2011), http://www.nytimes.com/2011/08/07/opinion/sunday/what -happened-to-obamas-passion.html?pagewanted=1&emc=eta1

71. Cooper, *supra* note 37, at 652.

72. *See* Smith, *supra* note 6, at 548–49 (Summarizing experiments conducted by H. Andrew Sagar & Janet Ward Schofield, *Racial and Behavioral Cues in Black and White Children's Perceptions of Ambiguously Aggressive Acts*, 39 J. PERSONALITY & SOC. PSYCHOL. 590, 596 (1980)).

7   A THOUSAND OBAMAS? BLACK ELECTORAL AMBITION
AND ACCOUNTABILITY TO BLACK VOTERS

1. Peter Wallsten & Krissah Thompson, *Obama Faces Uncomfortable Questions from Black Community, Lawmakers*, WASH. POST (Aug. 25, 2011), http://www.washingtonpost.com/politics/obama-faces-uncom fortable-questions-from-black-community-lawmakers/2011/08/25 /gIQAxV6meJ_story.html?hpid=z2.

2. Nia-Malika Henderson, *Waters Talks Tough on Tea Party*, WASH. POST (Aug. 22, 2011), http://www.washingtonpost.com/politics /waters-to-tea-party-go-to-hell/2011/08/22/gIQAb1UnWJ_story .html?wpisrc=emailtoafriend.

3. Interview with Jesse Jackson , Jr., in Wash., D.C. (July 27, 2011).

4. *Meet the Press: Gibbs, Daniels, Ford, Noonan, Dionne, Bartiromo* (MSNBC television broadcast Aug. 21, 2011), *available at* http:// www.msnbc.msn.com/id/44207023/ns/meet_the_press -transcripts/t/meet-press-transcript-august/#.TpFpp3LqKuI.

5. *See* Michael Powell, *Blacks in Memphis Lose Decades of Economic Gains*, N.Y. TIMES (May 30, 2010),http://www.nytimes.com/2010/05/31 /business/economy/31memphis.html?src=me&ref=general. ("Not so long ago, Memphis, a city where a majority of the residents are black, was a symbol of a South where racial history no longer tightly constrained the choices of a rising black working and middle class. Now this city epitomizes something more grim: How rising unemployment and growing foreclosures in the recession have combined to destroy black wealth and income and erase two decades of slow progress.") To be sure, Ford's current sentiment about Wall Street may be born of the fact that Ford has been able to parlay his stint in Congress into a lucrative Wall Street position. *See* Michael Barbaro & Louise Story, *Merrill Lynch Guaranteed Ford Annual Pay of at*

Least $2 Million, N.Y. TIMES (Feb. 25, 2010), http://www.nytimes. com/2010/02/26/nyregion/26ford.html.

6. Sekou Franklin, *Situational Deracialization, Harold Ford, and the 2006 Senate Race, in* WHOSE BLACK POLITICS? CASES IN POST -RACIAL BLACK LEADERSHIP 217 (Andra Gillespie, ed. 2010).

7. Ibid.

8. Ibid. at 218.

9. Ibid. at 220.

10. Ibid. at 220–21.

11. Ibid. at 221–22.

12. Ibid. at 231.

13. Ibid. at 233.

14. Ibid. at 234.

15. Ibid.

16. *Former Democratic Rep. Donates to Two GOP Candidates*, DAILY CALLER (Oct. 26, 2011, 1:51 PM), http://dailycaller.com/2011 /10/26/former-democratic-rep-donates-to-two-gop-candidates/.

17. Robbie Brown, *Black Congressman Eyes Alabama Governor's Seat*, N.Y. TIMES (June 4, 2009), http://www.nytimes.com/2009/06/05 /us/05davis.html.

18. Stephanie Condon, *Jesse Jackson Slams Black Votes against Health Care*, CBS NEWS (Nov. 19, 2009, 2:59 PM), http://www.cbsnews .com/blogs/2009/11/19/politics/politicalhotsheet/ entry5712116.shtml?utm_source=feedburner&utm _medium=feed&utm_campaign=Feed%3A+CBSNewsPCAnswer+% 28PC+Answer%3A+CBSNews.com%29.

19. *See* Brown, *supra* note 17. ("Mr. Davis has veered right of national Democrats on issues like gun ownership, late-term abortion and climate change. He attributes the defeat of every Democratic presidential candidate in Alabama since 1980 to the ideological gulf between state and national Democrats.")

20. Jeff Zeleny, *Alabama Voters Reject Coalition Bid*, N.Y. TIMES (June 2, 2010), http://www.nytimes.com/2010/06/02/us/politics/02elect .html.

21. Interview with Congressman Hank Johnson, in Wash., D.C. (Sept. 15, 2011). The precise exchange is as follows:

> *Hank Johnson*: So, in other words, you're saying without a runoff, then blacks would have been able to elect Cynthia McKinney once again to represent blacks?
>
> *Terry Smith*: That's correct. Do you disagree with that?
>
> *HJ*: No, I could not disagree with that.
>
> *TS*: But I think that the larger point that outside observers—by outside observers, the black—
>
> *HJ*: Keep in mind, however, that the process was implemented by the white folks who controlled the legislature,

white Democrats at the time. And they decided upon a run-off system, and that runoff system benefited their interests. And there was no thought to what it would do to African Americans, but it benefited their interests. And that's why we have a runoff system in Georgia. That system is still in place, and for—it does make it very difficult to defeat an incumbent. It makes it—it makes it more difficult to defeat an incumbent because you [have] to get 50 percent of the vote plus one. So it's actually an incumbent protection device. In the case of Cynthia McKinney, it did not work that way. It did work for other black representatives in Georgia. Why did it not work for Cynthia McKinney is because you can never ignore a substantial part of your constituency.

TS: You're referring to whites?

HJ: Yes. And so I told you from the outset of our conversation that taking care of home first and representing everybody, not just one part of the district but everyone in the district, and so that was a message that resonated and—.

In his 2002 upset of black incumbent Earl Hilliard, Artur Davis likewise appealed especially to white voters whom he perceived as being upset with the incumbent. "The first thing you do is isolate a community the incumbent has offended," Davis acknowledged after his election. *See* Michael Wilson, *In Alabama, How New Kid Won the Bloc*, N.Y. Times (July 3, 2002), http://www.nytimes.com/2002/07/03/us/in-alabama-politics-how-new-kid-won-the-bloc.html?pagewanted=all&src=pm.

22. Bruce A. Dixon, *How Sister McKinney Lost and What We Can Learn from It*, Black Commentator (Sept. 19, 2002), http://www.blackcommentator.com/12_mckinney.html#.TlsMJ3lgcIc.email (Detailing McKinney's 2002 loss to Majette).

23. Ibid.

24. The district was approximately 53 percent black. *See* Terry Smith, *Autonomy Versus Equality: Voting Rights Rediscovered*, 57 Ala. L. Rev. 261, 276 (2005).

25. Ibid. at 276–77.

26. Data on file with author.

27. Janai S. Nelson, *White Challengers, Black Majorities: Reconciling Competition in Majority-Minority Districts with the Promise of the Voting Rights Act*, 95 Geo. L.J. 1287, 1306 (2007).

28. *The Ed Show: A Stronger America: The Black Agenda* (MSNBC television broadcast Apr. 11, 2011), *available at* http://www.msnbc.msn.com/id/42553931/ns/msnbc_tv-the_ed_show/t/ed-show-monday-april-th/.

29. Ibid.

30. Ibid.

31. Ibid.

32. Jonathan Capehart, *Cornel West on Obama is No Better Than a Birther*, WASH. POST (May 18, 2011, 2:16 PM ET), http://www.washington-post.com/blogs/post-partisan/post/cornel-west-on-obama-is-no-better-than-a-birther/2011/03/04/AFcyUb6G_blog.html.

33. Kenneth T. Walsh, *Obama Reaches Out to Black Voters*, U.S. NEWS (Aug. 30, 2011), http://www.usnews.com/news/blogs/Ken-Walshs-Washington/2011/08/30/obama-reaches-out-to-black-voters.

34. Casey Gane-McCalla, *Round 2! Sharpton and Cornel West to Debate Again*, NEWS ONE (June 21, 2011, 9:51 AM), http://newsone.com/nation/casey-gane-mccalla/al-sharpton-cornel-west-obama-debate-chicago/.

35. Interview with Mayor Richard Hatcher, in Chicago, Ill. (Mar. 20, 2009).

36. Ibid.

37. Ibid. (Paraphrasing Julian Bond).

38. Ibid.

39. Ibid.

40. Joseph Williams, *Barack Obama Speech Reopens Rift with Black Critics*, POLITICO.COM (Sept. 29, 2011, 5:03 AM EDT), http://www.politico.com/news/stories/0911/64680_Page2.html.

41. President Barack Obama, Remarks at the Congressional Black Caucus Foundation Annual Phoenix Awards Dinner at the Washington Convention Center, in Wash., D.C. (Sept. 24, 2011), *available at* http://www.thegrio.com/politics/transcript-president-obamas-speech-at-the-cbc-foundation-gala.php.

42. Mackenzie Weinger, *Maxine Waters: Obama Remarks "Curious,"* POLITICO.COM (Sept. 26, 2011, 8:28 AM EDT), http://www.politico.com/news/stories/0911/64405.html. Even the nation's first black elected governor, Virginia Governor L. Douglas Wilder, himself no stranger to winning over the moderate white voters on whom Obama's reelection partially rests, took issue with the language and tone of Obama's speech: "I believe in the president's best intentions. I give him the benefit of any doubt.... But when he spoke to the CBC—and and by inference the people its members represent--and told them with an annoyed pitch to 'Quit whining!' he thundered words the dispirited do not need to hear during this difficult hour of America's history." *See* Williams, *supra* note 40.

43. Ibid.

44. Interview with Congresswoman Donna Christensen, in Wash., D.C. (Sept. 15, 2011).

45. Interview with Congresswoman Frederica Wilson, in Wash., D.C. (Sept. 15, 2011).

46. Interview with Congressman Danny Davis, in Wash., D.C. (July 27, 2011).

47. Lani Guinier, *The Triumph of Tokenism: The Voting Rights Act and the Theory of Black Electoral Success*, 89 MICH. L. REV. 1077, 1102 (1991).

48. Ibid.
49. Ibid. at 1127.
50. *See* ibid. at 1131. ("The authenticity assumption implicitly encourages black representatives to view their personal advancement as a group advantage and to position themselves to seek higher status based on the attendant privileges of seniority. Elected from 'safe' districts, black representatives can afford to spend less time 'at home.' Thus, black representatives may act even more independently than the responsiveness assumption contemplates.")
51. Kareem Crayton, *The Changing Face of the Congressional Black Caucus*, 19 S. CAL INTERDISC. L.J. 473, 497 (2010).
52. Ibid. at 495.
53. Ibid. at 498. *See also* Haya El Nasser, *Black Populations Fall in Major Cities*, USA TODAY (Mar. 22, 2011, 2:24:39 PM), http://www.usatoday.com/news/nation/census/2011-03-22-1Ablacks22_ST_N.htm (Noting that the 2010 census revealed that at least twenty of twenty-five large cities with a black population of at least 20 percent either lost black population or gained fewer blacks than in the 1990s. These cities include erstwhile black strongholds such as Atlanta, Chicago, Cleveland, Oakland, and St. Louis).
54. Guinier, *supra* note 47, at 1108–09.
55. Ibid. at 1108.
56. VALERIE C. JOHNSON, BLACK POWER IN THE SUBURBS: THE MYTH OR REALITY OF AFRICAN AMERICAN SUBURBAN POLITICAL INCORPORATION 141 (2002). Undoubtedly, part of the political division among blacks in Prince George's County reflects what Audrey McFarlane has described as the "Black-Black divergence":

    > One unavoidable fact is that middle class Blacks seek to avoid the disadvantages of poverty just as Whites do. Many Blacks who move to the suburbs do not want poor black kids in their children's schools, revealing a divide in racial identity based on class. But middle class Blacks are less successful at getting away. This is because of structural racial disadvantage in geographically concentrated black ownership. The domino effects are communities with less retail, inferior services, less commercial services. Thus the black middle class are not as successful at protecting their turf as white middle class are. So in effect this is a racial disadvantage but certainly a paradoxical one. It involves a disadvantage in escaping the poor and disadvantage in exercising privilege at the expense of the poor.

    Audrey G. McFarlane, *Operatively White? Exploring the Significance of Race and Class through the Paradox of Black Middle Classness*, 72 LAW & CONTEMP. PROBS. 163, 187 (2009).
57. Molly K. Hooper, *President Obama Told Me to Stop "Demeaning" Him, says Rep. Conyers*, HILL (Dec. 8, 2009, 6:00 AM ET), http://thehill.com/homenews/administration/71075-conyers-obama-told-me-to-stop-demeaning-him.

58. Alex Isenstadt, *Congressional Black Caucus Members Accused of Being Too Harsh on Barack Obama*, POLITICO.COM (Nov. 2, 2011, 4:55AM ET), http://www.politico.com/news/stories/1111/67386.html.

59. Ibid.

60. Glenn Thrush & Joseph Williams, *Black Leaders Turn Up the Heat on President Obama*, POLITICO.COM (Aug. 30, 2011, 4:35 AM EDT), http://www.politico.com/news/stories/0811/62284_Page2.html.

61. Isenstadt, *supra* note 58.

62. *See* Crayton, *supra* note 51, at 496. (Conducting a regression analysis of CBC votes from 1992 to 2004 and concluding that, with regard to party correspondence between CBC members and the president, "The CBC membership appears more divided during Democratic administrations. While one might expect Democrats to agree with members of their own party, the finding is quite consistent with the CBC's role in encouraging other Democrats to respond to issues of concern to the black community.")

63. Manu Raju & Marin Cogan, *Some Democrats Refuse to Back President Obama*, POLITICO.COM (Nov. 13, 2011, 6:10 PM EST), http://www .politico.com/news/stories/1111/68266_Page2.html.

8   DO AFRICAN AMERICANS NEED A BLACK PRESIDENT?
OF MOVEMENTS, NOT MEN

1. Interview with Representative Frederica Wilson, in Wash., D.C. (Sept. 15, 2011).

2. Ibid.

3. As he became more defiant after the debt-ceiling debacle, Obama himself seemed to belatedly acknowledge that Republicans and the Tea Party caucus had no interest in cooperating with him: "It's fair to say that I have gone out of my way in every instance, sometimes at my own political peril and to the frustration of Democrats, to work with Republicans to find common ground to move this country forward. Each time, what we've seen is games-playing, a preference to try to score political points rather than actually get something done." David Nakamura & Scott Wilson, *Obama Urges Bold Steps by Congress on Jobs*, WASH. POST (Oct. 7, 2011), http://www.boston.com/news/nation/washington/articles /2011/10/07/defiant_obama_challenges_gop_on_jobs_bill/. A November 2011 poll by Suffolk University showed that 49 percent of respondents believed that Republicans were intentionally stalling efforts to improve the economy in order to prevent Obama's reelection. Thirty-nine percent disagreed. *See* Greg Sargent, *Will Voters Buy the Idea That GOP Is Sabotaging Economy?*, WASH. POST (Nov. 3, 2011, 11:03 AM ET), http://www.washingtonpost .com/blogs/plum-line/post/will-voters-buy-the-idea-that -gop-is-sabotaging-economy/2011/03/03/gIQAJHziiM_blog .html?tid=sm_twitter_washingtonpost.

4. Michael A. Memoli, *Mitch McConnell's Remarks on 2012 Draw White House Ire*, L.A. TIMES (Oct. 27, 2010), http://articles.latimes.com/2010/oct/27/news/la-pn-obama-mcconnell-20101027.

5. Jackie Calmes, *Obama Draws New Hard Line on Long-Term Debt Reduction*, N.Y. TIMES (Sept. 19, 2011), http://www.nytimes.com/2011/09/20/us/politics/obama-vows-veto-if-deficit-plan-has-no-tax-increases.html?pagewanted=1&_r=1&emc=eta1.

6. The closest Obama's proposal came to the CBC's vision was to set aside $5 billion for job opportunities for low-income individuals. *See Breaking Down Obama's Jobs Plan*, WASH. POST (Sept. 8, 2011, 8:01 PM), http://www.washingtonpost.com/business/economy/breaking-down-obamas-jobs-plan/2011/09/08/gIQAaZpEDK_graphic.html. This was slightly more than 1 percent of the president's proposed expenditure.

7. In August 2011, after the debt-ceiling debacle, Obama's support among African Americans had fallen to a record low of only 76 percent. *See* Tom Jensen, *Obama Keeps Hitting Record Lows*, PUB. POL'Y POLLING (Aug. 30, 2011, 3:23 PM), http://publicpolicypolling.blogspot.com/2011/08/obama-keeps-hitting-record-lows.html. Realizing that the joblessness epidemic in the black community had taken its toll on black enthusiasm for Obama, the White House set about a program of broad outreach to African American voters. Nia-Malika Henderson, *As Joblessness Continues, Obama Faces Tough Challenge in Reengaging Black Voters*, WASH. POST (Sept. 23, 2011), http://www.washingtonpost.com/politics/obama-faces-growing-discontent-among-black-voters/2011/09/23/gIQA3vYurK_story.html.

8. *See* Charles R. Lawrence III, *The Id, the Ego and Equal Protection: Reckoning with Unconscious Racism*, 39 Stan. L. REV. 317, 340–41 (1987). ("Another manifestation of unconscious racism is akin to the slip of the tongue. One might call it a slip of the mind: While one says what one intends, one fails to grasp the racist implications of one's benignly motivated words or behavior.")

9. Ibid.

10. Jennifer Steinhauer, *Some in G.O.P. Find Soft Spot for Bill Clinton*, N.Y. TIMES (Oct. 7, 2010), http://www.nytimes.com/2010/10/08/us/politics/08clinton.html.

11. Greg Sargent, *What Coburn Really Said about Obama, Race, and Dependency*, WASH. POST (Aug. 18, 2011, 1:55 PM ET), http://www.washingtonpost.com/blogs/plum-line/post/what-coburn-really-said-about-obama-race-and-dependency/2011/03/03/gIQAdBywNJ_blog.html.

12. *Newt Gingrich's Legacy As a Political Commentator: Smears, Falsehoods, and Inflammatory Rhetoric*, MEDIA MATTERS FOR AM., http://mediamatters.org/research/201103020034#1 (last visited Oct. 18, 2011); Jake Tapper, *Newt Gingrich Defends Food Stamps vs.*

Paychecks Charge, ABCNews (Jan. 29, 2012, 1:56pm), http://abcnews.go.com/blogs/politics/2012/01/newt-gingrich-defends-food-stamps-vs-paychecks-charge/.

13. David Nir, *IL-14: Joe Walsh Says Media Will Protect Obama Because He's Black*, DAILYKOS.COM (Sept. 22, 2011, 12:12 PM PDT), http://www.dailykos.com/story/2011/09/22/1019312/-IL-08:-Joe-Walsh-says-media-will-protect-Obama-because-hes-black?detail=hide.

14. Nicholas Graham, *RNC Candidate Distributes "Barack The Magic Negro" Song*, HUFFINGTONPOST.COM (Dec. 26, 2008, 12:55 PM), http://www.huffingtonpost.com/2008/12/26/rnc-candidate-distributes_n_153585.html.

15. Ewen MacAskill, *Jimmy Carter: Animosity towards Barack Obama Is Due to Racism*, GUARDIAN (Sept. 16, 2009, 13.58 EDT), http://www.guardian.co.uk/world/2009/sep/16/jimmy-carter-racism-barack-obama.

16. For a recounting of Representative Doug Lamborn's reference to Obama as a Tar Baby, *see* Chuck Plunkett, *Outrage Follows Rep. Doug Lamborn Comparing President Obama to "Tar Baby*,*"* DENVER POST (Aug. 1, 2011, 5:04 PM MT), http://blogs.denverpost.com/thespot/2011/08/01/doug-lamborn-compares-obama-tar-bab/35111/.

17. Nick Wing, *Paul LePage: NAACP Can "Kiss My Butt" (VIDEO)*, HUFFINGTONPOST.COM (Jan. 14, 2011, 2:21 PM), http://www.huffingtonpost.com/2011/01/14/paul-lepage-naacp-kiss-my-butt-video_n_809234.html. Governor LePage also told a local chapter of the NAACP to "kiss my butt" when a dispute arose over his decision not to attend a Martin Luther King Day event sponsored by the organization. As LePage explained, "They are a special interest. End of story . . . and I'm not going to be held hostage by special interests." Ibid. LePage sought cover from the charge of racial insensitivity by pointing out that he has an adopted son from Jamaica. Ibid.

18. Lauren Victoria Burke, *Warning on House Floor: "Disparaging Remarks" Directed at Obama are "Inappropriate*,*"* JAMES RIVER J. (July 20, 2011, 7:29), http://www.jamesriverjournal.com/lauren-victoria-burke/16362-warning-on-house-floor-disparaging-remarks-directed-at-obama-are-inappropriate.html.

19. John R. Parkinson, *Texas Democrat Hints Obama Disrespected Because He's Black*, ABC NEWS (July 15, 2011, 6:10 PM), http://abcnews.go.com/blogs/politics/2011/07/texas-democrat-hints-obama-disrespected-during-debt-limit-negotiations-because-hes-black/.

20. Pete Kasperowicz, *Rep. Jackson: This President Treated "Differently" over Debt-Ceiling Vote*, THEHILL.COM (July 28, 2011, 5:31 PM ET), http://thehill.com/blogs/floor-action/house/174241-rep-jackson-this-president-treated-differently-over-debt-ceiling-vote?page=2#comments.

21. DeWayne Wickham, *Column: GOP's Disrespect of Obama Goes beyond Debt Fight*, USA TODAY (Aug. 3, 2011, 6:59 PM), http://www.usatoday.com/news/opinion/forum/2011-08-02-gop-disrespect-obama-debt_n.htm.

22. BARACK OBAMA, THE AUDACITY OF HOPE: THOUGHTS ON RECLAIMING THE AMERICAN DREAM 248 (2006).

23. Darren Lenard Hutchinson, *Racial Exhaustion*, 86 WASH. U. L. REV. 917, 973–74 (2009).

24. Nathan McCall, *At the Congressional Black Caucus, Obama's Sister Souljah Moment*, WASH. POST (Sept. 30, 2011), http://www.washingtonpost.com/opinions/at-the-congressional-black-caucus-obamas-sister-souljah-moment/2011/09/30/gIQAKoE9AL_story.html.

25. *See* Martha Albertson Fineman, *The Vulnerable Subject: Anchoring Equality in the Human Condition*, 20 YALE J.L. & FEMINISM 1, 15-18 (2008). (Advocating a systemic attack on structures of disadvantage that transcend identity groups, but acknowledging that "[o]f course, discrimination along identity lines unfortunately is likely to continue to occur; and, if it does, there will be an ongoing need to protest and remedy such discrimination.")

26. Caitlin McDevitt, *Morgan Freeman: Tea Party Is Racist*, POLITICO.COM (Sept. 23, 2011, 12:18 PM), http://www.politico.com/blogs/click/0911/Morgan_Freeman_Tea_party_is_racist.html.

27. Devin Dwyer, *Fewer See Improved Race Relations under Obama*, ABC NEWS (Aug. 24, 2011, 6:02 PM), http://abcnews.go.com/blogs/politics/2011/08/fewer-see-improved-race-relations-under-obama/.

28. Ibid.

29. Shannon Travis, *Poll Suggests Pessimism over Race as NABJ Opens*, CNN (July 29, 2010, 1:07 PM ET), http://politicalticker.blogs.cnn.com/2010/07/29/poll-suggests-pessimism-over-race-as-nabj-opens/.

30. Frank Newport, *Little "Obama Effect" on Views About Race Relations*, GALLUP (Oct. 29, 2009), http://www.gallup.com/poll/123944/Little-Obama-Effect-Views-Race-Relations.aspx#at.

31. Ibid.

32. Ibid. (Indicating a 10-point gap of 50 percent versus 60 percent).

33. *Blacks Upbeat about Black Progress, Prospects a Year after Obama's Election*, PEW RES. CENTER (Jan. 12, 2010), http://pewresearch.org/pubs/1459/year-after-obama-election-black-public-opinion.

34. Terry Smith, *Reinventing Black Politics: Senate Districts, Minority Vote Dilution and the Preservation of the Second Reconstruction*, 25 HASTINGS CONST. L.Q. 277, 281 (1998).

35. Darren Lenard Hutchinson, *"Unexplainable on Grounds other than Race": The Inversion of Privilege and Subordination in Equal Protection Jurisprudence*, 2003 U. Ill. L. REV. 615, 618.

36. *See* Adarand Constructors, Inc. v. Pena, 515 U.S. 200, 235 (1995). (Applying strict scrutiny, the highest—and hence most fatal—level of constitutional scrutiny, to a federal contracting program that sought to provide disadvantaged businesses with highway contracts.)

37. *See* Shaw v. Reno, 509 U.S. 630, 649 (1993) (Holding that the Equal Protection Clause prohibits the predominate and unjustified use of race in redistricting); *See also* Miller v. Johnson, 515 U.S. 900, 917 (1995). (Invalidating Georgia's congressional redistricting plan under the equal protection clause because race was a "predominant factor" in drawing the district lines.)

38. *See* Bartlett v. Strickland, 129 S.Ct. 1231, 1246 (2009). (Limiting the reach of the Voting Rights Act by finding that section 2 only applies in districts where minorities make up more than half of the population.)

39. Wal-Mart Stores, Inc. v. Dukes et al., 131 S.Ct. 2541, 2557 (2011). (Disallowing a gender discrimination class action suit against Wal-Mart on the premise that a "corporate culture" of discrimination cannot demonstrate a common practice of discrimination relative to the class members.)

40. *See* Lechmere, Inc. v. Nat'l Labor Relations Bd., 502 U.S. 527, 540–41 (1992). (Limiting union access to employer private property for purposes of organizing employees to those circumstances where "unique obstacles" impede alternative means of communicating with employees.)

41. *See* L. Song Richardson, *Arrest Efficiency and the Fourth Amendment*, 95 MINN. L. REV. 2035, 2068–72 (2011). (Arguing that the Supreme Court's allowance of consideration of race as part of the determination of reasonable suspicion allows for implicit biases in police officers' assessments.)

42. *See* McCleskey v. Kemp, 481 U.S. 279, 313 (1987). (Rejecting equal protection challenges to the imposition of capital punishment where statistical evidence in a state showed that defendants convicted of murder were more than four times as likely to receive the death penalty if their victims were white than if their victims were black.)

43. *See* Gonzales v. Carhart, 550 U.S. 124, 168 (2007). (Upholding the Partial-Birth Abortion Ban Act of 2003.)

44. *See* Ceballos v. Garcetti 547 U.S. 410, 426 (2006). (Holding that the First Amendment does not apply to government employees who speak within the scope of their official duties.)

45. Robert Barnes, *Justice Dept. Asks Supreme Court to Review Health-Care Law*, WASH. POST (Sept. 28, 2011), http://www.washingtonpost.com/politics/justice-dept-asks-supreme-court-to-review-health-care-law/2011/09/28/gIQAjCPK5K_story.html.

46. Terry Smith, *Rediscovering the Sovereignty of the People: The Case for Senate Districts*, 75 N.C. L. REV. 1, 10–12 (1996).

47. Ibid. at 20–21; 26–29.

48. Ibid. at 22–23.
49. Ibid. at 33–34.
50. Ibid.
51. Ibid.
52. Smith, *Reinventing Black Politics, supra* note 34, at 296-99.
53. Shani O. Hilton, *Herman Cain, Allen West and the Black GOP's Low Hopes,* COLORLINES.COM (Sept. 22 2011, 10:04 AM EST), http://colorlines.com/archives/2011/09/herman_cain_allen_west_and_the_black_gops_low_hopes.html. (Discussing historian William Jelani Cobb's account of the historical roots of black conservatism.)
54. *Top All-Time Donors, 1989–2012,* OPENSECRETS.ORG, http://www.opensecrets.org/orgs/list.php?order=A (last visited Oct. 19, 2011).
55. Ibid.
56. Ibid.
57. Dave Levinthal, *Business Executives Call for End to Anonymous Cash,* POLITICO.COM (Sept. 26, 2011, 3:13 PM EDT), http://www.politico.com/news/stories/0911/64448.html.
58. *See* NIELSON CO., THE STATE OF THE AFRICAN-AMERICAN CONSUMER 6 (2011) [hereinafter AFRICAN-AMERICAN CONSUMER], *available at* http://www.nielsen.com/content/dam/corporate/us/en/reports-downloads/2011-Reports/StateOfTheAfricanAmericanConsumer.pdf.
59. News Release, Sam Fahmy, Terry College of Business, *Despite Recession, Hispanic and Asian Buying Power Expected to Surge in U.S., According to Annual UGA Selig Center Multicultural Economy Study* (Nov. 4, 2010), *available at* http://www.terry.uga.edu/news/releases/2010/minority-buying-power-report.html#.ToQrBMHhIlI.email.
60. AFRICAN-AMERICAN CONSUMER, *supra* note 58, at 6.
61. Regina Austin, *"A Nation of Thieves": Securing Black People's Right to Shop and to Sell in White America,* 1994 UTAH L. REV. 147, 156 (1994).
62. Ibid. at 160 (internal quotations omitted).
63. Ibid. at 160–61.
64. *See* Fredreka Schouten & Paul Overberg, *High-Income Blacks Favor Obama,* ABC NEWS (June 14, 2007), http://abcnews.go.com/Politics/story?id=3277512&page=1. (Noting that as of June 2007, Obama had collected more than 2,200 donations from areas with an above-average share of black households and black household incomes. This amounted to nearly as much as Hillary Clinton raised in the first quarter from all sources.)
65. *Top All-Time Donors, supra* note 54.
66. *African Americans,* AM. LUNG ASS'N (Feb. 2010), http://www.lungusa.org/stop-smoking/about-smoking/facts-figures/african-americans-and-tobacco.html.

67. Ibid.

68. *See Top All-Time Donors, supra* note 54.

69. *Study: Many Blacks Boycott Sponsors When Offended by Programming,* TARGET MARKET NEWS (July 16, 2007), http://targetmarketnews .com/storyid07160702.htm.

70. Ibid.

71. Levinthal, *supra* note 57. ("[M]ost corporations have opted to funnel money to either 501(c)(4) or 501(c)(6) nonprofit organizations, which in turn spend the money on political advocacy without having to reveal their donors.") If a movie star's political comments and affiliations can affect Democrats' or Republicans' willingness to purchase a ticket to his movies, *see* Paul Bond, *Democrats vs. Republicans: Stars They Won't Pay to See; Movies They Hate and Love (Poll)*, HOLLYWOOD REP. (Oct. 6, 2011, 12:34 PM PDT), http:// www.hollywoodreporter.com/news/politics-box-office-democrats -republicans-244741, then corporations' political loyalties are a fair basis for consumers' purchasing decisions. Transparency is needed in order for voters to make these kinds of decisions.

72. W. Cole Durham & Robert West, 2 Religious Organizations and the Law § 17:13.

73. Adelle M. Banks, *Church Attendance Down, Congregations Getting Older, Report Says*, WASH. POST (Sept. 30, 2011), http://www .washingtonpost.com/national/on-faith/church-attendance-down -congregations-getting-older-report-says/2011/09/29/gIQA7jjvAL _story.html.

74. Terry Smith, *White Dollars, Black Candidates: Inequality and Agency in Campaign Finance Law*, 57 S.C. L. REV. 735, 747 (2006).

75. Interview with Congressman William Lacy Clay, in Wash., D.C. (July 26, 2011).

76. Ibid.

77. Interview with Congresswoman Eleanor Holmes Norton, in Wash., D.C. July 26, 2011).

78. Interview with Lenora Fulani, in New York (June 8, 2009).

79. Ibid.

80. Terry Smith, *A Black Party:* Timmons, *Black Backlash and the Endangered Two-Party Paradigm*, 48 DUKE L.J. 1, 70–72 (1998). (Illustrating how a black political party could succeed under fusion laws.)

81. According to New York University's Brennan Center for Justice, only seven states allow fusion candidacies. *See* ADAM MORSE & J.J. GASS, BRENNAN CENTER FOR JUST., MORE CHOICES, MORE VOICES: A PRIMER ON FUSION 1 (OCT. 2006), *available at* www.brennancenter.org /page/-/d/download_file_39345.pdf. (Listing Connecticut, Delaware, Idaho, Mississippi, New York, South Carolina, and Vermont.)

82. *See* Smith, *A Black Party, supra* note 80, at 51–52.

83. Clifford J. Levy, *It's Hevesi, Financed and Visible, against a Field That Isn't*, N.Y. Times (Sept. 28, 1997), http://www.nytimes.com/1997/09/28/nyregion/it-s-hevesi-financed-and-visible-against-a-field-that-isn-t.html?pagewanted=all&src=pm.

Conclusion

1. Sumi Cho, *Post-Racialism*, 94 Iowa L. Rev. 1589, 1595 (2009).

INDEX

Affirmative action
  black support of 52, 58, 60, 103
  race-neutral 4–5, 85–90, 93–94,
    96, 98, 157
  white opposition to 47, 52, 59,
    60, 103
African Americans/Blacks
  capture of, by the Democratic
    Party 3, 27, 46, 63, 69–71, 73,
    78, 120
  disposable income of 148
  experiences with immigration 73,
    76–78
  unemployment rates of 4, 19, 77,
    91, 111
  views of opposition to Obama's
    policies 12–13, 15–16, 98, 142
  *See specific topics for other
    discussions of African Americans*
Allen, George 5
Audacity of Hope 90, 140

Bachmann, Michele 42, 52, 126, 128
Bair, Sheila 87
Belcher, Cornell 101
Bennett, Robert 121
Biden, Joe 139
Blackmun, Harry, Justice 101
Blackwell, Ken 46
Bloomberg, Michael 111, 152, 153
Boehner, John 89
Breitbart, Andrew 114–15
Brown, Janice Rogers 59–60
Bryant, Phil 123
Bush, George H.W. 87
Bush, George W. 11–13, 27, 46,
    54–56, 59, 84, 86, 87, 121, 142

Butler, Charles 56

Cain, Herman 59, 60
Campaign finance
  African American/Black lack of
    participation in 38–39, 148–50
  impact on African American
    candidates 30–33, 37–39, 42, 150
  as means of wealth acquisition
    and maintenance 149
  and racial cuing 31, 33–38
Carnahan, Russ 21
Carter, Jimmy 126–27, 133, 139
Chait, Jonathan 89
Christensen, Donna 19, 128
Citizens United v. FEC 31–33, 36,
    148, 151
Civil Rights Act of 1964 53–54, 111
Clarke, Yvette 31
Clinton, Bill 1–2, 4–5, 9–10,
    54, 61, 84–87, 89–91, 96,
    102, 105, 110–11, 114, 116,
    137–38, 142
Clinton, Hillary 77–78, 107
Coburn, Tom 97, 138
Cohesion, black voters 3, 5–6, 9, 11,
    13–14, 19, 22, 36, 47–48, 55,
    61, 69, 83–84, 116, 129–30,
    132, 143, 155, 157–58
Colorblindness
  in elections 1, 21, 25–26, 67,
    105–6, 133, 149
Congressional Black Caucus
  (CBC) 2, 14–15, 17, 19,
    30–31, 39–41, 54, 73, 93, 95,
    98, 102, 116, 121–23, 125,
    127–32, 137, 139, 144, 148

Connerly, Ward 58, 60
Conservatives
    African American/Black 3, 6,
        29, 45–50, 55–61, 63, 71, 83,
        148, 157
    racial attitudes of 52–53, 56–57,
        59, 61, 93–94
Consumptive behavior
    African American/Black 148–50
Conyers, John 125, 131–32

Davis, Artur 14–15, 40–42, 122–23,
        130–31
Davis, Danny 128
Debt ceiling 88–89, 98–99, 136,
        139–40
Democratic Party
    over-reliance on African
        Americans 3, 21, 27, 53, 65,
        70, 72
Dinkins, David 73, 125, 151, 154
Discrimination
    in employment 34, 51, 53, 75,
        94–95, 103, 109, 145, 149
Dukakis, Michael 33–34
Dupree, Johnny 123

Economic versus political
        rights 148–50
Edley, Chris 86
Education, racial gaps in 75, 87–88,
        94, 111
Elections, racial polarization in 23,
        26–27, 48–49

Fineman, Martha 13, 75
Freeman, Morgan 141–42
Ford, Harold, Jr. 121–22, 124, 130
Fifteenth Amendment, U.S.
        Constitution 147
First Amendment, U.S.
        Constitution 32, 36
Fourteenth Amendment, U.S.
        Constitution 23, 25, 66, 74
Frank, Thomas 57, 110
Fulani, Lenora 152

Gates, Henry Louis 52, 112–15
Gay marriage, and African
        Americans 46, 55–58, 71
Gay rights, Obama's support
        of 75
Gerrymandering
    partisan 23–24, 28–29
    racial 3, 22–24, 28, 67
Gingrich, Newt 138
Giuliani, Rudy 125, 154
Goldwater, Barry 53–54
Great Recession of 2008 2, 4,
        87–88, 90–92, 121
Great Society, of Lyndon
        Johnson 1, 53, 120
Guinier, Lani 17, 39, 58, 129–30
Gutierrez, Luis 75

Health care
    disparities, Black versus
        White 96, 111, 142
    Patient Protection and
        Affordable Care Act of
        2010 53, 96
Hevesi, Alan 153–54
Hilliard, Earl 42
Horton, Willie 34–35, 104

Independence Party of New York
        City 152–53
Independent voters 3, 52, 58,
        64–66, 69–72, 137

Jackson, Jesse, Jr. 88, 98, 119–20,
        131–32, 140
Jackson, Jesse, Rev. 1, 15, 110–12,
        123, 126
Jackson Lee, Sheila 140
Jeffries, Leonard 106
Johnson, Hank 123–24
Johnson, Lyndon Baines 1, 5, 53,
        93, 120, 136

Kagan, Elena 86, 93
King, Martin Luther, Jr. 53,
        56–57, 142

Krugman, Paul 89

Latinos
    and immigration 66, 73–79, 127
    and Proposition 187 74
    social distance from African
        Americans 72–73, 76
    as swing voters 3, 64–65, 69,
        70–74, 78
Leadership Conference on
        Civil and Human Rights
        (LCCHR) 13–14, 39
Lee, Barbara 41 140
Long, Eddie, Bishop 56
Lott, Trent 106, 138

Majette, Denise 42, 123–24
Malebranche, David, Dr. 57
McKinney, Cynthia 41–42, 123–24
Medicaid 86, 88
Medicare 53, 86–89, 136–37
McConnell, Mitch 136
Meek, Kendrick 154

Nasheed, Jamilah 21
National Association for the
        Advancement of Colored
        People (NAACP) 13–14, 39,
        52, 114–15, 150
New Deal Coalition 52–53
Nixon, Richard M. 34, 53–54,
        96, 101
Norton, Eleanor Holmes 98, 152

Paige, Roderick 88
Paul, Rand 53
Paul, Ron 107
Perry, Rick 52, 126
Phillips, Kevin 53
Poverty, African American 4, 88,
        90–93, 121, 142

Race
    hydraulic conception of 124–26,
        129–31
    white exhaustion with 106, 140

Racialization
    definition of 96
    of health care 53, 96
    of Barack Obama 96–99, 133,
        139, 141
Reagan, Ronald 2, 48, 53–55, 59,
        87, 138, 145
Reed, Bruce 86
Reed, Kasim 125
Republican Party, racial attitude
        of 52–55
Richardson, Laura 131
Romney, Mitt 21–22, 32, 126
Roosevelt, Franklin Delano 96

Sanders, Bernie 132
Senate Districts, United
        States 143–48
Seventeenth Amendment, U.S.
        Constitution 146–47
Sharpton, Al, Rev. 38, 124–27,
        129, 132, 154
Shaw v. Reno 23–26, 28–29, 33,
        37, 144
Sherrod, Shirley 114–16
Sister Souljah 110, 141
Smiley, Tavis 125
Sotomayor, Sonia 127
Southern strategy, Republican
        50, 53
Steele, Michael 45–46, 48, 50–51, 57
Supreme Court
    discrimination against minority
        litigants 21–22, 25, 28, 36,
        42, 67, 83, 93, 144–45
    importance of, for protection of
        minority rights 145
Swann, Lynn 46

Tea Party 27, 35, 46, 50–54, 60,
        72, 74, 88, 115, 120–21, 128,
        133, 136, 138–39, 143, 153–55
Third Parties
    African American/Black 151–53
    fusion 152–53
    satellite 153

Thomas, Clarence 47–48, 59–60, 75
Thompson, Bennie 131
Transformative politics 111,
    114–15, 136
Triangulation
  Clintonian 1–2, 4–5, 9–10,
    13, 19, 61, 83–88, 92,
    99, 116
  post-racial 1–2, 4–5, 6, 10,
    18–19, 42–43, 61, 78–79,
    83–88, 101–18, 121, 136–37,
    141, 143, 157

Unemployment
  African American/Black 4, 19,
    77, 90–95, 109, 111, 116, 142
  white 4, 19, 91, 94–95, 111
United States Senate
  creation of Senate districts
    for 146

Vivian, C.T., Rev. 57
Vote dilution 26, 66, 147–48
Voter identification 27–28, 36, 145
Voting Rights Act of 1965 9, 13,
    25–26, 42, 49, 53–54, 58, 67,
    74, 111, 124, 147, 151
Vulnerability theory, applied to
    Black politics 10, 13, 75

Walsh, Joe 138
Washington, Booker T. 148
Waters, Maxine 95, 119–20, 123,
    125, 127
West, Cornel 2, 15, 124–25
Wilson, Frederica 54, 119, 128,
    135, 143
Wilson, Joe 98–99, 106, 139
Wilson, Pete 74
Wright, Jeremiah, Rev. 105–9, 112,
    115